# THE ROCK GARDEN

## AND ITS PLANTS

GRAHAM STUART THOMAS

# THE ROCK GARDEN

## AND ITS PLANTS

### FROM GROTTO TO ALPINE HOUSE

FRANCES LINCOLN

*To the memory of Reginald Farrer, whose writings enthralled me;*
*Clarence Elliott, who employed and encouraged me;*
*Gavin Jones, who inspired me;*
*Walter Ingwersen, who befriended me.*

Frances Lincoln Limited
4 Torriano Mews
Torriano Avenue
London NW5 2RZ
www.franceslincoln.com

*The Rock Garden and Its Plants*
Copyright © Frances Lincoln Limited 2004
Text copyright © The Estate of Graham Stuart Thomas 1989
Illustrations copyright © The Estate of Graham Stuart Thomas
1989 except where otherwise indicated

First Frances Lincoln edition: 2004

British Library Cataloguing in Publication data
A catalogue record for this book is available from the British Library

ISBN: 0 7112 2398 X

Printed in Singapore

9 8 7 6 5 4 3 2 1

# Contents

# Gratitude

After having written a book one of the most enjoyable jobs is to record all the help one has received from friends. First I must thank the Royal Horticultural Society for permission to photograph certain illustrations from books in the Lindley Library. The photography was done by Dr R. H. M. Robinson of the Harry Smith Horticultural Photographic Collection. The Librarian, Dr W. B. Elliott, has been most helpful in guiding me to old books on alpine plants and rock gardens. I think that these historic pictures show a very interesting evolution, particularly in the style of painting, through nearly two and a half centuries, from hand-coloured engravings to colour printing in this century. Besides being somewhat tired of colour-photograph reproduction, I felt that this book, being so much concerned with history, was worthy of having historical pictures.

And then, far away from plants, my deep appreciation goes to Terence Miller for his invaluable help with chapter 3. Although I have been interested in geology since schooldays, I felt very hesitant about including a chapter on this subject until I had Terence's assurance that he would peruse it; which he did, much to the chapter's benefit. I had also useful information on certain rocks from Professor R. J. G. Savage which I have gratefully incorporated.

Nor should I have been happy to launch these pages, so filled with plant names, had not Peter Barnes, Botanist at Wisley, kindly agreed to look through them – correcting my failings in taxonomy – nor without Joe Elliott's welcome help with the last chapter.

During the preparation of the book I made frequent trips to Kew, where Brian Halliwell and Tony Hall grow so many good plants; I am greatly indebted to the former – and to the Alpine Garden Society – for permission to reprint his article on the Alpine House at Kew. To the Director, Royal Botanic Gardens, Kew, and to the Regius Keeper at the Royal Botanic Garden, Edinburgh, I record my thanks for help with illustrations and the printed word. Further thanks are due to W. G. MacKenzie for his account of the oldest British rock garden, at Chelsea Physic Garden, London. It was a great privilege also to be allowed to borrow plants from Kew and from Wisley, in order to paint their portraits.

It is not until one starts digging into archives that one realises the amount of time that becomes absorbed; I am thankful to Peter Goodchild for doing a lot of 'digging' for me.

Next my thanks go to the Duchess of Devonshire and the Trustees of the Chatsworth Settlement – and their Librarian, Michael Pearman – for kindly furnishing not only photographs of some original engravings of Joseph Paxton's work at Chatsworth, but also records of the rocks as they are today. Similar help has come from the United States, where Brian Mulligan has kindly lent me photographs of rocks and plants in the wild, and Francis Cabot, Joel Spingarn, George Waters and Harold Epstein have also been generous with photographs. And I must thank Michael Warren for his photographic help. All photographs not credited otherwise are my own, taken during the last fifty years or so.

Here I must leave these acknowledgments, knowing I have recorded credit for many of the pictures under the captions. To all collaborators, my best thanks.

'As for several other Books that have been printed in our own Language, I have neither the Vanity nor Ill Will of censuring or condemning anything that is contained in them; but rather pay a great deal of Respect to the Memory of their Editors, and shall make use of those Writings wherever they agree with our present Method. But many of them being writ some Years ago, before Gard'ning was so bright as 'tis now; and others being of so mean a Taste as scarce to bear Reading at all, I cann't but after much Thought be of an humble Opinion that the present Undertaking will be of some Use to the World.'

Stephen Switzer, *The Nobleman, Gentleman and Gardener's RECREATION*, 1715

# Preface

My earliest enthusiasm in gardening was for rock plants, or, to give them their more aristocratic title, alpines. To grow these fascinating plants, rock had to be present in one form or another: in boulders to hold up the soil into imaginary cliffs and promontories, or in walls holding the soil in raised beds, or merely crushed to make rapidly draining screes. But there was no rock in my native town, Cambridge, nor in its immediate countryside except soft chalk, the harder clunch, and the attendant flints. Natural rock quarries were many miles away, much too far for cycling.

Imagine therefore the excitement that imported rock gave to one thirsting for knowledge of gardening – imagine the thrill of seeing the High Rocks near Tunbridge Wells in Kent, or the cliffs at Hunstanton, Norfolk, striped with white chalk, pink limestone and brownish Carstone! There was a rock garden of Hornton stone (from Banbury, Northamptonshire) at the University Botanic Garden and one of limestone from Derbyshire and Westmorland in Sydney Sussex College. A tiny textbook came into my hands, *Geology* by Professor A. Geikie, which was written in 1888; here was a fund of elementary knowledge that fed me for many years until later University lecturers opened the doors of the subject much wider. We had, however, a noted firm of stonemasons, Rattee and Kett, not far away. Mr Kett was a friend of my father's and he introduced me in early years to good building stone.

Subsequent holidays took me always to counties where stone abounded – to the Cotswolds, the Mendips, the Isle of Purbeck and North Wales; Cornwall, the Lake District, Yorkshire and Scotland came later. And wherever stone occurred the local flora gave me added interest, many of the plants being closely allied to or even identical with rock-loving plants from other countries, in which my interest was never assuaged. Horticulture is a lifelong friend, a never-ending interest, and rocks and alpine plants have never been far from my thoughts. Horticulture is like a fan, ever opening outwards, or like a diamond of many facets whose diversity of glints and colours are never-ending. Therefore I felt that, just as I had written books on trees and all kinds of hardy garden plants, I would venture one on rock gardens and all that the term conveys to me. Here it is, and it is but another of the many facets of gardening.

# Introduction:
## Setting the scene

Alpine plants are never found growing away from the influence of rock. The rock may not be large boulders; it may be in the form of gravel or sand: the small particles aid rapid drainage which is essential for the well-being of alpines. They do not grow in heavy clay or fat, greasy loams, nor are they kept in health by repeated deep digging and manuring; their culture is very special and is not to be regarded lightly. To us gardeners the term alpine plant covers many types of plants not necessarily from the Alps. Similarly 'rock' and 'stone' cover a multitude of different types of composition from volcanic and pre-volcanic to what are known as sedimentary rocks, such as sandstone, limestone, chalk and even coal. In a book about the history of rock gardening it is as well to know what this stone or rock is that plays so great a part in the lives of alpine plants. Thus my opening chapters will be little concerned with plants, but as the story unfolds the plants will be found to assume ever greater importance. So let us start with basic things which embrace the facts that, in addition to needing rock for their health, alpines are the only form of plant growth, together with mosses, lichens and the tiniest of shrubs – perhaps less than an inch high – which inhabit the high hills below the line of permanent snow and glaciers. And yet some of them may also be found in the sands and on the rocks of the seashore. With such a set of paradoxes and variables we must be prepared for some strangely dissimilar chapters.

\* \* \* \* \*

It is a well known fact that the face of the earth is covered by growth of some kind, except where conditions climatic or fundamental are prohibitive. This growth is entirely passive; it bends to the wind or current of water, and in almost every instance is pliable to some degree. It is alive, growing with an indeterminable and wholly mysterious power to exist and increase. It is supported by what we may call the crust of the earth which is its exact opposite. Over incalculable time this crust has been moved by interior convulsions and stresses, and battered by wind, rain and frost; in this process it has been broken, mixed and reformed into innumerable different assortments and compositions. Though we speak of 'stone dead', stone (rock) is not really completely static and without change, but only less dead than truly living things; the debris of rocks, the gravels and sands, accumulate and in course of time are re-made into fresh composite substances, compressed by their own weight and that of deposits above them, or the weight of the sea, into newer rocks. Where the disintegration is at its finest and mixed with vegetable and animal detritus it is a fertile hold for plant growth. But it is still inert, lying back on itself and held in place by gravity.

This partnership of rock and plant was little upset by the birth of animals; they are dependent on the partnership, but also help the plants, not only by their decomposing debris but also partly by their movements. Man merely exaggerates to a greater degree the effect of the animals. Whereas the plants simply use in a gentle way the inert masses beneath them – splitting them apart and transforming them – animals use in their turn the plants for food; outdoing them both, man in his turn uses and consumes the rock, the plants, the animals and their derivatives.

*       *       *       *       *

Though it is nature's way to make every living thing pliable and adaptable to the forces extant, it is man's way to create a rigid, lasting world. And yet, in spite of this, the impermanence of man's endeavours is in strong contrast to nature's flexible permanence.

To create his lasting world man had at first no knowledge and no tools, but gradually we may visualise his lot being ameliorated by the use of bones and timber – bones for digging and ploughing and timber for the construction of shelters. Sharp flints formed the first knives and tools, and after them followed metal tools and the consequent ability to shape wood and stone. Flints when split are extremely sharp and were an invaluable commodity, occurring in most of the great chalk seams in which areas the earliest colonisation proceeded in this country. But the wearing down of the chalk by glaciers had resulted in the hardest part of the seams, the flints, being carried away last, underlying the sandy, gravelly Breckland of Norfolk. I shall enlarge upon this in chapter 3.

It is significant that in that part of East Anglia there was no stone nor rock of other nature to be used for building – nor for use by chipping into sharp-edged tools. There in the neighbourhood of Thetford was the first mining undertaken, for flints, at Grime's Graves. A form of stone had come into its own as a needed commodity; its transference in bulk to one of the centres of Neolithic life at Avebury, Wiltshire, was possibly the cause of the Icknield Way being formed.

The farther west and north of these islands early man penetrated – long before Britain became an island – the more rock he found lying on the surface of the land and the less suitable was the land for elementary husbandry. By removing the rocks from the land-surface and using them for walls and the earliest dwellings – little more than what we should call pigstyes – the more suitable became the land for use; clearance of small trees and underbrush for use for fires, walls and roofing had the same effect.

Thus was rock first used to provide shelter. We know that in the south-east of England hard stone, which would be useful to provide rigid buildings, was eagerly sought. Apart from the use of clunch or hard chalk, or the later baking of clay for bricks, there was little to hand; even the adaptable Sussex sandstone which often lies near the surface was mostly out of reach on account of the heavy Wealden clay which was not only too obdurate for tools of bone or wood but was heavily wooded. On the surface, however, or lying shallowly below the vast area of gravels and clays which go to make up the London Basin, were what we know as Sarsen stones. There is quite an assembly of them in front of Ashdown House in Berkshire; from similar material was Stonehenge built. These great monoliths are the largest to be erected in these islands. The hard sandstone defied breaking or dividing until man had learnt how to make metal tools. Up to the present day such stones have been found by excavation or probing over many parts of the country west of London and have been used in their original sizes and shapes for building. Just as the earth's crust has been broken down and reformed, so these great blocks have been cut and used again and again until today when small portions will be seen in walls and gate pillars, churches and the quoins of buildings.

Stonehenge is an example of how stone could be assembled by brute force and used in an imposing way. As tools improved, the uses of stone became diversified. Remarkable achievement though Stonehenge was, the more stone became prepared, shaped and smoothed, the more was it used to create buildings of grandeur and beauty – the castles, abbeys and cathedrals. I like to think that no achievement in stone has surpassed the Perpendicular style of architecture, exemplified in walls, buttresses, windows and roof in Sherborne Abbey, St George's Chapel, Windsor, and at King's College, Cambridge. It seems a superhuman effort of man not only to have envisaged such a triumph of architecture, even while the Wars of the Roses were taking place, but to have achieved the crowning glory of the fan vaulting, merely with the aid of ramps, tree trunks and rope. Stone, when shaped, had thus become a thing of great beauty, but men could not use it to its greatest advantage without plant products – the scaffolding and ropes.

*         *         *         *         *

Still earlier in China, rocks themselves had come to be appreciated as objects of beauty, uncut and unpolished; in their natural shapes they were dragged out of lakes and rivers where the restless waters had scooped and hollowed and fretted them into fantastic shapes; they were used to create illusions of nature's vastness and variety. Much prized rocks were worth a fortune. Thus, apart from extreme formalism in Europe, the Far East had something to teach us whereby stone for its beauty alone was triumphant in the minds of mankind.

In between these two extremes, in Europe and elsewhere different types of stone were used in different ways, revealing contrasts of colour and texture. Glistening marble was used for the Taj Mahal at Agra, about a hundred years later than King's College Chapel, and of course marble has always been the favourite stone for statues from the days of ancient Greece to the present. From Greece a long progression of beauty was achieved with stone alone. Apart from statuary, with few exceptions – noted particularly in chapter 1 of this book – stone has been used in a formal way to provide that firm, permanent background to life which was needed to balance nature's pliability and caprices.

The appreciation in Europe of the beauty of rocks, singly or in their multitudes, was not reached until long after the taste for things Chinese had developed, late in the eighteenth century. Perhaps it was because Europeans had not learned the art of contemplation of nature. Though life was still hazardous in many ways, some stability and affluence had been reached and those wealthy enough were able to travel abroad in peace – or nearly so. The lure of art and antiquities took them to Rome. The travellers saw not only the majesty of the Alps, but also the compelling beauty of mountains and rocks which had given form and solidity to the great French pictorial masterpieces in oils of the previous century. Meanwhile poets and writers were extolling the beauties of nature, and Sir William Chambers in no small way called attention to all things Chinese. Not only the beauties of nature were brought to the fore, but as a contrast to the easier living, guarded by houses and walls, mankind could stand aside, as it were, and appreciate the savage grandeur of nature with its awe-ful crags, precipices, roaring waterfalls and the one thing that permitted and gave rise to it all – rock. And much of this was found to have caused the original grottoes to be made in the ancient world.

*   *   *   *   *

Unless it is purely for business, most of mankind would travel to see what the rest of the world was like, how the people lived, ate and worked, what animals and plants existed. In this way, often through commerce, bulbs and seeds were brought home by travellers. The French, Dutch and English started an accumulation of plants which continues to grow even to this day, particularly in England and Holland. It was manifest that such journeys would take the adventurers south, there being very little to the north of Europe to attract them. It is an odd thing that just as travel and the appreciation of beauty, launched afresh during the Renaissance, came to the fore in England, our gardens as such were being relegated to walled areas away from the great houses which were springing up in the midst of their parks. The most important views were destined to be composed of trees, grass and water with perhaps the odd building – classical, picturesque or even Chinese – which was given a place of vantage or ensconced in umbrageous grove. But the Picturesque or 'picture-like' style of gardening only applied to the surrounds of a great fashionable mansion. The craft of gardening, ever more expert, was carried on away from such expanses and developed in many ways. The hot-bed, long used as a means for forcing plants, gave place to the orangery – perhaps sparked off originally as a compliment to the House of Orange – exemplified by the great classical building at Saltram in Devon. Even before the early nineteenth century, great was the multitude of plants from warmer climates that had to be accommodated. The oranges and lemons had to be trundled outside for the summer. It was no small job if one remembers the assembly of palms, oranges, lemons and other exotics in huge *caisses* standing before the Orangery at Versailles. The plants had to have an airing outside for the summer mainly on account of the tiled or leaded opaque roofs of the buildings, which caused etiolation. Gradually the glass-roofed greenhouses evolved; heating by the old Roman method of flues gave way to hot-water pipes.

Whereas in earlier centuries the enthusiasm was for 'curious' flowers of real or supposed use to mankind, which could be grown in the open air, the taste turned to tender exotics, to be raised under glass and exploited to great effect in beds on Victorian lawns. The beds echoed in an eclectic way the formal patterns of the seventeenth century.

Among the new plants were those seen growing in the foothills of the Alps and other high ground in Europe. As exploration went on, and greater heights were conquered and enjoyed, the gem-like plants of the high mountains were observed and brought home. Because they would have been found in summer in hot sunshine, and because anything very choice would have been nurtured carefully under glass, they were at first often given the protection of the greenhouse. The first special feature made to accommodate them in England was a rock garden in the greenhouse at Chelsea Physic Garden in 1772; it was constructed of old building stone and basaltic lava from Iceland.

There is a strange sequence of events to be noted here. While we were journeying south for the plants, we went north for our rocks even though these islands contain such a diversified collection of native rocks. Our natural rock was not used until several decades later. In fact the one type of plant for which we might have gone north was the alpine or rock plant. Many of them do not necessarily have to come from great heights on the continent. The mountains of Scotland, even the hills of Yorkshire, the coast of Ireland, Iceland and other similar areas provide many of the self-same species. Even so there is no mountain range nor high hill in the Northern or Southern Temperate Zones which does not provide what we call alpine or rock plants; the same is true of a few great heights in countries nearer the equator.

*   *   *   *   *

Napoleon might well have called us a 'nation of shopkeepers and gardeners', so deeply interested were we in all the new plants which had been brought to our shores by his time. It is a stream which has been augmented ever since by exploration, and also by selection and hybridisation. The nation of gardeners loves plants, the beauty of plants, and the spirit of collection and competition.

Gardening is no static occupation. Its devotees are constantly exploring new sources of supply. Until about 1914 garden culture around great houses was much in the hands of the head gardeners. The introduction of the great conifers from North America and the Far East started a new fashion: that of enjoying trees for their own beauty and the excitement of watching them grow and speedily reaching to heights enjoyed in this country hitherto only by the elm. They came to be planted in collections (arboreta) regardless of design and gave the garden owner a means of indulging his gardening desires without much recourse to the garden staff. Likewise a similar enthusiasm prevailed for rhododendrons. To these enthusiasms we can surely add the fernery and the rock garden, which when once their building was completed, provided a hobby and entrancing occupation even for the ladies of the house. In addition, owing to the small size of most of its occupants the rock garden became a popular adjunct for the lesser gardens tended entirely by their owners. In this way has grown up the tremendous enthusiasm for alpine or rock plants – call them what you will – a movement which has given rise to the puissant Alpine Garden Society, the Scottish Rock Garden Club, the American Rock Garden Society, and many other similar groups.

During my life I have watched much of this unabated enthusiasm for alpines waxing ever stronger. Many growers of these plants now devote unheated glass-houses, frames, and raised beds with retaining walls to their treasures. It is a trend towards specialisation, and away from the great art in rock-building which had been achieved. It once again proves that many people are more fond of their plants than the art of displaying them. Hand in hand with this goes of course economics. At this moment the only successor to the upsurge of rock gardening that I can see in the history of garden art in this century is what I may perhaps call the ecological garden, where plants are grown for their own suitable association to avoid excess labour. This is undoubtedly the trend of the last thirty or forty years. On the other hand there is no doubt at all that the art of gardening – as opposed to mere cultivation – never stood higher than it does today. The Hidcote tradition is well to the fore and also the re-creation of parterres. I hope to show in the following pages how the art of using rock in gardens has reached great highlights in the past and how it may prove to be yet another lodestone in the future. The chapters have been simmering in my mind for many years and at last will be brought to boil. During this time I have handled much rock, in many ways, and alpine plants have never been forgotten since boyhood, when I made my first importations of plants from abroad – from British Columbia and Japan.

# 1
# The grotto

There is nothing to tell but how the sunlight is green – filtered and cool with the breath of falling water, how the trail follows the stream up and up, over fallen logs, with the summons of the hidden cascade rushing ever louder in your ears and the sense of green, light-hearted sacrosanct deepening as the rock walls rise.

Donald Culross Peattie, *Flowering Earth*, 1948

It so happened that our western civilisation had its beginnings in comparatively warm countries around the eastern Mediterranean, and that in some of these countries rocks abounded. The fact that the countries were populated was entirely owing to the presence of fresh water from springs and rivers. Water has the power of cutting its way through hardest rock and nowhere is this more obvious than where springs gush forth from some form of limestone, sometimes creating a hollow chamber or cave. Springs of this life-giving element would become hallowed and attributed to a water god, a nymph or Muse, without which life was thought to be pointless. A feeling of reverence and awe descended on those entering the cave. In Crete and Greece, countries of fierce sunshine, this entering into a cave would have been a relief and delight, especially when accompanied by this feeling of reverence: the exclusion of wind and light and the normal activity of one's fellow men, the only sound being the trickling or gushing of water.

Like a garden, as opposed to the regularities of a house, it was an escape from realities, entering a world of make-believe perhaps. (Possibly this is at the back of the minds of some speleologists today.) Man's fertile imagination imbued the cave and spring with divine powers, the seat of an oracle, associated with healing by lavation in the sacred waters. Apart from the other sacred element, fire, water was the starting point of all life from which growth flowed; when it was associated with rocks, cliffs and waterfalls, its influence was magical.

With the Grecian skill of creating beauty out of tooled stone, it is not a far cry from these humble, natural beginnings to realise that a particularly favoured spring might be enlarged into a small temple and suitably adorned in homage to the divinities associated with waters. Long before Moses struck the rock for water, Pegasus' hoof started Hippocrene, the spring on Mount Helicon, which became sacred to the Muses and was referred to by Keats in his *Ode to a Nightingale*. Apart from some of Housman's nostalgic poems, few poets approached so closely and in direct appeal to the unbearable sweet sadness evoked by thoughts free from the turmoil of life.

Elaboration of the buildings grew fast later in Rome where grottoes were a common adjunct of gardens. It was undoubtedly a case of natural beauty transformed by art into a feature of wonder and delight. It is here that we read of the first real divergence: away from natural beauty, art developed either naturalistically or architecturally. The grotto became a thing of surprise and entertainment, especially because many gardens were open to visitors, each carried away by the new 'conceits'. With Venus enthroned in beauty as the goddess of Love, further extravagant ideas were unleashed; she was sometimes depicted as riding on a shell, or posed in an apse with a shell-like overhang. From this, and the association of water, sprang no doubt the notion of decorating grottoes with shells, plucked not so much from fresh water as from the seashore. Not only shells were used for decoration, but all 'outlandish' rocky materials such as coral, lava, pumice and pepperino, spars and glittering mica, marble, tufa and travertine.

This is all rather far from a book which is mainly concerned with rock gardens, but I believe it is fundamental to it. In the time of the Renaissance, Italy was to the fore in the creation of elaborate gardens; elaborate in architectural design, the use of water and the notion of the grotto and all that was allied to it. There was a liberation of the architect to garden buildings and extravagances of all kinds, perhaps epitomised on the Isola Bella. Stone was the god upon which this adoration was lavished, with water and trees its main counterparts: the trees being particularly the vertical cypress and the round-topped pine. If plants of diverse kinds, native or exotic, were grown, they did not enter into the main garden, where design was paramount.

Far from remaining a dark, sacrosanct cave, the grotto assumed ever more extravagant liberation. The rigid geometry of stonework was contrasted not only by the free form of water and trees, but also by fantasies and illusions, jokes and tricks; these originated because hydraulics were now understood. Water was made to perform sometimes to one's discomfort! Thus there was the continued contrast of solemnity and frivolity, coupled with the contrast of stone with flowing water, and rock with foliage. The diversions were carried further, into the theatre. Wanting to add some verification to these generalisations, I was referred by Peter Goodchild to *Daphnis and Chloe*, a translation from the Greek of Longus by Angell Daye. Apart from calling attention to the paucity of appreciation of scenery by the Greeks, this 'novel' of the fifth century or even earlier specifically refers to a cave complete with 'a sweet fountaine, which raising itself, with a softe bubling gathered into a pleasant spring, wherewith the fresh and fruitfull grenes round about the same were continually watered' and 'in the inward part whereof were divers statues of Godesses and other Nimphs wrought finely out of stone'. To put it very briefly the story relates how the 'winged God' (Cupid) united Daphnis and Chloe, and those who had care of them 'agreed to go unto the cave of the nymphs, and there to offer sacrifices, for the better prosperitie and happy proceedings of their severall charges'.

The Italians were the first to introduce statuary into their grottoes. In turn statues were first used in British gardens by the Second Earl of Arundel in the early part of the sixteenth century. From this stems the popular trend today of buying reconstituted stone statuary and ornaments in garden centres – the outcome of visiting stately homes!

1 A water colour entitled *The Stables of the Villa Maecenas*, by Abraham Louis Ducros (1748–1807). It is fairly evident that the water has broken through the rear wall of the Stables, and has caused a collapse of the floor. Thus an accident has provided one of the most awesome effects of the strength of water, as so much admired by the lovers of the extremes of the Picturesque.

*Courtesy: The National Trust*

The Italians absorbed the writings of the ancients and all classical ideas; in their turn the traditions entered France and England, and formality in gardens was the ideal in the seventeenth century. Where grottoes were made they tended to be formal decorated buildings. But a change was on the way and urged on by writers and classical scholars, the English Landscape Garden gradually increased its hold on the great English landowners, and some small ones too. It is generally claimed that Alexander Pope, at Twickenham, created the first grotto in this country during the mid-eighteenth century, and he was one of the foremost in the new movement. His style was somewhat cramped as his plot was small and his grotto an excuse for a tunnel under the road, to open out into a view of the Thames. In spite of the semi-formality of his grotto, Pope was to the fore in a return to nature, giving her full rein; no doubt this was partly as an answer to the overweening Versailles-type of design, which was prevalent in the seventeenth and early eighteenth centuries. During the eighteenth century the English, on their big estates, idealised Italian *scenery* before turning wholeheartedly to the study of nature herself.

While on the continent the grotto and other garden buildings had become what we may call set-pieces, the final eye-catcher of a principal view, the English eye during the eighteenth century became more all-embracing and scorned the direct view. As the century proceeds this becomes the more apparent. We move from the first hesitant essays of Charles Bridgeman through the adaptation of military embankments and ditches to control the views, to William Kent whose softened architectural efforts led the way to the wholehearted naturalism of 'Capability' Brown, and thence to the Picturesque of Repton, Eames and Gilpin.

The triumph of this whole period was not the result of employing a garden designer, but was Henry Hoare's own grotto at Stourhead in Wiltshire, completed in 1748 by a Mr William Privett. Here was melancholy returned, to fit the mood of one who had lost his wife, son and two daughters. He turned to the embellishment of his great landscape for solace, and few can be other than moved by the way that buildings of classical form or the vernacular, the grotto, arches and waterfall, are met in a tour of that magical garden. Grottoes are not, however, to everyone's taste, and the gloom and dampness of the great grotto, inhabited by the traditional Nymph and River God, are far from the light-hearted formal grottoes of the previous century. Here was Nature restored in no small manner. The preparatory rocky arch, the darkness of the overhanging yews, the cavern entrance, the sound of water (from a spring that never fails) gushing around the sleeping nymph and issuing from the god's crock, the view of the lake and the rough steps eventually ascending to the tree-clad slopes are in themselves all a succession of experiences, just as the grotto itself is part of the succession of the landscape pictures. The local stone is rough and irregular and was accentuated by a strange natural waterworn limestone found in the Bath district, pitted with rounded holes of varying size and depth, as if fingers had been stuck into a lump of dough! This has been wrongly ascribed to tufa, a totally different kind of stone.

Pope's famous lines, written in 1731, may well have influenced Henry Hoare, who created Stourhead from 1741. Though they are hackneyed, I repeat them here:

> . . . To swell the terrace, or to sink the grot,
> In all, let nature never be forgot.
> Consult the genius of the place in all,
> That tells the waters or to rise, or fall.
> Or helps the ambitious hill the heavens to scale,
> Or scoops in circling theatres the vale,
> Calls in the country, catches open glades,
> Joins willing woods, and varies shades from shades,
> Now breaks, or now directs, th' intending lines,
> Paints as you plant, and as you work, designs.

In these few lines are all the instructions needed for envisaging an eighteenth-century landscape garden, of which it may be said that Stourhead is a supreme example. Hoare's grandson, Richard Colt Hoare, wrote that in the Stourhead grotto 'we see no finery, no shells, no crystals, no variety of fossils . . . but the native stone forming natural stalactites'.

Other designers did not follow these precepts. Just previous to Stourhead, the Hon. Charles Hamilton had constructed at Pain's Hill in Surrey a fantasy grotto of rough stone ornamented by all manner of exotic shells, spars, corals, etcetera. Many kinds of grottoes were constructed during the century, delight being taken by John Evelyn in the 'chalk grotts' at Cliveden; the cavernous tunnellings in the chalk at West Wycombe also come to mind, whatever their nefarious intentions were.

But, thanks to the exploratory writing of Christopher Thacker in his *Masters of the Grotto*, 1976, we have insight into the lives of two remarkable men, father and son, Joseph and Josiah Lane, both of Tisbury in Wiltshire. From about 1750 for some sixty years these two artists constructed or designed a series of remarkable grottoes in southern England, including Pain's Hill Oatlands (destroyed), Wardour (built above ground), Wimborne St Giles, Bowood, Fonthill and others. Ascot Place may be of their work also and is a true fantasy; with regard to the present grotto at Claremont it is known that the original was altered, and, judging by the similarity of the work and rock at Ascot Place, Temple Combe at Wargrave and

Claremont, I judge all to have been made by the same designer. Sir Walter Scott might be quoted very suitably here:

> Where midst thick oaks the subterranean way
> To the arched grot admits a feeble ray,
> Where glossy pebbles pave the varied floors
> And rough flint walls are decked with shells and ores.

It is significant that southern England – with some enthusiasm as far north as Yorkshire – was chosen for these extravaganzas. It seems to me that there are two reasons, one being the greater prosperity in the London ambience, and another the absence, at least until one reaches Dorset and thence northwards, of natural rock in any great quantity. Even had prosperity allowed it, I doubt whether anyone would have created grottoes where stone and rock abounded as in Wales and West Scotland. There is also the climate to be remembered; grottoes, to be effective, had to be dark and gloomy originally but however this may have been adjusted, a grotto remained a cold, roofed structure suitable as a contrast to sunny climes. The transport of rock was no problem; we know that even in the sixteenth century stone from Yorkshire was brought to Cambridge for college buildings.

A week or two spent finding and exploring grottoes in England would be a rewarding exercise. From tiny compilations of rocks which have a grotto connection, as at Clevedon Court, Somerset, to the neat and decorative niche at Clandon Park and superb Goldney Park there is much to see in the south; our journey would take us also to Curraghmore in Waterford, Ireland, where the owner and originator devoted years to its decoration with thousands on thousands of shells, and to Scotland to see the strange tunnel in the walled garden at Culzean.

Possibly the grotto at Goldney House may be considered as the most elaborate of the semi-formal type. Thomas Goldney inherited a house on a promontory at Clifton, Bristol, overlooking the Severn estuary. One can think of him, perhaps sitting on his 'terras' or in his rotunda in the 1750s, and watching his ships returning to port, hoping for ever greater consignments of exotic shells, until he had accumulated enough to decorate the interior of the roomy grotto and subterranean passage below the terrace. The grotto is absolutely encrusted with shells of every imaginable shape, size and kind, stuck on to the walls and pillars made of native stone. In spite of the decoration it remains a semi-formal series of rooms, complete with cascade and a marble Neptune. Fortunately it is owned by the University of Bristol and viewing is closely time-controlled. Though one has to put up with crowds, this results in safety from vandalism; the one skylight is scarcely enough to reveal all the exotic beauty, and the press of visitors reduces it still more. Neptune, however, has coloured lighting from above and the water is today moved by electricity whereas in the eighteenth century it was pumped by an engine in the adjoining tower. To what great lengths the wealthy went in those autocratic days! The grotto took twenty-seven years to complete, according to Barbara Jones' full account. The rooms are stuck with glittering spar or encrusted with shells wherever the rugged local limestone is not left visible. It is in excellent condition, having been restored recently by a team of experts from Bristol; likewise the marvellous little grotto at Hampton Court House, near Bushey Park, Middlesex. Designed by Thomas Wright

2 Interior of the grotto at Stourhead, Wiltshire, by F. Nicholson. 1813–14. It shows a portion of the Nymph of the Grot on the right, and the River God beyond the arches, both lit from openings in the roof. The walls are of deeply pock-marked waterworn limestone local to the Bath district, sometimes erroneously described as tufa. *Courtesy: The British Museum*

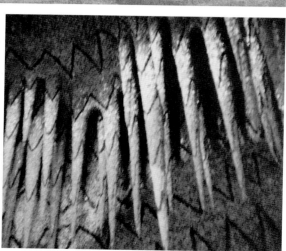

3 (*Left*) Deeply pock-marked limestone in the grotto at Pain's Hill, Surrey.

4 (*Right*) 'Stalactites' formed of laths coated with plaster in the grotto at Ascot Place, Berkshire.

5 Arches of the grotto at Ascot Place, Berkshire. Note the large keystones above each arch. This trick was repeated often, with very large rocks, by James Pulham.

6 (*Above*) The grotto arch within the walled garden at Culzean, Ayrshire.

7 (*Below right*) Goldney Grotto, Bristol. A work of masonry effectively disguised by shells and stones.
*Courtesy: University of Bristol*

8 (*Below left*) Goldney Grotto, Bristol. Restoration of shell-work in 1984.

*Courtesy: University of Bristol*

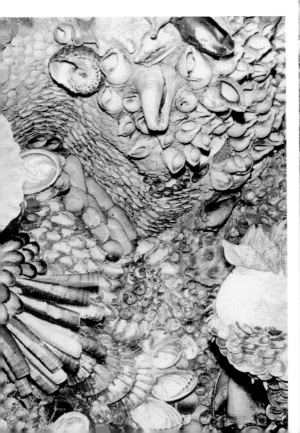

of Durham and built between 1757 and 1767, this was a glittering assembly of shells and corals but had fallen into disrepair. The story of its reclamation, and pictures in colour, appeared in *Country Life*, 18 December 1986; about 40,000 shells were required.

There is great variety among grottoes, but none of greater gloom or magnificence than that at Hawkestone in Shropshire, where an almost vertical cliff rises some two hundred feet from the grassy plain; it is of what is known geologically as Keuper sandstone. A tortuous path, cut in the face of the soft stone of the cliff, brings one to the top and explains the reason for the existence of the cliff: the stone is protected by a cap of much harder stone in the clefts of which grow aged pines. (This natural superimposition of ancient hard stone on top of the even more ancient sandstone is the geological basis upon which Pulham's rugged rockwork was founded a hundred years later.) The grotto itself is vast, a series of caverns and passages of great size, portions of which were once decorated with conventional materials. The contrast between the black caverns and the almost limitless scenery far away and below it are worth a long climb. There are also sham ruins to tempt you. It was all completed by the end of the eighteenth century by Sir Richard Hill.

Imitations of English grottoes were made during the late eighteenth and the nineteenth centuries in France, Germany and Russia. Their construction followed the same trend in fashion by returning to influence gardens on the continent, as did the *jardin anglais* of the previous century. In Germany they were given the most extravagant touch. In general they were looked upon as a variation of the Chinese taste, but imitations even went so far as using cast iron for cement-covered stalactites; in fact woodwork, hung with plaster, had been used at Pain's Hill and Ascot Place to enhance the awesome overhanging cliff-effects.

Early in the nineteenth century it was all over; grotto-making had almost ceased by 1840. This is a convenient date to consider; it was not long before public parks were made for the populace and a grotto would be exactly the opposite to what was thereby intended, i.e. to provide places where the dwellers in close confines of manufacturing cities might take the air. Another competitor had appeared on the scene: the head gardeners had their traditional walled gardens to superintend and to drain their energies, but the owners were discovering the freedom of planting the new great conifers and shrubs which were arriving from abroad ever more freely. This was but part of the new enthusiasm for plants apparent not only in large gardens but also in those of humble city dwellers. One of the great enthusiasms was for ferns, which are considered in the next chapter. Let us therefore use a few paragraphs to look into the Chinese influence.

As early as 1692 Sir William Temple had written about Chinese taste; slowly information about this great country, with so ancient a civilisation, trickled through to Europe. If plants came from there to the Middle East overland via the Silk Route from Tibet to Afghanistan, information must have followed. But Chinese gardening did not really influence England until Sir William Chambers published his *Discourse on Oriental Gardening* in 1772. Gradually since then we have come to know more about Chinese gardens and what prompted them. As with our own much younger civilisation, water was all-important; we find the same worship of it as the female element as in Eastern Mediterranean countries, and particularly in its connection

9 (*Above*) The soft Keuper sandstone cliff at Hawkestone, Shropshire.

10 (*Below right*) At Hawkestone. A drawing of the late nineteenth century by Emma Hill, showing the Castle on Castle Hill, with the steps hewn out of the Keuper sandstone on Grotto Hill (cf. Fig. 11)

*Courtesy: The British Museum*

11 (*Below left*) The path and steps leading up to the face of the cliff at Hawkestone, Shropshire.

12 Two of the arched entrances to the grotto at Hawkestone, Shropshire.

13 The waterfall at Bowood, the construction of which shows an early attempt at rock-stratification.

14 Ramshaw Rocks above the A53 in Derbyshire. It was no doubt this kind of scenic effect which inspired Joseph Paxton.

with caves and deities. Rocks of fantastic shapes were sought, revered and even worshipped as early as the twelfth century. Artificial mountains were built containing grottoes. It is recorded that Kublai Khan, the Mongol Emperor of the thirteenth century, had in his garden rocks of lapis lazuli, to tone with the green of water and trees.

The artificial mounts, grottoes and lakes were fashioned liberally by successive spendthrift rulers and were always totally informal, even when enclosed by a fence, over which distant trees and mountains could be seen and enjoyed. Long before we had started to use rocks in our gardens the Chinese were paying large sums for enormous rocks of fantastic shapes, mostly found in Lake T'ai, west of Shanghai, and in neighbouring districts. So great was the demand for these rocks that when supply ran short, likely limestone rocks were put in the lakes to become water-worn and smoothed.

The Chinese therefore had looked on stone with hallowed eyes for centuries and perhaps we may say created the first gardens of rocks. Their aesthetic appeal is more than a religious one. Much-prized rocks are set on end as an ornament in a courtyard; masses of them are joined and juxtaposed to give the effect of wild scenery; more sober blocks are used, often in simulated stratification, around lakes and streams. Everywhere they dominate their position, with a tuft of grass, shaped tree or bamboo as softening contrast, or standing where their shadows create a startling effect of fantasy and grandeur on a wall. It is amusing to read that in the late eighteenth century one emperor had some Europeans make for him a European folly, but this appears to be the sole example of a formal grotto in China. The Chinese taste was indeed only partially accepted in England. Let me quote from *Parks and Pleasure Grounds* (1852) by Charles H. J. Smith: 'Rockworks are pleasing objects when well executed. It is a very great error to construct them of all the curious, rugged, weatherworn stones that can be collected from the sea shore or the bed of a river'!

Dorothy Graham, in her book *Chinese Gardens*, has some highly relevant sentences: 'The intimate Chinese garden started twenty centuries ago. The idea of a garden was landscape reproduced in miniature.... The Chinese ideal remains unchanged. To turn aside from the current of life, to seek solitude for the refreshment of the soul.... Landscape became an obsession with the Chinese because each man perceived the problems of his own experience reflected in nature. To fortify his character he studied the time-worn rocks, the wind-bent trees....'

It was not to be long before the English vogue for the Picturesque, derived in part from the Chinese influence, left the dark and dank grotto and came out into the open. Josiah Lane had built by the end of the eighteenth century the grotto and great compound waterfall at Bowood, Wiltshire. Made of quarried local rock it has little pretence at geological exactitudes of stratification but provides perhaps our first glimpse of it. The whole *raison d'être* is the damming of Capability Brown's extensive lake and using the outpouring water to pass grotto arches and gush in a variety of falls some thirty to forty feet to a stream which disappears underground. Masses of rock were used to create the semblance of the water having caused the declivity to be made, but a glance soon shows that, as intimated above, the waterfall was the main object, not the creation of natural rockwork. Some three-quarters or so of the imported rock is built into small cliffs, walls and grots regardless of its stratification. The Picturesque reigns supreme, and certainly achieves a spectacle of importance when there is no shortage of water from the lake. As a gesture to his main life's work Lane provided a small cavern or grotto above the fall, and the fall itself is a construction of considerable ingenuity embracing ledges and small overhanging precipices to augment the spectacular gushing water. It is perhaps the largest and most 'natural' of artificial waterfalls in England.

Next we have an even more English creation – a direct imitation of nature. Above the great cascade at Chatsworth are many rocks of great size brought down from the hills above. In most of the literature they are usually described as Cyclopean, but they are certainly not 'one-eyed'! The giant cliffs, buttresses and promontories look out in every direction. They were built by Joseph Paxton in the second quarter of the nineteenth century and while they do not create an actual grotto, they have the illogical abandon of rockwork associated with grottoes and hence their inclusion here. As with those at Bowood and at Biddulph Grange, the niceties of geological stratification are mainly ignored; the desire of Paxton seems to be like that of most of the rest of his highly original endeavours, to be bigger and better. There is no doubt that his work at Chatsworth with rocks on the hillside has scarcely been equalled and certainly not surpassed in its awe-inspiring grandeur. He was obviously of the same mind as Salvator Rosa. As if this were not enough for his genius, he also erected in the grand conservatory which he created with so much verve and originality a towering grotto (alas, like the glasshouse itself, now gone) complete with waterfalls and attendant palm trees, bananas, rhododendrons and other shrubs. On a visit by Queen Victoria and Prince Albert after daylight the whole scene was lit by fairylights. Thanks to the Duke of Devonshire's generous inclinations, this wonderful creation was open to the public, free. There is no doubt that the visitors, totalling over 50,000 annually for fifty years, must have had a profound effect upon artificial gardening in this country alone. Paxton deliberately dwelt upon the scenic effect of the gigantic millstone grit boulders on the upper slopes of the garden, whereas it was the plants which were the main attraction under glass. There can be no doubt whatever that he was captured by the towering fangs and ledges which in that part of Derbyshire dominate the high ground with their gloomy magnificence. In fact in Paxton's *Magazine of Botany*, volume XII, 1844, there is an article on the use of rock in the garden. Here I will only quote the portion that applies to the Picturesque, where the rocks 'are . . . designed as imitations of the natural features of a wild and rugged scene . . . to copy the most picturesque assemblages of natural rock. . . . For, where a great thing is attempted – and a great thing it is to copy well the wild forms of natural rock – unless the means and material employed be perfectly adequate to, and in harmony with, the object attempted, the result must be puerile, and an effectual display of the impotence of the contriver. All the vegetation, moreover, which accompanies an extensive rockery [*sic*] should be subordinate to it.' In spite of its date I am able to bring in this inspiration of Paxton's in this chapter because millstone grit has little obvious stratification. One wonders what he would have done with the limestone of Yorkshire and Westmorland.

One of the most remarkable essays in rockwork in the country, very much of the Picturesque taste, is at Sezincote in Gloucestershire. The hillside has several

15 The giant rocks at
Chatsworth,
Derbyshire,
engraved for the
Art Journal,
c. 1851. Built by
Joseph Paxton.
*Courtesy: Trustees
of the Chatsworth
Settlement*

16 Paxton's rocks at
Chatsworth,
Derbyshire, in
1986.
*Courtesy: Trustees
of the Chatsworth
Settlement*

17 A painting by
Thomas Daniell,
R.A., of 1819,
entitled *Sezincote
Park*. Note the
giant rocks on the
right, placed in
awe-ful majesty.
They are still
exactly in place.

20 (*Above*) The Wellington rock and cascade engraved c. 1851, built by Joseph Paxton, at Chatsworth, Derbyshire.
*Courtesy: Trustees of the Chatsworth Settlement*

18 (*Below left*) Paxton's Wellington rock and cascade at Chatsworth, Derbyshire, in 1986. The masonry wall is obliquely tooled to resemble natural stratification.
*Courtesy: Trustees of the Chatsworth Settlement*

19 (*Below right*) Biddulph Grange, Staffordshire; entrance to the grotto tunnel.

21 (*Above*) Grotto and rock arch composed of Hertfordshire 'pudding stone' at Ashridge, Hertfordshire, by Humphry Repton, c. 1814. (cf. Fig. 28).

*Courtesy: Susan Gaze*

22 (*Right*) This little grotto, from *The Flower Garden* of 1838 by Charles M'Intosh, is a successful exposition of rock, water and imagination.

23 (*Below*) Fantastic compilation of limestone rocks to create a water feature in the Chinese taste at Oakworth Park, Keighley, Yorkshire.

*Courtesy: Maurice Baring*

springs, one of which has been used to create, with large pieces of local limestone, a series of waterfalls and pools. An engraving of 1819 (see Fig. 17) shows great restraint and devotion to the trees, rock, water and a few plants which help to indicate the Indian undertone of the whole delightful property. It is attributed to Thomas Daniell, though it may well be that Humphry Repton was consulted. During the last three-quarters of a century the stream-garden – or Thornery as it is called – has been enriched by modern planting. The rocks are used for effect and the major pieces have never been disturbed or altered. At the top is a small grotto of rough stones with three niches or caverns. In spite of its date this whole effort belongs, I feel, to the grotto era and not really to its successor, that of the true rock garden. In addition, the facts of geological stratification had scarcely been observed; that was to come later in the century.

At about the same time Repton was designing the garden at Ashridge, Hertfordshire. It suffices for this book to say that he created a grotto and rock bank composed of conglomerate or Hertfordshire Puddingstone, a natural stone formed by coarse gravel, imitated by Pulham at Bearwood, as I have recorded in the next chapter.

Finally I think we might look at a major work of 1842, namely Biddulph Grange, Staffordshire, before considering the immense output of words of counsel in books and magazines which poured out during the first fifty years of the nineteenth century – and indeed continued thereafter unchecked – about rock gardens.

The garden at Biddulph is one of the most remarkable in the country. James Bateman built his house in 1842 and made his garden in some 15 acres of rather swampy ground on the Knypersley estate, his father's property. By dint of moving soil into banks and heaps and planting shrubs, he divided the garden into several distinct compartments, thus antedating Hidcote by more than half a century. Only one portion of the garden was seen at one time – terrace, Egyptian garden, Chinese garden, lakes, rockwork and arboretum. We are only concerned here with the rockwork, which is of giant proportions complete with grotto arches. Very large pieces of local dark sandstone are used, scattered around in seeming abandon. But the more one examines the groupings the more one realises the artistry that has resulted in this array of caverns, precipices and arches. One particularly interesting feature occurs several times: some of the largest vertical rocks appear to have been split into two pieces, horizontally, and then fitted together again. There is also considerable use of tufa.

With its many features – and the surprising Indian buffalo above one's head – Biddulph takes a high place among gardens of grotto-character. It also creates a connecting link with this chapter and chapters 3 and 4.

Perhaps the Reverend Gilbert White may be allowed to have the last words to this chapter:

> Whence is this taste, the furnish'd hall forgot,
> To feast in gardens, or th' unhandy grot?
>
> *Invitation to Selborne*, c. 1765

# 2
# Ferneries, 'rockwork' and Mr Pulham

Rocks are generally considered as parts of the foundation of the
earth and their general character is that of grandeur, sometimes
mixed with the *singular, fantastic* or *romantic*. Their expression forms
a fine contrast to that of perishable vegetation and therefore they
have been eagerly sought after in gardens, both on this account and
as forming a suitable habitation for certain descriptions of plants.
Plant-rockworks are protuberant surfaces, or declivities irregularly
covered with rocky fragments, land-stones, conglomerated gravel,
vitrified bricks, vitrified scoriae, flints, shells, spar, or other earthy
or hard mineral bodies.

J. C. Loudon, *An Encyclopaedia of Gardening*, 1825

Even before the Prince Consort lent his considerable drive and enthusiasm to
the promotion of the study of the sciences and arts in the middle of the
nineteenth century, Loudon's incredible industry had enabled him to publish
his encyclopaedia. It gave insight and instruction into every sphere of gardening,
the science, the art and the hobby. With the cheapened printing and production of
books, an appeal was made not only to the professional gardeners, but to the rising
middle classes. They were educated people who thirsted for new knowledge and
engendered a spirit of competition among themselves, quite apart from the nobility
and landed gentry. The collecting spirit developed greatly during the century.
Books of pressed seaweeds, drawers and shelves of birds' eggs, shells, butterflies and
the like were equalled by the new enthusiasm for ferns. These were admirably
adapted, like the seaweeds, for drying and pressing. But the new enthusiasm among
ladies for gardening had a strong leaning towards not only collecting, but also
growing, ferns.

The collecting of ferns seems to me to follow quite naturally on the discovery
of the Picturesque in the previous century. Ferns in this country grow mostly in
the woods and stream-valleys and among rocks. Their collection took the seekers
into just those places which were a delight to see and no doubt awakened many
eyes to the beauty and savagery of rocky and mountainous scenery. The connection
with the grotto is thus most pronounced with this little section of gardening, which
grew suddenly to extreme enthusiasm and proportions for about thirty-five years,
until its collapse during the early 1900s. Meanwhile many big and small books on

ferns and fern culture had appeared. The recipe for growing ferns in gardens is the same in all of them – the use of loose soil and humus piled upon and worked between broken bricks in a shady or partly shaded place. As late as 1879 James Britten in his *European Ferns* claimed that 'There is probably no group of plants which has more numerous or more enthusiastic admirers than the fern tribe ... moreover they can be grown with the greatest ease in the back garden of a London house'. This was an inexpensive hobby: there was no costly spar or other material to be imported. Further, the collecting together of British ferns was a conveniently small hobby because only about seventy species are native to Britain.

Fern collectors scoured the country for every species and aberrant form that could be found; whole districts were denuded of one species or another and unscrupulous vendors cleared up what the amateurs had left.

It was, however, the age when foreign plants were being brought into cultivation ever more freely, and many foreign ferns were too tender to grow in the open air in this country. The enthusiasm spread to greenhouses; gentle or generous warmth – in cool houses or 'stove' – made ideal controllable conditions for tender ferns. It was all very well for the head gardeners to grow them in ranks, according to size, in pots on benches, but I think the extraordinarily satisfying contrast between the delicate filigree of fern and the solidity of rocks soon led to rockwork being made to present a raised bed and to show one kind above or below another.

As an aside, connected with ferns, we may note that while greenhouses were rich men's hobbies, due to the heavy tax on glass, this tax was removed in 1845 – and coal was cheap. Everything seems to have played into the development of gardening connected with rocks and stones – though this was only one little effect within the whole of horticulture, which among professional gardeners and amateurs alike was to experience a boom until 1914. The beauty and delicacy of ferns had taken a hold on gardeners just when the pursuit of gardening in general was due to reach its most vulgar and ostentatious forms, typified by carpet-bedding.

Mr N. A. Hall, writing in *Garden History*, Spring 1983, recalls the firm of W. & J. Birkenhead of Sale, near Manchester, which in 1888 listed no less than 1400 species and varieties of ferns, both hardy and tender. In the same town, at the same time, F. W. & H. Stansfield made 'a speciality of British Ferns of which our collection is without a rival in the Trade'. Even as late as 1914, H. B. May & Sons Ltd of Edmonton, who had taken over the Birkenhead collection in 1910, listed many hundreds of British fern varieties. Though longer in its duration than the Dutch tulip mania, and without its commercial overtones, this passing delectation for ferns has its only parallel in England perhaps in the much longer and all-absorbing enthusiasm for auriculas and gooseberries.

Though fern collecting as a hobby gradually declined, the construction of rockwork for ferneries continued until well into the last quarter of the nineteenth century in England. This was due almost entirely to Mr James Pulham. It was his imagination and industry that resulted in his firm's work which for fifty years and more provided the link between the Sublime and Picturesque of the eighteenth century, through the vogue for ferns, ferneries and rockwork, to the rock gardens and all that pertains to the culture of alpine plants today.

24 Imitation rockwork
   by James Pulham &
   Sons in Battersea
   Park, London. The
   'rock' was first built
   with pieces of
   concrete, broken
   bricks, clinker etc.
   and then carefully
   covered with a
   cement mixture,
   being brushed,
   fingered and tooled
   to represent natural
   rock. Built between
   1868 and 1876, from
   *The Garden*, 1873.
   *Courtesy: Royal
       Horticultural Society*

25 The same outcrop
   today. One of the
   characteristics of
   Pulham's work was
   the naturalistic
   weaker stratum under
   the heavier rocks.
   Battersea Park.

26 Tufa built against a
   fernery wall at
   Lessness, Belvedere,
   Kent.
   *Courtesy: Royal
       Horticultural Society*

Like the present author, Pulham attributes much of his efforts to a love of geology from his school days. In his commercial booklet – hard covers and gilt edges – printed to interest and educate his potential clients of the future after only twenty-eight years of work in gardens up and down the country (from Sandringham, Battersea Park and Fonthill Abbey down to tiny villa gardens) he wrote:

> I was brought up as an architectural modeller, etc., succeeding my father; I have made [architecture] a study, as essential to success, and hence also I acquired practical experience in the use of various cements, so necessary to ensure durability.

This is the crux of the matter concerning Pulham's efforts: the new very hard and durable 'Portland' cement had only been known and generally used since 1840. However great his ingenuity and artistry might have been, he owed all his initial success to cement, as might be inferred from the title of his little publication *Picturesque Rock Garden Scenery, Ferneries etc.* or *The Pulhamite System of forming Rocks*, c. 1877. Pulham's father, also named James, had been connected with the firm of Lockwood who had pioneered the manufacturing of Portland cement. (It was so named from its resemblance to the Portland stone, *primus inter pares* among native rocks.) It was our James Pulham who started the firm of Pulham and Son at Broxbourne, Hertfordshire, in 1820 which finished in 1939, at which time the address was at Elsenham near Bishop's Stortford, also in Hertfordshire. There was a London office in Newman Street, off Oxford Street. The third Pulham, Mr J. R., was for many years honorary secretary to the Horticultural Club, London, and I came across him as a consequence from time to time. They were Royal Warrant holders to King Edward VII and King George V and the expertise had resulted in a lucrative business. Much of this information was given to me by Mrs William Robinson, Mr Pulham's daughter, but Dr W. Brent Elliott has also supplied some in his article in *Country Life*, 5 January 1984. This followed on a visit with him to Merrow Grange near Guildford, Surrey, where I first introduced him to Pulhamite Stone.

There is no doubt whatever that this long-standing business had much effect on the building of rock gardens in this country, for in many of their later works the firm used natural stone. There is also no doubt about the sort of rockery extant through the country when the firm started. To quote from their booklet again:

> In Kew Gardens, the chief rock-work to be seen is composed of bits of old building stones, burrs, lumps of brick-work, and a very few small bits of rough stone packed up, forming sloping banks – that is for hardy ferns and Alpines – and connected with a ridiculous artificial ruin.

Some of Pulham's more extensive works contained grottoes, as at Madresfield Court, Worcestershire, but whatever the aim, they always strove after the eighteenth-century ideal of the rugged and the Picturesque.

> To those who do not appreciate the beauty of picturesque scenery, I may venture to say it is because they have not a taste for such: for it is where rocks most abound that the artist loves to dwell, the admirer of nature and tourist delight to ramble.

He quotes from Wordsworth:

There is a spot, as you may know,
If ever you to Langdale go:
Into a chasm a mighty block
Hath fallen and made a bridge of rock.

The gulf is deep below
Worn by the force of water so,
And in a basin, black and small,
Descends a lofty waterfall.

None having a taste for the picturesque, can travel through our lovely valleys, as the Derwent, Wye, Dove, Severn, Dart, Tamar, Dee – sometimes passing over rivers, chasms, or between high cliffs, without feeling emotions of the sublime, in admiring the charming variety of the landscape, varying from the lovely sylvan beauty to the romantic, in its varying degrees of change and sublimity; in the magnificent effects of the rock, the beautiful windings of the rivers . . . ; so unlike the serpentine form, or line of Hogarth's system of beauty, too often adopted, making artificial streams of parallel width.

. . . Ivy clad ruins form another element of the picturesque, and can be and are so closely imitated as to be apparently real. They may be built of the same kind of stone as the rocks of the locality, where there are such, on a plateau of elevated rocks. At the same time these ruins are a very convenient means of concealing unsightly walls or other objects near or distant . . . a ruin of a tower may enclose a water cistern above a small room . . . the ground floor may serve as a garden retreat, tool house, stable etc. . . .

As to appearance, those who know the effect of bold projections and depth of shadow will understand that it is the same in architecture: there must be the projection to produce light and shade.

By this naturalistic system of forming rocks, we try to avoid doing anything contrary to nature or to what is consistent with geology, to appear natural and possible, so as to have the appearance of natural ferneries, etc. altogether different to ordinary rock-work, which is generally called rockery, sometimes made of clinkers; hard refuse from gas-works, etc., holds no moisture, so needful to the well-being of plants. Sometimes pieces of stone are set up on end to make a lot of pinacles [*sic*], or any way that seems to fit best. In this Cockney tea-garden style of arches, mounds, circular rustic ponds, waterfalls – often like mill-weirs, etc. – are made formal and smooth, instead of irregular and rugged, as in nature.

But it was just this rough, waste material coupled with bricks – and slates for recessed stratifications – that Pulham found ideal to form his artificial outcrops, so deceptively like the real thing:

Where no real stone or rock exists, or too expensive to get it to the place, it may be artificially formed on the spot, with burrs, rough bricks, or concrete for the core, which is then covered with cement, to imitate the colour, form and texture of the real rock as of red, yellowish, grey or brown sandstone; also limestone and tufa, whichever is desired or most consistent with the geology of the district.

Where the ground rises sufficiently to form a rock-cliff, a cavernous recess may be made for a boat-house, with landing-place on the rock, as at Sandringham, Denmark Hill, Westerham, Champion Hill, Darlington, etc., thus making an interesting feature. . . . Mr Broderick Thomas says, writing me from Sandringham, of the boat-cave thus formed there ''Tis quite a work of art; "picturesque art" the editor of the *Art*

*Journal* calls it'.... The rocks should all be consistent with natural formations, to imitate
something wonderful, interesting, grand, curious, or beautiful in nature, combining the
elements of picturesque beauty of landscape scenery – of rock, wood and water – as
real waterfalls, caves, rocky-streams, cliffs, etc., ... to be overgrown by the ferns,
Alpines, and other rock plants, as much as can be required: indeed, so much, that after
a few years to need cutting away, to shew the rock beneath, as at Highnam, Hutton,
Taplow, Fonthill, Lockinge, Southgate, etc., being so much overgrown.

How far I have succeeded in this picturesque art, as Mr S. C. Hall terms it, I beg to
invite your inspection of some of the works, executed during the last twenty-five
years, many of them under the difficulties enumerated of adapting it to places ill prepared
for it. To do all this well, a staff of men have been instructed and grown up in it, many
from their youth, and it must be so, for only those will do who have been found to
have some taste for this kind of work ... it is rare to find a brick-layer or plasterer
who understands the proper use of cements, though most of them think they know ...
anyone who thinks they do, should test their knowledge by trying to stick twenty
bricks flat, one before the other, against a wall, which the writer has done successfully....
I invariably supply the cement (then I am enabled to guarantee the durability), some
of which I have manufactured especially for the purpose.... The soil taken out may be
used to form undulations on either side, giving more depth and effect:

> To appear as if primeval earthquake's sway
> Had rent a shattered circuitous way
> Through the rude bosom of the hill,
> Telling of the great convulsion still.

These four lines Mr Pulham attributes to Byron, but he could not avoid adding a
couplet himself:

> Making charming nooks for cosy bowers,
> To grow the ferns, heaths, and Alpine flowers.

It is astonishing what spendid masses some Alpines, usually so insignificant in pots,
make when planted in nooks and corners of rock-work, where, small as they are, they
often become too large for the places assigned to them.

Mr William Robinson's excellent work, *Alpine Flowers* will be found very instructive
and interesting; giving descriptions of hundreds of varieties, and the mode of
cultivation. Until these came out, little was heard of Alpines; hence the question asked
by some, What are they?

These extensive quotations show to what detail the firm went in their specialised
subject. The quotations merely refer to the firm's first twenty-eight years.

One particularly impressive covered fern house, heated by pipes under a mosaic
walk, and connected with outlying rockwork and tunnels, is at Merrow Grange,
near Guildford. It was built by Pulham for Francis Baring-Gould about 1907. A
smaller version is at Old Warden, Bedfordshire.

Work alongside the lake at Sandringham, Norfolk, and also around the lake at
St James's Park, London, is on a similar scale. That at Sandringham was constructed
between 1868 and 1876 and includes a boathouse, whereas there are two islands in
St James's Park much loved by the pelicans in summer.

These examples are, however, completely dwarfed by three others which I have
seen: at Bearwood, Wokingham; Madresfield Court, Worcestershire, and in London

at Battersea Park. All three are of very large proportions and were wonderfully conceived and constructed essays in the Sublime. The earthworks alone are a monument to the imagination because they are on initially flat ground, while the extent of the 'works', with the main outcrops, caves, streams etc. are echoed in an appealing way by outlying groups of rocks decreasing in size the farther they are from the stupendous centres. Stupendous is not an extravagant word to use, for the divergence between depth and height may be some 30 feet, and the rocks may measure 10 feet in height and width. All of this was done, of course, by hand, so to speak, no earth-moving equipment being then available. The fact that the examples at Madresfield Court and Bearwood are now rather overgrown with vegetation matters little; though Pulham's choice plants have gone, the overgrowth merely makes them appear to be even more natural than they were. At Battersea, at the time of writing, the site is overrun by children, the 'rocks' are being worn away and the clinker and brick are becoming evident, though I hear news of its restoration. This great effort is meant to strike awe from across the lake which is now stagnant because the engine for pumping the water is out of use. Water occurs as a stream through the Bearwood construction, though in a limited way. There is no doubt that these and maybe other examples are of national importance, representing a unique achievement.

Only a firm which had made such a study of geology through the country could have applied their findings to such expert representations of nature. In fact it was an abortive beginning to the art of rock-building, which later was awakened by John Wood with real and naturally weathered stone in and after 1900. Phase one of our increasing delight at growing alpines in 'natural' rock settings had begun. This phase is reserved for chapter 4.

Even so a further word about the firm of Pulham must be written. Their work, like that of any other pioneer, had detractors. Some correspondence in the *Journal of Horticulture, Cottage Gardener and Country Gentleman* of 1872 denigrated the use of artificial rock, but Pulham triumphantly replied. Indeed, in another article Pulham's work at Battersea Park in the late 1860s was eulogised. It is sad that there is no catalogue of their work after 1877 when some of their biggest contracts were completed; the Madresfield Court work dates from 1877–1880. *The Gardeners' Magazine* of 1888, conducted by Shirley Hibberd and others, praises this work to the full: 'This is a noble construction in agreement throughout with the characteristics of the new red sandstone or triassic. The imitation is so perfect that we have to assure ourselves of its artificiality, the great blocks being admirably modelled.'

It is obvious from some of the quotations above that the Pulham firm had studied nature in various parts of England, and also that they were extremely careful to make something that would last. In fact durability was *guaranteed*. Seeing some of these creations today makes one realise how successful they were aesthetically and geologically, and they were also permanent. It is only occasionally that a slight flaw or chip reveals the brick or other material so skilfully covered. Covered, that is, not by simply pouring a slurry of tinted cement mixture over the foundation, but by fingering, tooling, brushing the surface, and by other techniques, to make them so deceptive that a visitor to one of their great works at Brighton Aquarium (now unhappily gone) remarked that the stone used was the Old Red Sandstone. And

27 (*Left*) Pulham's imitation rock-work at Madresfield Court, Malvern, Worcestershire. Note the large pieces of rock perched over the opening and the tooling to represent a stratum of shale. Constructed in 1878.

28 (*Below*) The Pulham imitation rock-work at Bearwood, Wokingham, Berkshire. Besides the typical overhanging strata, this effort shows a thick stratum of falsified conglomerate stone, effectively finished with river gravel. (cf. Fig. 21).

he was 'a gentleman of the British Association', says Mr Pulham, triumphantly!

Up to about 1877 many of the grottoes and rock gardens contained ferneries, or were principally made for ferns. Listed are numerous British and European ferns and their varieties, both large and small. Little aspleniums for small crevices; *Osmunda cinnamomea* and *Onoclea sensibilis* from North America, several forms of polystichums, polypodies, hartstongues, are recommended. It is surprising to find three special small ferns included: *Asplenium marinum*, which I know to my cost will only grow within smell of the sea; *Hymenophyllum tunbridgense* and the Parsley Fern. The hymenophyllum or Filmy Fern will only grow in dark damp caves and I know it was established at one time in the small dripping cavern on the Wisley rock garden, one of the few portions left of the Pulham creation of 1911. As to the Parsley Fern, *Cryptogramma crispa*, this grows by the million in North Wales in slaty and shaly banks but disappears abruptly where limestone occurs. For years my old friend A. T. Johnson in North Wales had tried to grow it, finding it usually failed after a few years, until he observed how its roots were frequently nine inches or more down between slates. Planted so, it flourished, also in my garden in Surrey.

Although Pulham was so devoted to his geology, he loved his plants. Sometimes, creating a wild effect he would use little but ferns, sedges, rushes, grasses, wild arums, acanthuses, *Eryngium bromeliaefolium*, small bulbs and the like, with *Aspidistra lurida* in sheltered spots. Elsewhere in perhaps sunnier rock gardens places would be found for many alpine plants, soldanellas, pyrolas, *Philesia*, *Berberidopsis corallina*, *Oxalis lobata*, *Cyananthus lobatus*, *Schizostylis coccinea*, cortusas and pulmonarias, aubrietas, *Epigaea repens* and even *Eritrichium nanum*! Also listed by them is *Reineckia carnea foliis var.*, and *Tritoma (Kniphofia) burchellii fol. var.*, both of which I should like to find somewhere today.

It was Pulham's contention that their kind of construction of rockwork, with its skeleton framework, allowed them to make plenty of rooting places, whereas had they used gigantic rocks which they simulated, it would have been necessary for these rocks to have been anchored far into the soil to balance the dramatic projections which he loved.

Reverting to an earlier paragraph, where local stone was available, the Pulhams used it. A good example is at Waddesdon, Buckinghamshire, where good Portland limestone was uncovered when the top of the hill was levelled for the approach drives and house. The construction of the imitation outcrop and cave are unmistakably in the Pulham *genre*. The main waterfall at Sheffield Park, Sussex, has a foundation of native Sussex sandstone which was augmented by further rocks, quarried locally, by Pulham. Later the National Trust commissioned Mr Ian G. Walker to extend the rockwork in the late 1970s. Mr Walker was one of the few great rock builders who may be said to have revered more the effect of the rocks themselves than the plants concerned.

Thus had the overtones of the Picturesque and the Sublime been carried into the twentieth century. Though we shall take a step backwards in chapter 4 to the earliest phase of the art of rock gardening, the progress went hand in hand with the special delight of cultivating alpine plants. Before we consider this hobby it will be as well, I think, to delve a little into geology, so that we have some knowledge of the origin of the rock or stone which we shall contemplate using – what we can do with it and indeed what it can do for us.

29 (*Left*) Part of the rock garden at Wisley, constructed in 1911 by Pulham & Sons. The main material was Sussex sandstone; the shelving rocks, so typical of their work, was of Bargate sandstone from Surrey. *Courtesy: Royal Horticultural Society*

30 (*Below*) Pulham's work at Blakesley Hall, Northamptonshire, showing the characteristic stratum of shaly rock underlying the bolder strata. From an old postcard by Judge's. The garden is now overgrown with weeds.

31 (*Right*) The cave at Wisley in 1911, wherein Filmy Ferns used to grow. Constructed by Pulham & Sons.
*Courtesy: Royal Horticultural Society*

32 (*Below*) The shelving Bargate Sandstone today; (cf. Fig. 30).

33 (*Above*) Portland stone, quarried on the spot at Waddesdon Manor, Buckinghamshire, and used by Pulham & Sons with their usual aplomb, with receded weaker strata.
*Courtesy: The National Trust, Waddesdon*
*Manor*

34 The cave at Wisley today.

# 3
# The origins of the rocks

A rounded time-worn shoulder of granite thrust itself through the
grass a little way off down the field: a bit of the body of the earth
lying unchanged and uncommunicating beneath the changing
vesture of tree and grass. A pair of chaffinches were flirting upon
it, uttering their glad little cry, *spink, spink, spink,* the busy transient
creatures, wearing out their brief living upon that fragment of the
huge under-lying inertia that had seen and would see many of their
kind come and go.

Howard Spring, *The Houses in Between,* 1970

This country was in the van of geological exploration and classification in the
late eighteenth and through the nineteenth centuries so it is perhaps appropriate that a British book about rock gardens should have a chapter devoted
to geology. To support this I may mention that my father, while at school in about
1875, drew a geological map of Britain which I still possess.

Most countries have rock in them somewhere; in Britain they are concentrated
mainly in the west and north. There is no shortage of rocks in certain parts of Italy,
nor in France, and of course in Italy and Greece is found that most prized of all
rocks – marble. It was formed by the pressure exerted on limestone by the intrusion
of hot magma. Magma is generally considered to be more or less fluid material that
pushes up through volcanoes and other world-crust disturbances; an example is the
granite of Cornish tors. Marble is therefore a very precious and specialised kind of
rock in more ways than one. Like the timber of Linden or Lime trees used for its
close smooth grain by that master-carver Grinling Gibbons in the late seventeenth
and early eighteenth centuries, marble takes most kindly to the chisel and polishing.
In its whitest state it gleams in the sunshine but in cooler, duller climates it
can appear cold and lifeless. Our nearest approach to this classic white limestone
is the coloured or tinted Purbeck 'marble', in reality an ordinary sedimentary
limestone, capable of taking a polish. Purbeck marble, full of fossils, can be seen in the
vestibules of the Festival Hall, London. But no polished marble is suitable for use
out of doors. Some of our coarser, duller limestones, and also sandstones,
appear to be more permanent in our climate and they certainly are best as a
background for plants.

Let us begin at the beginning. It is estimated that it has taken as much as four
thousand five hundred million years for the world to reach its present state; we
know from its still occurring subterranean rumblings that the process is not

complete. Indeed, in addition to volcanoes and earthquakes, coasts are being eroded year by year, and mountain ranges decrease in size, their stones being carried away by rivers to the sea. During this unimaginably long span of time, what we call the 'crust' of the earth has been hardening and settling, but in a confused way. Risings and sinkings of the land (whether under the sea or dry) and extremes of cold and heat have alternated, rivers have come and gone, and what we call continents have shifted; at least they have altered shape again and again. The extreme force and power of water-flow is undoubtedly shown best in the Grand Canyon in Colorado, some four hundred miles in length, and from four thousand to seven thousand feet deep. It has cut through layer after layer of rock amounting to at least seven hundred million years of sedimentary deposit. Recently we have had small disasters from mud and water at Lynton in Devon; another occurred in 1985 at Watsonville, California. Frost is very damaging to exposed, somewhat soft rock, as in the screes at Wastdale, Cumbria, and Eglwyseg in North Wales. From all this it is obvious that rocks are 'mortal' like ourselves.

If we look at a map of Britain the Great Glen in Scotland from Mull to the Moray Firth is conspicuous. In studying the rock formations throughout the country, more or less parallel oblique lines crop up again and again (such as the Menai Straits), despite the multiple foldings of rocks and their superimposition onto others. In fact, leaving Scotland somewhat in the wings as it were – though not forgotten – we can take our best look at British geological irregularities by journeying at least in thought at right angles to the Great Glen or Caledonian 'rift', from Anglesey to Kent. Practically all the different rocks, clays, gravels and sands are visible somewhere along this line.

The oldest rocks lie mainly along the entire west coast of Britain. They, the igneous rocks, basalt, granite and their derivatives, form much of the higher mountains and also obtrude in the Malvern Hills, the vertical stratification of the Long Mynd and the Wrekin. We may visualise these ancient rocks being pushed up by alternate shrinkings and expansions of the 'crust' of the world, through the waters of the earth and later through what had accumulated above them – the first sedimentary rocks – which were derived from particles broken from the ancient igneous rocks by wind and water, frost and ice and deposited elsewhere. It was this huge tilting of our western seaboard mountains that not only pushed through the younger rocks but in general caused a tilting of the whole land downwards to the east. In North America rocks of a comparable period are those composing the Appalachian Mountains; red sandstones and many carboniferous strata occur.

Of these igneous rocks only granite is ever used for rock gardens, and even then only rarely, though we must bear in mind that any local rock may be used for *rockeries*. A rock garden, or garden of rocks, is something more deliberate and artful than a mere pile of pieces of rock on a mound or bank. Figure 35 shows a natural outcrop of vertical well-weathered granite on St Michael's Mount, Cornwall. It is in granite that the glass-like mica occurs, which provided 'glitter' for grottoes and was used for the first miniature windows. Particularly grey granite is quarried near Aberdeen and that of a reddish hue at Peterhead farther north, and also at Borrowdale in the Lake District. Granite is also found in many of the eastern parts of the United States and in California.

35 (*Above left*) Granite, split and moulded vertically by the weather, on St Michael's Mount, Cornwall.
  *Courtesy: P. R. Miles*

36 (*Above right*) An outcrop of granite in North Wales. It will be noted that the joints follow no regular pattern except for somewhat vertical splitting, but there is superb form in each boulder.

37 (*Right*) A tiny quarry in shaly rock near Talycafn, North Wales, with almost vertical strata. This photograph is included because it would serve as a model for a miniature rock garden and pool if built with different rock.

38 (*Right*) New Red Sandstone, exposed and weathered but not glacier-worn, between Shrewsbury and Oswestry, Shropshire.

# Scotland and Ireland

Turning now to Scotland and Ireland, the same lines of rock from north-east diagonally to south-west are still apparent. The outermost north-west portions of the two countries, and indeed the whole of north Scotland down to a line from Loch Fyne across to Aberdeen, are composed of ancient metamorphic and igneous rocks, including granite and sedimentary rocks in considerable mixture. Just below this is a broad band of mixed schists and slates, some of which are limy, which are found again in north Donegal. There is then ample Old Red Sandstone down to the Forth of Tay. It is interesting to find this old sandstone forming the bulk of the Orkneys and Caithness, and also the promontories in the south-west of Ireland. Carboniferous Limestone is found over all the central parts of Ireland with outcrops of the Old Red Sandstone here and there, in fact wherever you stand on the limestone, the sandstone in small quantities is seldom more than fifty miles away. The Edinburgh and Glasgow regions have an indescribable mixture of rocks including Carboniferous Limestone, but there is no Magnesian Limestone in either country.

More broad bands of lime-free schists extend from Dunbar across the Irish Sea to County Down and beyond, while the south-east of Ireland closely links in composition with North Wales. The vast area of Carboniferous Limestone which contributes more than half of the central land-mass of Ireland reaches its most dramatic phase in the Burren, on the west coast of County Clare and the Rock of Cashel, while just south are the mighty cliffs of Moher, seven hundred feet, and reputedly the highest vertical cliffs in Europe. These are composed of the immensely hard Millstone Grit which extends some fifty miles south until it meets the Old Red Sandstone in Kerry – including the imposing Macgillicuddy's Reeks – and County Cork. Ireland has been compared to a shallow bowl with mountains all round it, the bowl threaded with slow rivers and placid lakes and meres. There is no lack of rocks and stone. The Wicklow and Mourne Mountains are of granite.

# The Limestones

Having moved away from the ancient igneous rocks and their relatives, we come to the first conspicuously different stone – the limestone of Wenlock Edge. Wenlock stone is angular and grey and is more used for walls than rockeries, but more of this anon. While this grey limestone accumulated under water the next ridge is of sandstone, and from some parts of Britain is reddish brown. It is what is known as the Old Red Sandstone, though in some places it is anything but red. Again, its fossils indicate a living atmosphere, but its redness is due not to coloured water but more likely to a hot and sunbaked climate – desert conditions indeed. There is a great area of it in Herefordshire and away to the west in southern Wales and also in north Devon. It is comparatively soft and presents no escarpments, though it is the next ridge to be traversed from Wenlock. It is used locally for rockeries and may be seen, exposed, at Dudmaston, Shropshire, in the neighbourhood of Bridgnorth.

In geological time our next important rock is also the most important in the

39 (*Right*) An example of an Old Red Sandstone outcrop in County Kerry, Ireland. The rounded outline is due to weathering, not glaciers.

40 (*Left*) Deep grykes on the Burren, in the shelter of which Hart's Tongue ferns, grasses, bluebells and orchids grow.

41 (*Right*) Carboniferous limestone on the Burren, County Clare, Ireland. A limestone 'pavement of rather angular and irregular grykes The wind from the Atlantic (with which it is almost level in places) is so strong at times that pieces of stone are lifted and tossed aside. A great variety of alpine and lowland plants grow wherever there is enough shelter, including *Gentiana verna.*

42 (*Below*) Nearly vertical carboniferous limestone strata, exposed in a new garden at Kenmare, County Kerry, Ireland. Rainwater, seeping through turf, has dissolved much of the stone, which has never been subjected to smoothing by glaciers. Excellent, deep root-run will be found between the layers.

history of rock gardening in this country – the Carboniferous Limestone. But it is almost non-existent in our journey: we have to go to southern Cumbria and the Pennines and Derbyshire, to find it in its plenitude. The 'grey, waterworn limestone' of the rock garden makers comes mostly from those areas; hundreds of tons of it have been carted to the south-east of the country. The fact that it is Carboniferous indicates that it was laid down in much the same time as the coal seams – but even before – and it is similarly the product of a warm moist climate. Besides the area around Carnforth, it extends west of Ingleborough for miles and is of course on what Reginald Farrer was brought up. Ingleborough itself rears its noble head not because of the hardness of its agglomeration of rocks, but because of its capping of Millstone Grit. For all its hard appearance the limestone is comparatively soft; water is its doom, dissolving it away wherever it can flow and seep, particularly because the water from the uplands drains in many places from huge areas of acid peat. The 'pavements' around Ingleborough and at Hutton Roof are very noted features and well worth exploring, but treacherous on account of the deep clefts or 'grykes' between the roughly rectangular blocks or oblique cracks in the surface. The grykes may be more than ten feet deep but only a foot or two wide at the top. In addition to the often more or less parallel grykes are secondary joints, oblique, to which I refer on page 98. The flora is fascinating; all the plants – except a few shrubs blown flat by the everlasting winds – grow in the clefts or grykes, sheltered, damp and cool. Here are lilies of the valley, orchids and dwarf ferns.

I must use a separate paragraph here for this, to us, all-important stone. In the first place, as an addition to Mr Pulham's travels and observations through the country, no less famous a gardener than Canon Ellacombe, who lived, gardened and wrote at Bitton, near Bath, is said to have called attention in 1876 to the limestone pavement at Ingleborough, noting the plants growing in it. Secondly, this and all other limestone is so susceptible to acid water that it has given rise to some peculiar formations: fretting, declivities, caves and sinkage. Thus even rainwater has been responsible for widening and deepening the grykes on the pavement; on the Burren can be seen large areas which have sunk owing to subsidence below. Small subsidences in Derbyshire and elsewhere are known as swallow-holes or potholes and give our speleologists much interest – and danger. On the Dalmatian coast they are known as dolines, and one such was made, with only limited cultural success, at Cambridge. The Yugoslavian region is known as the Carso district and from this the term 'karst' is derived which is applied also to southern districts of China. In Chinese paintings we see, frequently, those almost unbelievably vertical cone-shaped hills which have always struck me as being artists' licence. But no, they may be due to harder portions of limestone of vertical stratification which have remained while their softer surroundings have dissolved over millions of years and have been swept away by rivers to the sea. Small trees and bushes grow in their clefts completing the picturesqueness of the Chinese paintings.

Much of the high land in Derbyshire is of the same formation but is not similarly exposed and fretted; on the coast of County Clare in Ireland, on the Burren, vast areas of similar pavements may be seen – moreover it is a noted area for true alpine plants growing at sea-level, such as *Gentiana verna*, *Dryas octopetala* and mossy saxifrages, also *Thalictrum* and *Adiantum*, *Arctostaphylos* and *Potentilla fruticosa*. It is an unparalleled assembly of highland and lowland plants. Parts of the Great Orme Head, in North Wales and at Cemmaes Bay, Anglesey, are covered in blue spring scillas on outcrops of the same rock which also occurs on the Gower Peninsula and on the Mendip Hills. These Mendips have equal claim to fame for rock gardens as their mostly more northern relatives. Whereas the Westmorland and Ingleborough limestones are grey and inclined to horizontal stratification, the Mendip stone is of a warmer colour. The Cheddar Gorge is a dramatic drop, cleared it is believed by a river, deeper and deeper down in its fissures and hollowing out its caves. On its topmost ridges grows the Cheddar Pink; below ground its caves are hung with stalactites and were the depositories of bones of animals left there by prehistoric hunters. It is worth noting here that the big area in Northumberland underlain by the same limestone has across it – breaking through it – a more or less continuous line, the Whin Sill. It is a narrow outcrop of dark younger rock, basalt or dolerite, with its escarpment facing north. It was therefore a blessing to the Emperor Hadrian who used its elevation as an added fortification to parts of the Roman Wall. It also causes the spectacular waterfall at High Force in Teesdale.

Water, indeed, has a very great part to play, always, in soluble limestone. In Derbyshire and in Gloucestershire may be found what we gardeners call tufa. This is a quite recent, soft, coarse textured 'stone' formed by calcareous water dripping on to moss and all kinds of detritus which it covers and gradually solidifies, totally distinct from the deeply dimpled rock in some eighteenth-century grottoes mentioned in chapter 1.

At its hardest, Carboniferous Limestone will appear as hills, witness Housman's 'high-reared head of Clee'. Even so, what it would have rested on in the confused and uptilted or down-dropped Lake District, wore away – an accumulated depth of some thirty thousand feet. The intervening strata, known elsewhere under this limestone, had gone.

It is difficult to visualise, and still more to realise, that were the ancient rocks and this limestone laid one on top of the other in their original ordered sequence, a thickness of some seven miles would be reached – encompassing a span of some two hundred million years.

Lime is an important ingredient of rocks and soils to us gardeners, and I have long wondered how it originated, as we usually consider the oldest rocks to be free of it. Here Terence Miller came to my help. Apparently the primary source of calcium carbonate must have been the most ancient crystal rocks. This would be gradually transferred in solution through rivers to the seas. In the course of untold millennia, as life grew in the seas the primitive algae were able to secrete calcareous filaments etc. on a rock-forming scale. As life increased in both quantity and variety, multicellular plants and animals deposited ever greater quantities, forming the various familar limestones of the less ancient world. Over countless millions of years these creatures produced lime and the countless billions and billions of their dead bodies, sinking slowly to the sea bed, accumulated into a hard rock. In addition, some limestones seem to have been formed by direct chemical precipitation, and others are simply limestone sands produced by erosion of pre-existing limestones. Journeying from ancient Anglesey and North Wales the car rides over a narrow pass through Wenlock Edge in Shropshire, with notices at the roadside about the

43 A band of hard sandstone forms ledges over which, in times of flood, waterfalls would form. If some of the smaller pieces of washed-down rocks were removed it could well form the model for a valley rock garden. Rocks do not always presuppose a mound. Northumberland.

44 Ingleborough, West Yorkshire. The hill of carboniferous limestone is capped by much harder millstone grit, hence its flat top. Below it very large areas of nearly flat limestone occur, known as 'pavements' Rain seepage has formed innumerable 'grykes' in places, splitting the surfaces into fairly regular sections. The grykes may be 1–2 ft wi at the top but may descend by as much as 10 ft. Seedling of all sorts germinate in the ledges of the grykes but tend to be blown flat on exposure to the wind. Lily of the Valley foliage can be seen to the right of the middle foreground. Ash, elder and thorn are the most frequent shrubby growths; Bird Cherry also occurs.

45 The weathered and waterworn Westmorland limestone prized above all others for the making of rock gardens. The grykes are wide and shallow, permitting each piece of rock to be weather-fretted. The portions of the rocks below the turf are much less fretted and as a consequence this rock is not suitable for building one piece above another, and is best used on flat or slightly sloping ground. (cf. Fig. 71).

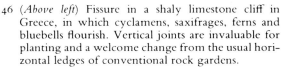

46 (*Above left*) Fissure in a shaly limestone cliff in Greece, in which cyclamens, saxifrages, ferns and bluebells flourish. Vertical joints are invaluable for planting and a welcome change from the usual horizontal ledges of conventional rock gardens.
*Courtesy: W. George Waters*

47 (*Top right*) Irregular outcrops of carboniferous limestone on the Great Orme, North Wales. The joints are wide apart and irregular, but nevertheless are visible.

48 (*Second top right*) A carboniferous limestone 'pavement' on the Great Orme, North Wales, with narrow grykes. The prostrate bush is an ancient *Cotoneaster integerrimus* blown flat by the wind and no doubt nibbled by animals.

49 (*Right*) Cheddar Gorge. The vertical cliff shows horizontal stratification. It is believed that the opposite side of the gorge, with sloping stratification, is due to sinkage through the tunnelling of underground streams. The formation gives an indication how valley rock gardens can be made to accommodate plants which prefer shade and coolness, or hot sunny slopes, on the opposing sides of a valley.

50 (*Below*) High Force, Teesdale, Yorkshire. The force of the constantly running stream has cut through much of the very hard sandstone of the Whin Sill. It should be remembered, when making streams in rock gardens, that the water must fall over the lowest part of the rock-headland, and never be made to fall over the highest rock merely to get a deeper fall. (cf. Fig. 104)

danger of falling rocks. Nowhere else, to me, is this astonishing fact of the accumulation of ancient limestone more arrestingly brought to notice. There are two
upturned ridges on the Edge – literally they are rocks which, laid originally on the
flat, have been tilted so as to form an 'edge' in the landscape; this is the first edge
or escarpment that we meet in our journey to the south-east, and sets a pattern
followed again and again with other sedimentary rocks, clays, gravels and sandstones
and yet more limestones all the way to the London Basin.

From the heights of Wenlock, looking west towards the Long mynd and the
Wrekin, Housman composed some of his most graphic lines:

> On Wenlock Edge the wood's in trouble,
> Its forest fleece the Wrekin heaves;
> The gale, it plies the saplings double,
> And thick on Severn snow the leaves.

He was visualising a great gale, and how gales had been blowing the old gnarled
trees and saplings as they did in Roman times – but that, long history though it
may be to us, is merely a recent minute in geological time.

Surrounding the Derbyshire limestone region is a broad belt of Millstone Grit,
a hard, dark, rough rock, free of lime, which provides an acid soil. On the table-
lands above it are acid peat bogs often covered with White Cotton Grass. The rock
seams project high up above the valley roads and have a dark brooding significance
typified by Ramshaw Rocks above Matlock Gorge. Much of the centre of Devon
is of the same material, but of a lighter colour. Somewhat later geologically is the
Forest of Dean sandstone, south-west of Gloucester. This is closely aligned with the
coal seams, and is a smooth, warm, greyish fawn colour and has been much used
also for rock garden building. While the Millstone Grit was used for the purpose
its name suggests, the Dean sandstone was smoother and made excellent grindstones.

Not far north of the Forest of Dean are the Malvern Hills 'containing the most
ancient rocks of all the Welsh Borders.... When you stand on the Worcestershire
Beacon, above Great Malvern, and look south to the Hereford Beacon, you are
upon rocks of perhaps the oldest generation in England, and in time your retrospect
is far beyond five hundred million years, perhaps a thousand million or more, into
the huge mist and obscurity of the beginning.' This is how, dramatically, Terence
Miller puts it in *Geology and Scenery in Britain.*

Before we return to our journey south-east, I must mention another area of
limestone which occurs in a fairly neat triangle on the coast of Yorkshire, south of
Durham, and also forms the ridge of the Pennines. Though not used except in local
rockeries, this is Magnesian or Dolomitic Limestone and its chemical properties are
not so markedly limy as the Carboniferous strata, being tempered, for lime-
intolerant plants, by the presence of the magnesium. Referring to *Rhododendrons in
the North* published by The Northern Horticultural Society in 1970, I find there
are, strangely, no noted rhododendron gardens in the area; yet it is recorded that
*Rhododendron* species of the Triflora Subsection are native on the same formation in
Western China. Though light of colour, this east Yorkshire stone is not of a rosy
colouring like its close relatives in the Dolomites in South Tyrol, extolled by
Reginald Farrer in *The Dolomites*, 1913. It is an interesting aside to mention that

though the acid (non-limy) soils in Britain and in the Alps support only a limited flora, in gardens just the opposite obtains: we can grow far more on a neutral or acid soil than on one which is markedly limy.

51a & b  Two views in a limestone quarry in Gloucestershire. In the figure *above* can be seen a seam of thin stratum, in a style so much copied by Pulham.

# Sedimentary Mixtures

After the long digression on limestones, let us return to our journey, coming across the New Red Sandstone in large areas from the Severn to the Mersey and clearly to be seen in architecture in Stourbridge, Albrighton and Chester. It is a comparatively soft stone and therefore does not 'outcrop' dramatically. Some of the beautiful Devon and Somerset churches like Broadclyst and Bishop's Lydeard are typical. Again the colour of the stone denotes an arid desert origin, and for this reason gives rise to some of our underground seams of salt, and indeed the extraction of which in Tatton Park near Macclesfield caused a sinkage of the land and a resulting lake, as mentioned in my *Gardens of the National Trust*. Further beds are found in Yorkshire.

Successively on our journey there have been escarpments of hard rock interspersed with low-lying land composed of clays and soft sediment. This will be our pattern henceforth.

The mixed geology of Dorset will be our pivot from which many layers of limy rocks and clays extend north to Middlesborough. After the incredibly mixed assembly of rocks hitherto scattered seemingly at random, and their ages being confused owing to the washing away of thousands of feet of sedimentary accumulation by tumultuous seas, a new line is struck by Lias Clay over which is an escarpment of limestone that is rough as opposed to the three classes we have already looked at. It is mainly of a light colour from a warm honey-tint at Ham Hill near Sherborne through varying tints of cream to grey in the north. It is not a simple ridge, but much branched and with fretted inlets; broadly speaking it is of oolitic material – that is, granular, but with fossilised shells and fragments of shells included. It is in the whole of the well-known Cotswold escarpment, conspicuous at Bath and Birdlip, but it gradually peters out as it goes north, eventually to reappear in force as a limy sandstone in the Clevedon Hills at Sutton Bank and then farther north to Whitby. The oolitic stone in the Cotswold area, unless bedded correctly and well weathered, is soft and prone to frost damage; even so, when exposed for centuries in walls, it is very hard and is used at Hidcote vertically as 'cobbles' for path-making. It is used extensively for local rockeries.

Two extremely mixed areas are around Bristol and Bath – famous for its warm-coloured stone – and in Dorset. Near Portland are the noted beds which take their name from it; here is gathered our very best building stone. It is generally considered to be too hard for rock garden work. The Normans brought much stone of the same geological era for building from Caen. It is very lasting (if weathered and bedded properly) and is also suitable for delicate carving. It is wonderful to think that the skill of the Renaissance builders was just in time to put up the unequalled British expression in architecture ready for the unequalled flowering of British choral music in the following century.

On each side of the Cotswold ridge there is a wide trough of clays which extend in varying widths as far as Hull; they are the Lower Lias and the Oxford clays respectively; following this is the interrupted band of Kimmeridge clay. It takes its name from a position on the Isle of Purbeck, but is most in evidence on both sides of The Wash. A hard sandstone, brown from the iron it contains but sometimes a

52 The hard chalk headland, ending Ballard Down, Dorset. The successive layers of chalk can be seen clearly on the isolated pinnacle ('Old Harry'); it is between these layers that flints mainly occur.

dark green, occurs in the Lias, particularly at Hornton (from which it takes its name) near Banbury. Being one of the stones nearest to the London area, and lime-free, it has been used for rock gardens but does not make a conspicuous ridge anywhere. It was a favourite material of Henry Moore, for his sculptures.

The Greensands, both Upper and Lower, describe a similar course but the Upper finishes at King's Lynn, near The Wash. They weather into a rich medium loamy soil, on which nearly everything grows well except roses. If we step aside at Stourhead, Wiltshire, which is already some five hundred feet above sea level, and walk up through the village a hundred feet or so, we have before us a great high ridge (Chalk) which is our next objective and a major step up from the undulating clays. A more dramatic example is seen at St Catherine's Point on the Isle of Wight, where a thin cliff of Chalk lies on top of the steep cliff of greensand and clays. The Needles and 'Old Harry' at Swanage, Dorset, are of hard Chalk and contain bands of flints.

## The Chalk and the Thames Basin

... To the west the bare, lone downs in tireless permutation of shape and contour, stretch on and on into the dormitory of the sun.

H.J. Massingham, *English Downland*, 1936.

The area underlain by Chalk is the largest of all the geological areas in Britain. While not a hard stone – only its hardest type, clunch, is used for building and none of it is used for rockeries or rock gardens – it gives great character to the contours of the land carved out of it. The River Thames meanders through it and here and there it presents a high, dramatic, white escarpment, particularly in its southern reaches. From Bridlington in Yorkshire to The Wash it is some thirty to forty miles wide; it is even wider in eastern Norfolk and lies from there in a continuous south-westerly band to Wiltshire. An arm goes farther into Dorset, and two arms go east: these are the North Downs finishing on the coast of eastern Kent, and the South Downs – 'so noble and so bare' – finishing at Beachy Head, near Eastbourne, Sussex, in cliffs nearly six hundred feet high. At Hunstanton in north-western Norfolk the cliffs display chalk at the top; below this is a harder pink limestone, and at the bottom a brown ferruginous sandstone, called in these parts Carstone. It is allied to the Lower Greensand but here is found in thin layers and in mostly small hard pieces, much used in local buildings and at Sandringham.

The vast area of Chalk, extending to northern France, once covered most of southern Britain, an indication that at one time the whole area was under sea. For the Chalk is composed of a precipitation of lime from sediment from marine creatures. It is about a thousand feet thick at its greatest and took, it is estimated, some thirty million years to accumulate. We must try to visualise then that sub-sequently the western chalk areas were washed away; the chalk that is left having a general eastern trend downwards; also extending below London and joining in France. Some twelve thousand years ago, the sea broke through making the English Channel and further washings down from the west tended to fill up the London area with mixtures of clays and gravels.

It remains to mention The Weald and East Anglia, where much sand accumulated and also – from the Chalk – flints, derived ultimately from the remains of fossilised sponges. These, because they were so hardy and split readily into cutting edges, and lay comparatively near the surface, were the first stones to be mined – as at Grimes Graves in Suffolk.

To look at The Weald we will make our imaginary journey from London southwards. A considerable area of Bagshot sand lies to the north-west. Gravels and coarse sands slope up to the first ridge of Chalk – the North Downs which originally

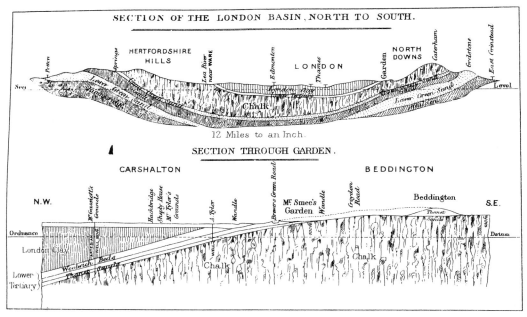

53 A geological sectional map of the London Basin, from *My garden: its plan and culture* by Alfred Smee, 1872. His book is probably the largest and most exhaustive account of any single garden. The diagram shows how chalk underlies the whole area, to rise again in East Anglia and Surrey.
*Courtesy: Royal Horticultural Society*

sailed up and over, joining the South Downs. The dome cracked about ten million years or so ago, was washed away, exposing immediately under the Chalk the rocks we have looked at in our journey across the Midlands, and which by exposure and erosion have produced the heavy soils of The Weald. First was what Farrer referred to (in his search for sand to make tractable his Yorkshire clays) as 'the coarsest of Redhill grocers' sands'. The colour of the sand no doubt is indicated in the 'red hill'. Thence the Chalk slopes upwards, with a washed-away escarpment facing roughly south, as at Box Hill on which box or *Buxus* grows wild happily, and looking over the greensand heights as at Leith Hill, almost a thousand feet high. We reach ironstones again in this section which is known as The Weald, stretching from Haslemere in eastern Surrey to Eastbourne and Folkestone. It was an area of considerable oak woodland. The trees provided the charcoal for early smelting, recorded in many 'hammer-ponds' and in Bloomer's Valley at Wakehurst Place near Haywards Heath.

After the Chalk was scoured away, deeper erosion exposed older, smooth, comparatively soft sandstone in several places. Two of its most conspicuous elevations are the hard veins of the High Rocks at Tunbridge Wells and the valley edges at Wakehurst Place. The valley, caused by the stream, leading down to Westwood Lake, has this great escarpment of sandstone for more than half a mile. Part of the same escarpment, though widely separated, is to be seen on the Forestry Commission's Gravetye estate, at one time owned by William Robinson. He valued this outcrop in his undulating and partly wooded land and recalls how he had the brushwood cleared from it, so that it could be seen as a feature in the landscape.

It is said that this soft sandstone holds twice its own weight of water. In dense shade under yews at Wakehurst Place it provides one of the habitats of the delicate Filmy Ferns. So long as it is used when weathered and laid on its original line of stratification, it is good for building and is an extremely popular stone for rock gardens. It remains just to mention Kentish Ragstone, a hard limy formation which crops up at Hythe and Folkestone; it contains many fossils and splits unevenly; even so it is used for building and for paths as at Batemans, East Sussex. The Romans used it for foundations of buildings in London. A softer version called 'hassock' gives its name to the place so called, south of Haywards Heath, Sussex.

But we have not quite finished. We have seen how above the Chalk was formed a sandy covering which has filled up what we call the Thames Basin. (In his book *My garden: its plan and culture*, 1878, Alfred Smee offers us a wealth of information; particularly I would call attention to his diagrams of the stratification of the Thames Basin, here reproduced in Fig. 53.) Here and there the sands and gravels remain on top of the chalk hills which account for the comparatively lime-free capping at Polesden Lacey, Headley Heath and Epsom Downs, all in Surrey. Over much of the chalk rather more to the west the finer sands coagulated into a hard, smooth sandstone. Much has even been found in the Bagshot area of Surrey, in fact the great waterfall at Virginia Water, in Windsor Great Park – first built in 1790, repaired in 1946 – is made of this stone which used to be discovered by prodding the sandy ground. Its greatest manifestation is in Wiltshire and provided mankind, long ago, with ready-made stones for the great outer ring of Stonehenge. It occurs much in the area, especially to the north near Marlborough; pieces lie in quantity in front of Ashdown House near Lambourn. They are known as 'grey wethers' (because in the distance they look like sheep) and as Sarsen stones. From earliest times this convenient rock has been used for building and for road-setts. Thus we may say that the 'youngest' of our rocks provided the material for our oldest building.

In places where the sedimentation was coarser, the firming into rocks reveals many pebbles. This is known as Hertfordshire Puddingstone or conglomerate and it is found in many places from Sussex to Hertfordshire. Repton used it to create his rockwork at Ashridge and isolated pieces are used on the grotto at Claremont and elsewhere.

I have permitted myself to include these sands and gravels in these notes on our British strata, because they are, of course, what rocks in due time are made from. One such gravel, of an orange-brown colour, composed of a binding sand or sandy clay and rounded pebbles of all sizes, occurs in thick beds around the gravel areas south of London, and also in Hampshire where another valley – through which runs the River Test – gave them resting place. This material is known as hoggin and has always been in great demand for drives and paths. In fact it was the favourite path gravel, sometimes screened to remove large stones, before the days of crushing machines.

The latest sedimentation in these islands occurs where moisture is prevalent over acid soils. Here sedges and sphagnum moss grow and build up into peat. Vast areas are found in Scotland, Wales, Lancashire, in Ireland and (the sedge-peat in particular) on Sedgemoor in Somerset. King Alfred's Isle of Athelney was here, indicating a little how much drainage has been effected over recent centuries, for few areas are now under water. The photograph (Fig. 160) shows the peat being dug by hand in pre-war days at Shapwick; the top layer is loose and suitable for gardening; the second is firm and like almost black gingerbread – the best peat for fuel; beneath this is an apparently bottomless mass of leaves and twigs and plant debris, undecomposed owing to the extreme acidity. In all probability the whole lot, all three layers, had never been dug before and the bottom layer is therefore a thousand or more years old. But we shall be returning to the peat in chapter 9.

However, this is only another minute in geological time. Even the last Ice Age occurred, geologically, only recently, its gradual ending coinciding with what we consider in our limited knowledge as the first appearance of man. The last ice sheet melted over most of Britain about twenty thousand years ago. It is such thoughts as these that make us realise our own impermanence and what a tiny part each one of us plays in the life of the world.

> As dreams do slyde, as bubbles rise and fall,
> As flowers do fade, and flourish in an hower;
> As smoke doth rise, and vapours vanish all
> Beyond the witt or reach of human power;
> As somer heat doth parch the withered grasse,
> Such is our stay, so life of man doth passe.

> Epitaph to Anthony Underhill, Ettington,
> Warwickshire, 1587

# 4
# The rock garden and its history

Times have wholly changed for the rock-garden. Fifty years ago it was merely the appanage of the large pleasure ground. In some odd corner or in some dank, tree-haunted hollow, you rigged up a dump of broken cement blocks, and added bits of stone and fragments of statuary. You called this 'the Rockery', and proudly led your friends to see it and planted it all over with Periwinkle to hide the hollows in which your Alpines had died.

Reginald Farrer, *The Rock Garden*, 1912

The 'grotto' of the late 18th century became the 'rockery' of the 19th and we have not yet grown out of this pertinacious habit which creeps in at inopportune moments and ruins an otherwise good scheme.

W. H. Godfrey, *Gardens in the Making*, 1914

We find a stumbling block at the outset – a very large boulder, forsooth. What is a rock garden and how does it differ from a rockery? Rockwork is another term used. James McNab, the famous curator of the Edinburgh Botanic Garden, writing in *The Garden* in 1871, claimed that rock gardens could be looked upon as comparatively modern institutions, while rockeries were of ancient date, constructed so as to produce a landscape effect. Today I think the terms, in part, have been transposed. Let us therefore decide, for the purpose of this book, that 'rockery' is a belittling term denoting formless heaps of soil and stones; that rock gardens can be made to produce a landscape effect, where stone is laid as it might be in nature, or can be a building without strict geological observance but where rock plants thrive. As to 'rockwork', I think this belongs to Mr Pulham and the grotto.

The rock garden as we know it today, together with its peat banks, screes and bogs, is generally considered as the newest art in the long history of gardening. I call it an art (though in many ways it is a science or craft) because I consider that, when all the possibilities are brought together – the geology, the effect, the cultivation – no word other than art will do. Art is defined in dictionaries as 'skilful execution as an object in itself', and 'skill applied to imitation and design'. And I hope that the illustrations of constructions in this book will make this claim irrefutable. Occasionally, if we take a hint from Japan or China, the rock in itself may be considered supreme, in which case the aim might be described as a garden of rocks, plants being omitted. This is perhaps not such a distant ideal as it might seem; here and there I have observed a beautiful piece of Westmorland limestone being used in a garden solely for its own beauty. I shall return to this in my last chapter.

\*     \*     \*     \*     \*

> The garden then unfolds a beauteous scene
> With flowers adorn'd and everliving green,
> There silver lakes reflect the beaming day
> Here crystal streams in gurgling fountains play:
> Cool vales descend and sunny hills arise
> And groves and caves and grottoes strike the eyes.

The above lines by Torquatus Tasso, the famous sixteenth-century Italian poet, seem to me to add together all the beauties of the rock garden complete – and indeed cover what I am trying to convey in these pages.

But it was not until rather after his day that mountains and rocks, waterfalls and grottoes became accepted by the *avant garde* aesthetes in this country. The Renaissance was the outcome of national eye-opening, encouraged by travel and learning. The germ of rock gardening was born and gradually assumed importance in the horticultural scheme of things towards the end of the eighteenth century. Father Attiret, a French missionary, wrote in 1743 that rocks were built in gardens in a rude and rustic way 'with different Pieces of Rock, some of which jut out and others recede inwards and are placed with so much Art, that you would take it to be the work of Nature'. His writing had little effect but gradually towards the end of the century ideas began to crystallise. The influence first seems to have come from the beauty of water falling down rocky escarpments. In the mid-eighteenth century Herbert Mackworth, MP, created a masterly cascade near his house, The Gnoll, at Neath, South Wales. In 1777 it was claimed to be of unparalleled beauty. And then in 1778 Joseph Pocklington, the son of a Newark banker, decided to build himself a house on an island in Derwentwater. It is stated that to him must be ascribed first the idea to settle in the Lakes for the beauty of the landscape. But he did more and he built another house, Barrow Cascade House, sited near to the famous cascade, and set about building follies and increasing the height of the cascade in about 1795. One might imagine that Reginald Farrer was describing the Barrow Cascade when writing his book *Among the Hills* in 1911:

> The upper stream is wholly different from the brawling whiteness of the lower one. It slides sheer and calm down into the foaming mass beneath it, like a sheet of smooth glass falling into another of broken glass. And thus together, in a roar of splendour, they plunge into the misty profundities of the gorge, and the bridge and the rocks and all the hill vibrate with the intensity of their unresting magnificence.

Water has always been a plaything of 'children of all ages' and it is not surprising that these two examples exist, showing, I think we may claim, the earliest marriage between the Picturesque in garden art and the rock garden. However, the construction of real rock gardens did not follow for at least another fifty years.

There were, however, others who had observed nature, in particular Thomas

Blaikie, who was sent to Switzerland to observe alpine plants and wrote the following in his *Diary of a Scotch Gardener* about 1775 from the French Court: 'The Duc de Chartres has recently bought the Park of St Leu ... the gardens which were laid out by Mr Prescott are composed mostly of a shrubery ... ; the vue from every part is most agreable ... ; here is a Rever which proceeds from a Spring in the park and formes a Cascade nearly 30 feet high where there is an artificell rock very well done and the destribution about it done with taste ...'. It is of course possible that he was alluding to something which approached a grotto more than anything else, but he is one of the first writers to travel through to Switzerland specifically to see plants on the mountains. His thoughts were therefore trained more to cultivation than fantasy. Indeed we have travelled far already from what in 1830 was dubbed 'The Lapidium, commonly called rock work' (James Main: *The Villa and Cottage Garden Directory*).

How to describe the remarkable work during the 1830s at Hoole House, near Chester, is another matter. I think I will let the illustration (Fig. 54) speak for itself. Lady Broughton, besides having an obviously beautiful and extensive garden, was intent upon imitating the craggy outlines of the Savoy Alps. The construction took many years to complete. The foundation was of red sandstone and had an imitation glacier of fragments of white marble to represent snow, and grey limestone, quartz and spar to indicate ice. A great effort was made with various mulching materials: dark gravel to foster warmth and white gravel for coolness, and also moss. In addition to its astonishing outline it was a genuine attempt to grow rare alpines including such choice items as pyrolas and pinguiculas from the Alps, *Coptis trifolia* from Japan, *Calceolaria fothergillii* from Patagonia and the Falkland Islands and *Jeffersonia diphylla* from North America; *Rubus arcticus*, cyclamens, soldanellas, campanulas, *Dryas octopetala* and *Cortusa matthioli*, all from Europe. This rock garden was epoch-making in all ways and nothing approached it until Sir Frank Crisp created his Matterhorn. It was a real alpine garden in advance of its time.

Only a few years later, by 1839, Mr William Wells developed something quite different at Redleaf, at Penshurst, Kent. Both this and Hoole House were described by J. C. Loudon in *The Gardeners' Magazine*; here at Redleaf Wells inherited small outcrops of Sussex sandstone, probably with conspicuous iron veins in it, as it is described as 'red' in one account. It was perhaps more a case of making good use of what was there than rock garden construction, but the distribution in a completely informal way of rock, plants and shrubs on an informal lawn was an innovation in a period devoted to rather vulgar formality, judging by our standards.

In spite of the collection of plants at Hoole House these two gardens owe more to the Picturesque spirit of the late eighteenth century than to serious attempts to cultivate a representative collection of the many plants that were becoming known.

The Picturesque spirit in gardening continued through much of the nineteenth century alongside the trend towards ornamental formality, some of it eclectic but mostly horrific to our eyes. But before writing about rock gardens made specifically to cultivate alpine plants, I should like to refer to some of the many writings about the subject. J. C. Loudon, in *The Gardeners' Magazine and Register of Rural and Domestic Improvement*, has many references to rockwork, such as the rocky scars on steep banks at Blenheim Palace, and he noted that good work had been done at

54  The rock garden at Hoole House, Cheshire, constructed in 1838. From J. C. Loudon *The Suburban Gardener* of that year.

*Courtesy: Royal Horticultural Society*

55  The rocky garden of William Wells at Redleaf, Kent, was described by J. C. Loudon in his *The Gardeners' Magazine* of 1839. Natural outcrops of sandstone were revealed and supplemented.

*Courtesy: Royal Horticultural Society*

Pain's Hill, Ascot Place, Fonthill, Clumber Park and Wardour Castle. In 1831 we come across the first reference to geology – apart from Pulham's – in an article by S.T.B. The writer calls attention to the value of a study of geology in order to be able to construct rockwork with a painter's eye and thus to achieve acceptable garden scenery. In 1838 there are notes on covering the ground between the rocks with plants or a mulch of stones. Here we see the effort to make the work look settled and natural as well as avoiding labour in upkeep – a foretaste of today's preoccupation! In the 1840s Paxton's outcrops at Chatsworth (see Figs 15, 16, 18 and 20) were being formed as recorded in *The Gardeners' Chronicle* and there is reference to turning a chalk pit into a garden, moreover an injunction that in any such work we should 'follow nature'.

In *The Floral World and Garden Guide*, another great Victorian writer had his say in 1877; the editor was Shirley Hibberd whose name, like that of Loudon's earlier, is difficult to avoid in accounts of this sort. He opined that 'the rocks should be used in huge blocks in piles and mounds, not to imitate caverns and rude cairns, but strictly as ornaments.... This is rockwork, not rockery ... and it conveys the idea of artistic repose, not natural and rugged sublimity.... While a *rockery* may be a most fantastic, gloomy, romantic, or savage scene ... rockwork must be artistic or elegant ... and the rough unhewn material used simply, because *that*, in the hands of an artist, may be made as appropriate and beautiful as the exquisitely sculptured forms which the chisel *might* have obtained from it.' It seems to me that his ideas were considerably muddled and when we read that a year earlier he had advocated the making of artificial coral by means of dipping twigs or cinders into a yellow rosin perhaps we can leave Hibberd on the shelf for the time being. On the other hand, to be fair, I must mention that in the same publication he gave great credit to the building of rock gardens and claimed that the best was in Yorkshire at Backhouse's nursery, composed of 500 tons of millstone grit, and that their catalogue was very interesting; moreover that the noblest rockwork was at Chatsworth: it was stupendous and being formed in 1844. He also ridiculed the 'pocket' as a place and receptacle for growing alpine plants on account of its inadequacy. A little later, in 1875, a contributor to *The Gardeners' Chronicle* advocated the imitation of cromlechs as a diversion. All writers, however, were unanimous that all foreign matter – vitreous slag, clinker lava, brick-bats, shells, bits of masonry – should be excluded in favour of genuine rock; these oddments had been much to the fore in grottoes and sometimes in ferneries.

Finally, before passing on to real rock gardens, I must mention the extraordinary rock wall erected in 1847 at Lamport Hall, Northamptonshire, in 1847 by Sir Charles Isham, tenth baronet. By building a wall of undressed stone running north and south, extending from the house, he conceived the idea of an east-facing rockery. Broader at the base than it now is, this took the form of a cliff of rock complete with recesses and small caverns, and was planted mainly with dwarf evergreen trees and shrubs. I have never seen anything like it elsewhere. It was originally peopled – in the caverns – by tiny china gnomes with ladders, barrows and tools, all to scale. The gnomes and their impedimenta have now gone but perhaps they left their mark on horticulture all those years ago, and have been reincarnated in the plastic horrors of today. This amazing piece of work completes my notes which are mainly concerned with the Sublime and Picturesque.

I must ask forgiveness for the confusion of dates adopted in order to try to give the best picture of the decades; in 1838 that prolific writer J. C. Loudon issued his *Suburban Gardener and Villa Gardener* and as far as I can ascertain he gives the first real drawing of a supposedly natural outcrop of rock. In fact, as usual in his books connected with the history of gardens and garden design in this country, J. C. Loudon provides us with the mainspring, so to speak, of the construction of rock gardens. It was his contention (as ours) that 'In general, no rockwork of any kind whatever can be put together in a manner satisfactory to the man of taste, except by a workman who has the eye of an artist.' This is what my book is about and launches us into the second part of this story.

\*    \*    \*    \*    \*

Sweets of the wild, uncultured blowing
Neglected in luxuriance growing;
From the dark ruins frowning near,
Your charms in brighter tints appear,
  And richer blush assume
You smile with softer beauty crowned,
While all is desolate around,
  Like sunshine on a tomb.

So James Lothian, in 1845, envisaged a definite turn towards his *Practical hints on the culture and general management of alpine or rock plants*. There is no dividing date, of course, but just that the trend was towards plants instead of horrific rocks – for the time being; we shall return to this later. Meanwhile, as we shall see in chapter 6, botanists and travellers had been at work and many of the floral gems of the Alps had been discovered. Some much earlier volumes by Charlotte Murray, *The British Garden*, 1808, and Charles M'Intosh, *The Flower Garden*, 1838, had already pointed the way with surprising lists of alpine plants. M'Intosh was at one time head gardener to the King of the Belgians at Claremont, Surrey.

But besides still having Pulham with us, as it were, we are entering, after 1850, into a much bigger stage, dominated by the nurseryman James Backhouse of York, William Robinson, and later by Farrer, and all who sprang from them. The Backhouse firm was established in 1859 and continued until 1955, having during this period had an immense influence on gardens and indeed other nurseries, and on young men who worked there for a time. One of his men, W. A. Clarke, joined a Cambridge firm about 1925 to specialise in rock plants and I had the privilege of learning from him. A dark flowered form of *Saxifraga oppositifolia* bears his name. A glance at one of Backhouse's old catalogues will reveal at once how advanced they were among nurserymen. In the early 1880s Ellen Willmott of Warley Place in Essex had commissioned James Backhouse of York to make for her an imposing alpine garden, in the shape of a deep gorge. It was composed of millstone grit from Yorkshire and is still intact, though its rare plants have gone. The encouragement had not only come from Charlotte Murray, James Lothian and other minor writers, but from examples by national institutions.

We have to go back to 1772, in which year a rock garden was made at the Chelsea Physic Garden, London (founded in 1673), expressly for the growing of alpine plants. During his curatorship of the garden, Mr W. G. MacKenzie sent me the following information:

> From the Memoirs of the Botanic Garden at Chelsea dated 1820 there is the following entry under the year 1772:
>
> 'Mr Stanesby Alchorne, Honorary Demonstrator, presented about forty tons of old stones, brought from the Tower of London, for the purpose of raising an artificial rock, in order to cultivate those plants which require such a soil, and to this rockwork was afterwards added a large quantity of flints and chalk given by Mr John Chandler, and also a large quantity of lava from a volcano in Iceland, presented by Joseph Banks Esq. These materials being considered fully adequate to the purpose, the rockwork was undertaken and was finished in the course of the summer of the following year.' On the existing rock garden today there is a lead plaque with an inscription 'Basaltic Lava brought from Iceland to the Chelsea Physic Garden by Sir Joseph Banks in 1772'. It might also be of interest to you to state that the year the rockwork was completed William Curtis [of the Botanical Magazine] was elected to the vacant office of Demonstrator of Plants and *Praefectus Horti* at the Garden.
>
> No doubt slight alterations have taken place over those long years but I doubt if these would amount to much as it was constructed around the remaining indoor lily pond which was built and commented on by John Evelyn in 1685, and it is still serving that same purpose today. In my time I have removed much of the Tower of London stone which was Portland and had weathered, as can be seen around the City, to an almost pure white. This against the black basaltic lava was too much of a contrast to live with or serve as a background for any plant. I did, however, leave some as steps to the pond and in so doing kept the records straight.

The stone used was in great part useless to the plants, but the rock garden's erection under glass calls for some comment. All 'exotic' plants imported into England came from warmer countries than ours, with few exceptions. The sunshine in the heights of the Alps is very warm at flowering time which is when the flowers would have been seen and collected; they were therefore given every care under glass.

In 1800 a mound-like rock garden was constructed in the National Botanic Garden at Glasnevin, Dublin, with weathered stone from the Howth peninsula, just north of Dublin; it was the very ancient Cambrian sandstone. We read in the *History of the City of Dublin* (1818) that the mound was constructed on the most elevated part; the rocks were piled together without any apparent order so as to give the appearance of a natural rocky mound. Indeed in *The Dublin Magazine* of July 1800 it was claimed that probably 'no Botanic Garden in Europe can boast of so well-constructed, highly finished and useful piece of artifical rock-work; not to mention how highly gratifying and instructive it must be to the scientific cryptogamick botanist, who may make lichens his study ...'. It is nice to feel that a botanic garden was so much to the fore in this work.

Only three years later than at Glasnevin, the City of Liverpool opened its botanic garden, complete with rock garden, the leading spirit being William Roscoe, after whom the genus *Roscoea* is named. By 1808 there were over a thousand different kinds of plants, shrubs and trees growing in the garden and four hundred and sixty flourishing in the extensive greenhouses. The stone there was also foreign, which had been used as ballast in ships returning to the Mersey. Perhaps an experienced geologist will one day list the rocks thus procured.

56 (*Above*) The earliest ro
garden constructed by
James McNab, the Cu
at the Royal Botanic
Garden, Edinburgh,
about 1870.
*Courtesy: The Regius*
*F*

57 (*Left*) A drawing from
*The Gardener* of 1872
showing an early effor
at growing alpine plan
at the Royal Botanic
Gardens, Kew.
*Courtesy: The Director,*
*Royal Botanic G*

These two gardens were followed by Cambridge University and Kew. It is not certain when the original one at Cambridge was started, but it probably had a small beginning when the garden was laid out from 1831 to 1846, its opening date. At Kew a rock garden of Reigate sandstone was built in 1867, but it was not on the present rock garden site. The first one here was built in 1882. But before this Edinburgh looms. Here an original type of garden was made with a minimum of stone, as will be seen from the illustration (Fig. 56). It speedily housed a vast collection of plants. The Curator, James McNab, may be quoted as follows from his article in *The Garden* of 6 December 1871:

> In the construction of the rock garden here, I got the stones of the old wall split up longitudinally, and arranged in a piece of sloping ground facing the north, which I had previously laid out in an undulating and somewhat geometrical form, and which I had divided into uniform sections, separated by stone paths and steps. These sections were then divided into angular compartments of various sizes, and each filled with soils suited for the various plants to be put into them. The compartments of the various sections were afterwards filled with various species of a genus, such as the sections of Sempervivums, Sedums, Saxifrages, also of Primulas, Silenes, Aubrietias, Gentianas, Androsaces, etc. Other sections were filled with plants of a uniform height, particularly of kinds of which only a few species exist, while others were arranged in geographical order. The success of the early part of this experiment was such as to induce me to transfer a very large proportion of our alpine plants from pots to the rock garden; and I am happy to say that I have never had cause to regret it.
>
> The rock garden recently constructed at the Edinburgh Botanic Garden, and still in progress of extension, contains upwards of four thousand compartments, of which 2,200 spaces are filled with various species and varieties of alpine and dwarf-herbaceous plants, besides numerous dwarf, shrubby kinds, from all temperate parts of the globe.

In 1893 James Backhouse of York was to put up a rock garden of 250 tons of millstone grit at the Birmingham Botanical Gardens.

It is easy to see that a considerable 'movement' had begun, nationally, and hence the demand for alpine plants from Backhouse and other nurserymen. The demand and interest were accentuated by much quicker travel; from mid-century onwards ever quicker and more extensive railroads were made and soon Switzerland could be reached from London in two days. Holidays became popular and foreign plants were often brought back as a result. Geology and botany were encouraged and taught, thus everything conspired to further horticulture, and, at this juncture, its youngest department, the rock garden.

William Robinson, famous gardener and writer, was widely travelled and in 1870 published *Alpine Flowers for English Gardens*. In its pages was much good advice on every aspect of rock-building and cultivation, besides a lengthy, fully descriptive list of plants, many of which are still scarce today. Let me make two small quotations from his closely printed pages:

> Many persons who arrange rock gardens doubtless fear the sun burning up their plants; yet the sun that beats down upon the Alps and Pyrenees is fiercer than that which shines on the British garden. But, while the alpine sun cheers the flowers into beauty, it also melts the snows above, and water and frost grind down the rocks into earth; and thus, enjoying both, the roots form perfectly healthy plants. Fully exposed plants

do not perish from too much sun, but simply from want of water. Therefore it cannot be too widely known that full exposure to the sun is the first condition of perfect rock-plant culture – abundance of free soil under the root, and such a disposition of the soil and rocks that the rain may permeate through and not fall off the rocks, being also indispensable.

A small rock-garden can be so arranged as to appear as if naturally cropping out of the shrubbery. With a few cart-loads of stones and earth excellent effects may be produced in this way.... An irregularly sloping border with a few mossy bits of rock peeping from a swarming carpet of Sandworts, Mountain-pinks, Rock-cresses, Sedums and Saxifrages, Arabises and Aubrietias, with a little company of fern fronds sheltered in the low fringe of shrub behind the mossy stones.

Though we eulogise Reginald Farrer's immense influence on the cultivation of rock plants, we should remember what he thought of William Robinson as a precursor: 'Then suddenly, flaming and audacious, arose Mr Robinson with a crash among the Lobelias of the late Victorian era. Like all true prophets, he arose magnificent, passionate, unguided and unguidable.'

Besides actual rock gardens he advocated using alpines on walls, in border edges and in pots and window boxes. Here was a whole world of new treasure for the keen gardener. And far from the old days when all was run by the head gardeners of great establishments, by 1870 innumerable small houses – villas – were being built, each with its small garden in which the owners could indulge their fancies.

Across the Atlantic, rock gardening was also budding and what is usually considered to be the first rock garden of any consequence was made near Boston, Massachusetts, in the early 1880s. It was extensive and housed a great collection of native and foreign plants, gathered together by General Stephen Minot Weld.

By the turn of the century – or even before it – we are among the 'big stuff'. It is stated that the Backhouse rock garden was composed of five hundred tons of millstone grit, a hard dark type of sandstone. The firm constructed many large rock gardens and started one for Sir Frank Crisp at Friar Park, Henley on Thames, which eventually was composed of 7,000 tons of Yorkshire limestone, with an imitation Matterhorn on top made of shining quartz and with a grotto by Pulham below; the whole covered three acres. But it had its rivals, for McNab's regimented beds at Edinburgh had been altered and enlarged to a considerable size by the use of great irregular lumps of rock with no thought of stratification partly because they were pieces of conglomerate rock without any 'bed'. The same was true of Sir Frank Crisp's at Friar Park, and I cannot imagine the millstone grit at York being any different. The rock at Edinburgh was a conglomerate from Callender, in Perthshire; some Old Red Sandstone from Dumfriesshire was also used. The work started in 1906 but ceased in 1914.

The site of the present rock garden at Kew was first given to this type of cultivation owing to a gift of 2,630 kinds of alpine plants from a Mr George Curling Joad in 1882. It was constructed mainly of Cheddar Limestone, but oolite was also used, and because the matter was urgent (to house the collection of plants) various other abandoned stones were collected from elsewhere in the Garden, including the Arboretum; logs and tree stumps were included. By 1925 the Curator, Walter Irving, had published his little book *Rock Gardening*, and recorded that remodelling

58 A limestone outcrop constructed at Kew prior to 1883. Here we see unmistakable efforts at geological stratification.
*Courtesy: The Director, Royal Botanic Gardens*

59 The same outcrop some years later, well clothed and softened with plants. Note *Pinus strobus* 'Prostrata' near the centre of the picture.
*Courtesy: The Director, Royal Botanic Gardens*

60 A gentle suggestion of rock garden – a few rocks laid unobtrusively at the edge of a shrubbery. From William Robinson's *The English Flower Garden*.
*Courtesy: Royal Horticultural Society*

61 Mendip Limestone at Kew, photographed c. 1930.
*Courtesy: The Director, Royal Botanic Gardens*

of many parts had been undertaken and that Carboniferous Limestone from not only Cheddar but Derbyshire, Yorkshire and Westmorland was used as well as oolitic limestone from Gloucestershire. It was well built from the point of view of the culture of plants. I became familiar with it in the late 1920s when I was a student at the University Botanic Garden at Cambridge. Here there were two rock gardens: an old one composed of all sorts of stone, some of it tooled masonry, backed by a rough stone wall and sham gothic stone arch. It is sad that these period pieces were removed in the 1950s; they may have been built in the very early days of the garden's design, but in any case against the wall throve *Rosa × hardii* ( × *Hulthemosa hardii*), also *R. stellata* and *R.s. mirifica*. The main rock garden, of brown Hornton sandstone from Oxfordshire, was constructed under the guidance of F. G. Preston, Superintendent, between 1911 and 1920. It was, once again, made principally to house plants that liked all sorts of conditions. It had a scree, and was of the valley persuasion, like that at Kew, but comparatively small. With this I was of course also familiar.

At Graigue Conna, Bray, not far from Dublin, is a rock garden created by Lewis B. Meredith. His book *Rock Gardens, how to make and maintain them* appeared in 1910. He provided not only photographs of his work during the placing of the rocks but also an interesting plan of the general concèption of a man-made ravine with jutting crags to frame the views. The rock used was rather angular, a hard local stone. I am glad to say the garden still exists and is cared for in no small way by Mr and Mrs J. R. Brown, who inherited Meredith's superb shrubs and trees.

But I have written nothing about the rock garden at Wisley. Originally built by James Pulham in 1911, after the Second World War it had become necessary to overhaul it. It was constructed mainly of Sussex sandstone, with some thinner strata of Bargate stone in Pulham's usual highly original style. Over the years much of the Bargate has been used for paths and much of the somewhat crumbling Sussex stone has been replaced with freshly quarried rock. The unfortunate result scenically has been to lose much of Pulham's rugged grandeur, though as homes for plants the terracing is highly successful. The major loss is the traditional Pulham overhang, with its dramatic dark shadow.

We shall return to the national botanic gardens later but I feel I must break into the narrative with early twentieth-century events. In fact, this whole era is dominated by Reginald Farrer and his influence. I would go further and say that though he died in 1920 at the age of forty, his influence is still with us.

While William Robinson's book *Alpine Flowers* (1870) gave much information that was necessary for their successful cultivation, his writing has a rather dictatorial bias. He did not enthuse his readers in this particular branch of horticulture, though the opposite is true of others of his publications. It is recorded he had recently been to Hoole House; perhaps what he saw there chilled his blood. The book made no impression on me as a youngster, whereas directly I picked up a book by Farrer I was fully enthused. Starting with *Alpines and Bog Plants* and *My Rock Garden* followed by *The Rock Garden*, I read the lot. If one can stand the erudite, racy, often purple prose there is no putting down any of the volumes. One cannot but wonder what heights he would have achieved had he lived longer instead of dying in Burma so early in life, like Purcell and Mozart. In writing his obituary in the

Bulletin of the Alpine Garden Society, Clarence Elliott wrote 'There never has been, and I do not think there ever will be, another who will leave so vivid a mark in his passing on any horticultural subject'.

Farrer's greatest influence was felt among the plants whose beauty he extolled in such a wonderful way. Many of his word-pictures remain engraved on my memory. We must not forget the influence we have had from the North – first Backhouse and then Farrer, to say nothing at the moment of other worthy folk. Farrer lived at Ingleton, under the great hill of Ingleborough, with the most beautiful limestone in the world all around him. The Craven Highlands of Yorkshire, his home, carried the seams of this lovely stone through to Westmorland. It was natural that he should use this stone to the exclusion of all else, and he told how to use it in his little book *The Rock Garden* of 1912:

> All limestone, except the most friable and crumbling ... is unparalleled in value for rock-work. By far the best of its forms, though, is the wonderful weather-worn rock of the Craven Highlands and Westmorland, which has so singular a beauty, alike of colour and outline, that a rock-garden so built is well furnished in itself already though never a plant has yet been inserted ... block fits block like the sections of a jigsaw puzzle, so that the merest child at work with these could hardly help compiling ... a rock-work that shall really look all of a piece, the creation not of man, but of the untrammelled forces of the world at work since the hills first were ... Stone, of course, can be as entrancingly attractive in itself as any flower. The joy of a noble boulder rightly placed, is something complete and perfect.
>
> Never think you are going to get a dignified result by humping a quantity of stones indiscriminately together. And never think, either, on the other hand, that you can't get the noblest and grandest effects, just because your ground is no more than a quarter the size of a small bedroom. In spaces no bigger, any Japanese townsman will have at the back of his house some apt and perfect little valley or mountain dell. This is done by nothing more than an exact sense of proportion....
>
> Stone, in nature, is never disconnected; each block is always, as it were, a word in the sentence. Remember that urgently; boulder leads to boulder in an ordered sequence. A dump of disconnected rocks, with discordant forms and angles, is mere gibberish.

The very fact that his stone was so beautiful led him astray. His own garden did not display any real observance of geological rules. He pontificated to no small degree – and certainly with considerable success – about rock garden building, nevertheless. In *The Rock Garden* are examples of types of rock building which he scorned (see Fig. 63). He felt the 'Devil's Lapful' was the title that might be given to the arrangement of rocks at Edinburgh: 'The plan is simplicity itself. You take a hundred cart loads of bald square-faced boulders. You next drop them all about absolutely anyhow; and you then plant things among them. The chaotic hideousness of the result is something to be remembered with shudders ever after.' In *Among the Hills* he states that 'few people seem to have any adequate sense of the beauty of rock as mere rock. Without consideration of garniture or surroundings, rock itself can be one of the most beautiful things in all beautiful nature.... They bash it down with hammers ... or hew steps in it ... they have neither sight nor reverence; yet gods as surely dwell in rock and cliff as in the oak or the glittering waters.' It is worth reflecting here upon the examples of rock work by Pulham; but of course, Farrer was, first and foremost, a plantsman.

I think I might quote here a few other sentences to show that Farrer was not the only guiding light. In 1908 F. G. Heath, in his little book *Garden Rockery*, wrote: 'Nature's arrangement is the most picturesque and the most beautiful method as well as the most useful, and yet Nature is not followed in nine out of ten cases of rock building. Rockery is the most delightful and suggestive of all garden adjuncts, a microcosm of mountain and valley.' And again, Walter H. Godrey in his *Gardens in the Making*: 'Let the stones of which it is to be composed resemble in some degree the natural stratification of the quarry, for Nature seldom tosses her material in a confused heap, save in her angry and volcanic moods.'

We must now take another small step backwards to record the beginnings of what we may call the rock gardening of today. There was no doubt that the efforts of Pulham, no less than Robinson's book, had had effect, but the real influence came from the Horticultural Society. Before the Royal Charter was awarded in 1861 the Horticultural Society had been gaining in strength from its inception in 1804. In 1912 it helped to sponsor the Royal International Horticultural Exhibition held in the Temple Gardens; it was an auspicious decision to hold this first great spring flower show on the self-same spot that factions of the Houses of Lancaster and York had quarrelled over the Red Rose and the White in the reign of Henry VI, as told by Shakespeare. Be this as it may, from our present point of view the show was remarkable for two exhibits of rock gardens that came from Yorkshire, one from the Craven Nurseries of Clapton, owned by Reginald Farrer, which was no doubt filled with good plants, and the other by a Mr John Wood of Skipton, Yorkshire. I believe this was the first exhibition rock garden that showed unmistakably geological stratification of Yorkshire limestone. In *The Gardeners' Chronicle* it was recorded that it was 'by general consent the most natural piece of rockwork ever exhibited' and that the planting was 'careful as it was really subordinated to the beauty of the general workmanship'. In Farrer's words, 'his creation shows the sense, shapeliness, dignity and balance of Mr John Wood's almost orientally perfect composition'. Those with very long memories still recall its epoch-making occurrence. Other exhibitors were Pulham, Backhouse, Tucker, Whitelegg, Reuthe and Wallace, all well-remembered names today. It is noteworthy that Pulham, always with an eye for effect, included in his foreground bergenias and hostas – an idea taken out of eighteenth-century landscape pictures, where such bold foliage increases the sense of perspective.

The first show at the Royal Hospital, Chelsea, was held in the following year, 1913, and from that date – apart from war periods – until the 1960s, the Society sponsored the creation of full scale competitive exhibition rock gardens on the famous 'rock garden bank' at the annual Chelsea Show in May. There is no doubt that they have had a great influence on this branch of garden art. In my opinion the making of a scenic rock garden is without doubt in the highest rank of art.

Frank Kingdon Ward in his *Common Sense Rock Gardening* (1948) was in no two minds about it. (He was not only an ardent plantsman but also deeply steeped in geography and geology.)

It is perhaps the most artistic of all man's creations, the highest expression of his artistic sense.... Here is no crude imitation of nature but rather a fastidious selection and

62  Sussex sandstone at Kew, built by George H. Preston, c. 1961.

*Courtesy: The Director, Royal Botanic Gardens*

*(a)*

The Almond-pudding System
(The wrong arrangement of spikes)

*(b)*

The Plum-bun System
(The wrong arrangement of Humpety-Dumpeties—
haphazard and disconnected)

*(c)*

The Right Placing of Spikes
(With evergreens)

*(d)*

A More Tolerable Way of Using Humpety-
Dumpeties (With evergreens)

63  Diagrams from *The Rock Garden* by Reginald Farrer, 1912.

combination of line, form, and colour, like a Chinese painting, to produce a completely satisfying harmony. Many people seem to think that ... they are imitating nature. They would be quite hurt if you told them that the final result is nothing like Nature's handiwork. They might feel less so if you told them, what is perfectly true, that the rock garden they have created is more beautiful than anything nature could have designed. A rock garden is a work of art, and man has at his beck and call resources embracing all nature. Man's artistic sense is sublime. Nature alone can make the lack-lustre raw diamond in the furnace of the earth's crust. But man's art cuts the jewel to set free the sparkle therein imprisoned like a djinn.

My first visit to Chelsea Show was in 1929 and I remember standing spellbound before the rock gardens – which, with alpine plants, constituted my first love in horticulture. At once it was apparent that, as throughout these pages, there were two ideals: the scenic rockwork and the rock garden made almost entirely to show off plants. The two ideals were realised by two firms, Gavin Jones and Clarence Elliott.

Once again we have to step backwards in time, for Clarence Elliott had worked for a spell with the Backhouse firm of York. He established the Six Hills Nursery, Stevenage, Hertfordshire, in 1907. He was an exceptionally keen-brained alpine plant enthusiast with a spicy sense of humour. After the war Gavin Jones and Walter E. Th. Ingwersen became his partners. In due course Colonel Gavin Jones left Elliott and started with Walter Ingwersen a nursery at Letchworth, Hertfordshire. But this combination also foundered and Ingwersen began Birch Farm Nursery in 1929 on William Robinson's Gravetye Estate near East Grinstead, Sussex. There were of course many other firms in these islands specialising partly if not wholly in the rock garden and its plants; too many to name, but the names of Stormonth of Carlisle, Hayes of Ambleside, Hodson of Nottingham, Whitelegg of Chislehurst, Prichard of Christchurch come readily to mind. My illustrations of Chelsea and Southport Shows will recall others, notably Reginald Kaye of Carnforth who had spent some years with Ingwersen and had there been infected with both sides of this section of gardening. Pulham was there, too, in fact this firm was the first to *excavate* on the rock garden bank.

Clarence Elliott usually chose Westmorland Limestone for his exhibits. Gavin Jones liked something more severe for his scenic efforts – ably and subtly planted by his wife – and used Welsh granite; subsequently, his manager Geoffrey Chalk used Forest of Dean sandstone. Mrs Jean Chalk, his widow, tells me that Gavin Jones absorbed much from the teachings of Symons-Jeune, and Chalk in turn profited by Gavin Jones' examples. It was left to Marcel de Smet and a Mr Jacobs to use to perfection Mendip Limestone which is more rugged than that from Westmorland. Walter Ingwersen remained true to the absorbent, but quarried, Sussex sandstone, which outcrops in various parts of The Weald. His gardens, like Elliott's, were always the mecca for the ardent plant lover.

If I have seemed to give too much space to the efforts of these three pioneering spirits in the field, it is because they so well illustrate the story I am trying to tell and because I have known them all, and those who came after them. It was during his spell at Letchworth that Walter Ingwersen hit on the idea of covering the corrugated iron roof of a shed with some three inches of gritty, poor soil and planted it with sempervivums or House Leeks. The idea took my eye and I repeated it at Cambridge as told in my book *Three Gardens*. I am amazed that the idea has not become more common; it is not only highly successful, but increases the growing space of small gardens, and gives interest throughout the year. Likewise we must lay to Elliott's credit the idea of trough and sink gardens, an idea which was instantly popular and has many devotees. They were first exhibited at Chelsea in 1923. I believe he was also the first to use tufa; by boring holes in this soft stone he proved how easy it was to establish saxatile plants directly in it.

These great works of art, put up at Chelsea and Southport in particular, have been criticised by many, being called 'stockbrokers' rock gardens'. This was an opprobrious way of saying they were only for the rich; of course they were, but one exhibit might result in orders for three or four. No two would be exactly the same owing to the dictations of the various sites. But all would require extremely time-consuming upkeep, particularly in the mowing of grass on awkward slopes between rocks. The turf was really to create immediate soft green contrast at the show against the rocks. In the garden – or in nature – there would be screes and carpets and tussocks of dense ground-cover plants and tiresome mowing would be obviated. The fact is that these great natural exhibits were really the result of a desire to show off the rock-placing; the fussy little alpine plants were merely show decoration. One exhibitor, Ian G. Walker of South Godstone, preferred to do just this; to have magnificent rocks set among nature's rough turf. In this way 'the London dweller could have the countryside' not on his walls but in his garden.

From 1949 onwards Sussex Sandstone was chosen for rebuilding the Kew rock garden, largely done by George Preston, son of F. G. Preston of earlier mention. The limestone previously used had proved not only hard and non-absorbent, but in London had been kept almost white in the sulphur-laden air. The sandstone has proved the exact opposite, but being freshly quarried, it lacks the weathered and waterworn finish of the Carboniferous Limestone. On the other hand, being of more or less rectangular blocks it has the advantage of being suitable for building up to considerable heights, one block serenely fitting over another. A hundred tons of it were used to construct the portion at Cambridge which was given lime-free soil, when the new rock garden was built around the lake.

The same claim for success at Cambridge cannot be made for the use there of five hundred tons of Westmorland Limestone. As will be seen from the illustration (Fig. 71), this favourite stone of Farrer's weathers above ground fairly speedily (in a geological sense) but where its bases are sunk in the ground it has a very different appearance. Whereas the outlying groups of rocks are admirably done, the 'cliff' is not successful for the simple reason that the stones do not join one above the other. Considering there was so much other land available when the garden was enlarged after the Second World War, it is a pity that this outlandish rock garden was allowed to intrude on the peaceful classic design of over a hundred years' standing.

The Alpine Garden Society was started by a handful of keen spirits in 1929, followed by the Scottish Rock Garden Club in 1933. In addition to all that I have written so far I must pay tribute to the enormous encouragement that these two societies have given to our craft and art, just as the American Rock Garden Society has done across the Atlantic. The Alpine Garden Society held jointly with the Royal

64 Scenic rock garden of Mendip Limestone at Chelsea Show by William Wood & Son in 1937, showing careful alignment and assortment of rocks.
*Courtesy: Denis Wood*

65 Westmorland Limestone scenic rock garden at Chelsea Show in 1956, by Geo. G. Whitelegg. Distinct and effective stratification and assortment of rocks.
*Courtesy: Harry Smith*

66 Reconstruction of the rock garden at Wisley in 1986, showing the new use of Sussex sandstone to form terraces for growing the maximum number of plants. While this is satisfactory to the cultivator it is at variance with geology since the rocks presuppose a shelf of rock stretching away under the next layer. Compare such false planting places with Figs. 92, 99, 100 and 101.

67, 68 Westmorland
Limestone scenic
rock gardens at
Chelsea Show
c.1955 by Geo. G.
Whitelegg.
Although there is
little detailed
consecutive
stratification the
rocks are grouped in
like assortments
creating a pleasant
whole.
*Courtesy: G. G.*
*Whitelegg Ltd*

69 A great layer of thick
Westmorland
Limestone protecting
weaker layers which
gave way to screes and
pools. By Reginald Kaye
at Southport Show in
1934.
*Courtesy: Reginald Kaye*

Horticultural Society a Conference in 1936. In her opening remarks, Lady Rockley, author of a useful little book on *Historic Gardens of England*, claimed that this was the 'great age' of rock gardens. Among other speakers were Gavin Jones and Walter Ingwersen, with Captain B. H. B. Symons-Jeune. Gavin Jones said that a rock garden 'ought to look alright *before* it is planted. . . . What I like is a surprise outcrop of rock or group of outcrops in situations where Nature would permit them. This gives the illusion that the rock was there before the garden.' Without some sort of refreshment, the mind was like 'a London dweller with no picture of the countryside on his walls'. (These ideals were precisely what Pulham had in mind.)

The influence of all this enthusiasm, skill and art spread to the Continent, just as the eighteenth-century Landscape Garden did, but the spread was less owing to the two world wars. Rock gardens were made by British firms in France, Belgium and Holland, and farther afield.

It may be asked whether it is in good relation in today's preoccupation with conservation that hills should be stripped of their rocks, or quarries made, in order to create a garden in counties far away. The stripping of hillsides of stones has been going on since the Saxons started farming; quarries have been made since building started. And is it worse to cart limestone from Yorkshire to Surrey than Welsh slates to any other county? There is also the aesthetic sense that may be upset. But here again is it worse than having a Himalayan rhododendron or a Japanese maple in our gardens, or mahogany from the West Indies for furniture in our homes? There is no single answer to all of these questions except to say that in the pursuit of art all is fair and permissible.

The one popular stone I have not really given due observance to is tufa, but for details I refer you to chapter 11.

Those who live in the north and west of these islands have no need to cart stone about the country, for their counties abound in rocks. In some places great artistry has been used gently to expose an outcrop or uncover a ledge. The largest 'rock garden' of this or any kind is at Cragside, Northumberland, where an untold area of beautiful Carboniferous Limestone has been exposed and enjoyed. This kind of thing started with William Wells at Redleaf (Fig. 55) but its most successful and remarkable appreciation was early in this century at Brockhurst, near East Grinstead, where cliffs and ravines were made the homes of many a choice plant by Frederick Hanbury. This garden has been restored. At Rowallane in Ulster the dark shale and sandstone, smoothed by glaciers, were cleverly exposed; both Cragside and Rowallane belong to the National Trust. The Scottish Trust has worked with the same shale and sandstone at Threave in Kirkcudbrightshire, where some beautiful effects have been achieved simply by uncovering glacier-worn formations. A friend wrote me after a visit in 1986 that he was 'fascinated to see a natural rock outcrop; added stones, without plants, used as a deliberate feature, with a small bridge over it. Both the stone and the surrounding plants enhanced each other.' The photograph (Fig. 77), kindly supplied from Threave, shows the skilful work which harks back to what is known in Japan as 'dried-up water scenery'.

Many other initial efforts at rock garden making and the cultivation of alpine plants were made in the Eastern States of North America, as recorded in the 50th Anniversary Issue of the Bulletin of the American Rock Garden Society in 1984.

70 (*Top right*) Full use of markedly stratified and worn Westmorland Limestone on T. R. Hayes & Son's rock garden at Southport Show in 1956.
*Courtesy: Hayes Garden World*

71 Westmorland Limestone unsuccessfully used to create a cliff effect: the rocks have bases not weathered and worn and thus do not fit on to one another.

72 (*Below*) Forest of Dean sandstone effectively arranged at Chelsea Show, 1961, by Gavin Jones. Though the vertical placing of the upper rocks is at variance (geologically) with the lower courses, the picture as a whole was never surpassed.

73 In this Chelsea rock garden of 1964, Gavin Jones Nurseries contrived to make it appear that the gushing water had burst through a weak spot in the escarpment of Forest of Dean sandstone.

*Courtesy: Harry Smith*

74 Brown Hornton sandstone used by Geoffrey Chalk of Gavin Jones Nurseries at Chelsea Show in 1959.

*Courtesy: Harry Smith*

75 Natural rock uncovered and used with great effect in Harold Epstein's garden at Larchmont, New York State.
*Courtesy: Gottscho-Schleisner Inc. New York*

76 Natural rock and watercourse retained as a satisfying feature at Stonecrop, the garden of Francis H. Cabot, New York State.

*Courtesy: Joel Spingarn*

Notable among such gardens are those of Harold Epstein at Larchmont, and
Stonecrop, belonging to Francis H. Cabot; both are in New York State and are
examples of superlative use of natural rock formations.

One of the most remarkable efforts in rock-pictures is the quarry garden at
Belsay, Tyne and Wear. While sandstone was being extracted for the building of
the house in the early years of the nineteenth century, care was given to the shaping
of a series of 'rooms' in the quarry connected by narrow passages and openings.

77  (*Right*) Silurian rock, lime-
free, smoothed by glaciers,
exposed at Threave (The
National Trust for Scotland),
Kirkcudbrightshire. Water-
rounded pebbles and grassy-
leafed plants have been added
to create the effect of a dry
river bed.
*Courtesy: W. Hean*

78  (*Below*) Silurian rock exposed
and augmented in the stream
garden at Logan,
Wigtownshire.
*Courtesy: Royal Botanic
          Garden, Edinburgh*

Though it has been neglected for some years, the newly installed head gardener, Mr Stephen Anderton, took at my request a photograph of it as it is today (see Fig. 81). Its general effect perhaps approaches more closely to the ideals of chapter 2, but it is unadulterated natural rock and therefore I include it here. It is noteworthy that in it is a tall Chusan Palm, *Trachycarpus fortunei*, surely the most northerly example on the eastern side of Britain?

Whatever sensations these efforts may engender, I think nothing surpasses the surprise and delight at Steadstone, Dalbeattie, Kirkcudbrightshire. On passing through the house one is confronted by the small mountain of granite in Fig. 80, carefully planted so that the maximum effect of harsh rock and the delicacy of plants is most strongly contrasted. With it one would seem to have the best of both worlds. At Logan in the same county much rock has been exposed, and I came across a startling formation of limestone in Kenmare in the south of Ireland, where acid peaty soil had been cleared from unweathered limestone.

In spite of all that had been written over a hundred years, in spite of all the rock climbing and observation, and in spite of Pulham's examples and John Wood's earliest attempt at stratification; in spite of Farrer's injunction that each rock laid should look 'as if it belonged to the next, and had been its bed-fellow since the foundations of the hills were laid' – in spite of all this, nobody had really explained how rock garden building was to be done according to the rules of geology until Captain B. H. B. Symons-Jeune wrote his book *Natural Rock Gardening* in 1932. He practised what he preached, too, and laid his rocks according to Nature's rules. We had all learnt about stratification by then but not about the joints and vertical fissures; graphically his book explained it all. After reading it one looks at rockwork and Nature's rocks with new eyes. I set about photographing outcrops on my travels about the country and the examples appearing in this book, and the diagrams, stem directly from Symons-Jeune's original instruction. He used to come to me for help in planting his contract work, mostly in Mendip Limestone. As an interesting, even amusing, aside I may mention that his daughter, on marrying and becoming Lady Loder, inherited a Pulham rock garden built in 1890 at Leonardslee, Sussex.

In the foregoing pages we have explored many avenues of thought, artistry and expertise, and have noted how our subject has all along been the plaything of horticultural advancement. I suggest we let Jason Hill have the last word in this chapter by the following passage from his *The Curious Gardener*, 1932:

This practice of making rock gardens may be fairly regarded as complementary to the modern recreation of climbing mountains; for in both we seem to be looking back, with a kind of sentimental nostalgia to the wilderness from which, by means of our civilisation, we have at last succeeded in escaping. In the rock garden we recreate a little patch of that wilderness which stands to us, now, for freedom. The success of an illusion does not depend upon the size of the stage, and in a square yard it is possible to make an excerpt of Alpine scenery which will reproduce the authentic quality of the mountains as truly as the largest rock garden can do: perhaps even more successfully, for it is too small to be felt as an incongruous part of the surrounding landscape. . . . Within this little compass we can have a flowered boulder, a grey scree set with jewel plants or a patch of Alpine lawn. . . .

79 The first use of
Mendip Limestone
at Chelsea Show by
Captain B. H. B.
Symons-Jeune. *The
Gardeners'
Chronicle*, 1923. The
slabs are placed
nearly vertically,
providing excellent
interstices for
planting. (cf. Fig.
82)
*Courtesy: Royal
Horticultural Society*

80 The 'small mountain
of granite' at
Steadstone,
Kirkcudbrightshire,
skilfully planted
with shrubs and
ferns by Bernard
Maxwell.
*Courtesy: Jonathan
M. Gibson, Country
Life*

81 Going from one
'room' to another
in the remarkable
sandstone quarry-
garden at Belsay,
Tyne and Wear.
The rock was
quarried skilfully to
achieve this effect.
*Courtesy: Stephen
Anderton*

# 5
# *Creating a rock garden*

In place of the dismal mess of oddments that formed the old-time
'Rockery', with its wretched inhabitants pining beneath the drip
of trees, smothered among common ferns, ivy and periwinkle, we
find a new creation, in which numbers of the choicest alpines can
flourish with a vigour almost equalling, and indeed sometimes
surpassing, that of the plants on their native hills.

J. Bretland Farmer

To talk of imitating nature, as so many vainly do, is to encourage a
rank and empty delusion. To make a thing look 'natural' is by no
means to imitate nature. Nature often looks more artificial than
the worst form of artificial art; nature in the mountains is often
chaotic, bald, dreary, and hideous in the highest degree. By making
a rock-garden look natural, then, we mean that it must have a firm
and effortless harmony of hill or vale, cliff or slope.

Reginald Farrer, *The English Rock Garden*, 1925

From what I have written it will be realised that the rock garden is largely a
British invention; to put it more explicitly I should say it is an art due to the
British interest in alpine and allied plants. It had a considerable fillip from
Henri Correvon in Switzerland in the early years of this century and this we should
not forget. It has been a very great movement within general horticulture and as I
have seen so much of it happen I felt I wanted to make a record of how the
enthusiasm has spread and how so much of it has come to stay. Further, it is opening
out into a number of separate enthusiasms and is proceeding just as horticulture in
general does. Horticulture has been likened to a fan, ever expanding outwards and
rock gardening in its smaller way does likewise. It will also be realised that this cult
of the alpine plant has come a long way; a book of twice this length could be
devoted to listing and describing all the suitable plants for the art. Because the list
is so very long I thought it best not to try to cover it completely, but to leave the
plants to other writers; a glance at the bibliography at the end of this book will no
doubt be helpful.

If I were asked, I suppose I should have to admit that I am an impatient gardener.
I tend to garden in a hurry, aiming to see the lawns laid and cut, and the plants
burgeoning as soon as possible. This would not lead me to plant what are known
today as semi-mature trees. To start with, the term is wrong: 'semi' means 'half'
and there is not a tree that is planted from nurseries which even approaches semi-

maturity; further, little time is gained by this operation. A sapling will usually catch up and surpass in height the larger specimen unless the latter is particularly well prepared. Of all gardening, perhaps rock gardening pays the least dividends from hurrying.

If we accept that the creation of a 'natural' type of rock garden – one which copies the serenity and beauty of nature as far as is possible, at least to the eye – is in reality an *art*, it is manifest that it would be unwise to do it in a hurry. Art cannot be achieved in a hurry. But apart from this there are the practical matters to be considered: the thorough preparation of the ground, the attention to drainage, the analysis of the soil and the additions needed to make it fertile; all these points and more need to be given priority before a stone is laid or a specimen is planted, because it will be impossible to deal with this kind of basic treatment when once the stone is in place. And when it is planted, a rock garden cannot be dug and manured as we might seek to improve a border of perennials and shrubs.

First, however, there are some fundamentals to think about before doing any designing or planting. In the smaller garden of today – where a rock garden may take up the majority of the space – there is usually some formal boundary: wall, fence or hedge. It is essential to be able to get at all of these for practical repairs or maintenance. Therefore do not plant shrubs or climbers against the *uprights* of a fence, which, if of wood, will need renewal in due course. Wood always rots at ground level, though it is almost everlasting when exposed to the air. Climbing plants on fence or wall will need pruning and a hedge needs clipping; for these reasons a space should be allowed for the work. Rain-water sumps should be located and borne in mind because sometimes they may become choked and have to be renewed. This can be a great nuisance, as I found in an earlier garden.

There may be trees on the site, or in next-door gardens; the size to which they will get and how far their roots will spread must be assessed. The shade they cast may appear to be an inconvenience but it is by no means disastrous as long as it does not result in completely shading the only areas for sitting in the garden. (I am dreaming that we all look upon our gardens as an outdoor room, whether we like to sit in sun or shade.) Overhead tree-shade is the last thing to be given to a rock garden. It is a mistake to allow a tree to remain because it is young and small, or because its removal will make the plot unbearably empty; trees and shrubs grow much bigger and faster than any of us anticipate as a rule. What looks small today may need drastic reduction in a few years, causing havoc and resulting in ugliness. Some new houses have been built very near my garden but between us – on *their* plots – are oaks and sycamores, youngsters now but which will achieve seventy to eighty feet in height and certainly eighty feet in width and will be poking into my neighbours' windows before long. This example shows what little care and thought planners give to their sites.

Next, whatever sort of rock garden you design, it will probably be necessary to have a garden shed and a corner for rubbish, compost-making, storing of peat bales, making of bonfires etc., and a firm path will be needed between these and the house. This path will provide access to various areas for weeding and other maintenance, and watering.

There are further practicalities to be considered. Is there to be an area for children's games? Are dogs to be kept? How do you keep your own cat or dog away from choice and tiny alpine plants? For believe me, cats and dogs can do much damage, and the peregrinations of neighbours' small animals are not, according to law, the responsibility of their owners. The subjects of small trees, shadows, sitting places and the like I discussed fairly fully in my book *Three Gardens*; they all need careful thought. There is no need for a garden to be always in full sun; the passing of shadows across it on sunny days can be a wonderful addition to the design of a garden, in fact, I would almost add, an advantage and even a necessity. Light and shade are the two fundamentals with which any picture is made.

This brings me to the oft-repeated phrase 'the genius of the place'. Would a rock garden as a work of art be appropriate to the site? If not, alpines can still be grown in other ways, which are explored in a later chapter. Should the rock garden be large, more or less to fill the garden, or only to fill a portion of it? Should it be visible as a great feature from the house windows? If it is to be built of very beautiful rock this might be permissible, but many rock plants are not conspicuous in winter, being deciduous. I think I like best to look upon lawn and evergreens in winter, but I have compromised by keeping these for the front garden through which I pass daily, leaving most deciduous shrubs and plants for the back garden into which one need not go during inclement weather. On the other hand, of course, more varied colour and interest can be achieved from a mixture of evergreen and deciduous shrubs and plants throughout the year.

The size of the rock garden will be governed by the size of the whole garden and a sense of scale; the 'genius of the place' covers all this and also the general 'feeling' and surrounds which may be beyond our control. (I think that any real work of art can be achieved in untoward surroundings so long as the sight of the surroundings is softened by the growth of shrubs – or even trees, or climbers on a fence.)

Before going further into the 'genius' let us return to the size of the rock garden. If it is to take up nearly the whole plot, all that is needed, therefore, is to obscure the boundaries with shrubby growth. Many of the greatest works of garden art are in the Far East, and may be in miniature relationship to a loved view. I quoted Reginald Farrer about Japanese gardens in chapter 4 to show how in a tiny plot a completely satisfying landscape in miniature could be made. But to do this with our rock garden in a portion of the garden we need to have it out of sight, to come upon it suddenly, and as suddenly to realise that all the surrounding foliage, and that of the rock plants, is in miniature. It would be no use trying to achieve a miniature landscape and using at the same time a large-leafed hosta in it; we should have to choose that tiny variety 'Thumbnail' if we were determined to include a hosta.

The 'genius' also concerns the soil, which so far we have scarcely considered. The soil very often governs the surrounding landscape and its trees and plants. I consider it would be folly to try to make, for instance, a heather garden on a heavy clay soil; it would be worse than folly to try to achieve it on a limy soil. A rock garden can be predominantly limy, or its opposite, acid, and there are plenty of rock plants – and indeed carpeting plants which would give a moorland effect – which will thrive on a limy soil without having recourse to heathers. But a rock

82 Rock formation at Hart's Pass, Whatcom Co., Washington, U.S.A. Stratification in three distinct directions in a small space. The top and lower left angles of stratification would make good homes for plants but the middle layers would not because they would lead moisture away from roots in crevices. If the illustration is turned half on its side with B at the bottom, the middle sloping rocks provide admirable cool planting crevices. (cf. Fig. 79)
*Courtesy: Brian O. Mulligan*

weak rocks

strong rock

disintegrated rock

D

scree formed from disintegrated rock above, flowing down slope

B

C

A

A, B, C, D fallen rock, disintegration joints
D is the base

83 Mendip Limestone. A weak rock has fallen in front of an outcrop of strong rock. A scree has started to form.

*of strata, leaning against the hill*
*ondary joints*
*primary joints are hidden under the turf*

84 Very steeply tilted strata of Carboniferous Limestone at Cashel, Ireland.

85 The same tilted strata as in Fig. 84, seen from the far end.

86 Gentle outcrop of almost horizontal strata on the Great Orme's Head, North Wales. Carboniferous Limestone.

A *top stratum*
B *primary joints*
C *fallen rock*
D *rock has been protected by B*
F *weak seam protected by G*

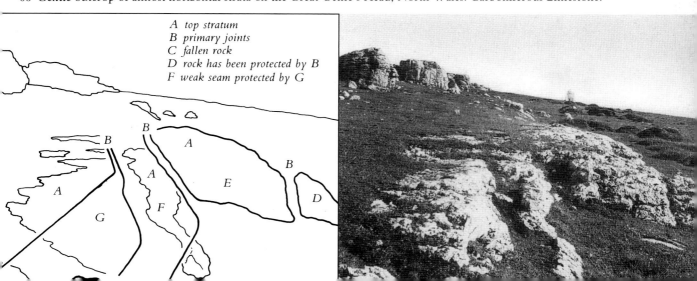

A *firm closely integrated bed of rock, holding up (B) loosely integrated bed of similar rock*
C *places for scree*

87  A steep slope on the Isle of Purbeck where the limestone is holding up the bank.

88  View of Fig. 87 from the right side. It shows a ledge such as could be used for a footpath bringing the loosely arranged rocks above into easy reach for planting.

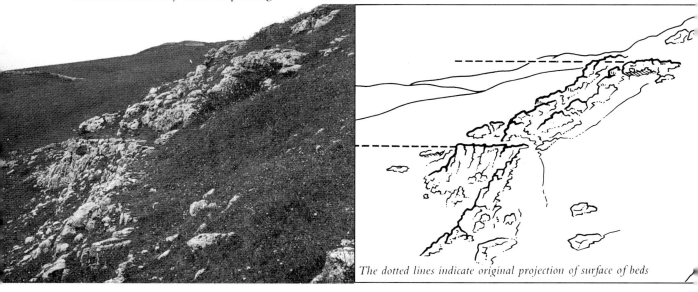

*The dotted lines indicate original projection of surface of beds*

89  A closer view, from the left side of Fig. 87.

*The central portion of Fig. 88, at X, is similar to formation at A in*

garden, if made with an eye to art, can easily absorb as its neighbours shrubs of all kinds, and woodland plants if trees abound, or marsh plants if there is natural water, whereas it would destroy its art if its immediate neighbours were beds of roses, rows of vegetables or prim summer flower bedding. There is no 'genius' in them for our purpose.

## The Soil

Let us now consider the soil. It is an unfortunate truth that building contractors are very prone to play havoc with the lie of the land around new houses. Subsoil from the footings are often spread over the neighbouring topsoil with disastrous results. In addition, heavy machinery and lorries often compress the natural soil – or this extra soil – until it is difficult even to get a fork into it.

If the garden is on flat clay it would be necessary to import suitable soil to build up the outcrops of rock, for the simple reason that to dig and delve and make a valley in order to form a hill with the surplus soil would result in drainage problems; and rock plants do not thrive on clay. On the other hand, if the clay is on a slope all will be well.

Sands, gravels and chalk offer good drainage for sunken paths and other excavations, but much skill will be needed to ensure that the subsoil is either removed altogether or used in exchange for the topsoil under portions which are to be raised. This applies to flat as well as sloping ground. Apart from these extremes it is wonderful how plants, shrubs and trees from all over the world will thrive on what we call 'normal' soil. Our own soil often appears to be normal but two plots are seldom alike. Enough has been said, I think, to prove that great care must be taken to ensure that, in whatever extreme medium we are to work, we must bolster the character of weak soils to make them good and fertile. The strange thing is that very light (sandy, gravelly) soils and very heavy (clay) or chalky soils all benefit from an admixture of the same thing – humus. This can be in the form of leafmould, peat or garden compost plus, if necessary, a general fertiliser. If we accept that for alpine and rock plants – as for lilies – the first and second essential is drainage, with drainage also for the third, we shall not go far wrong. Sloping ground is more advantageous than flat from our point of view, but much can also be done on the flat. So that now we have attended to surrounds, approach, fertility and drainage and have dug and thoroughly turned and mixed all the soil to be used.

I have read somewhere that a rock garden follows no rule of design. This must surely be disputed. If one is putting up a work of art its siting is very important, and involved in the siting is the vision of an outcrop here and a valley there, with all the variations between the two that one can conjure up. Perhaps the writer of that early sentence was visualising what he would do when his wagon load of rocks arrived. Undoubtedly really beautiful weathered and characterful stone dictates its own placing and rock joins rock in an ordered way. But to visualise what one can do on a flat or sloping site, much can be achieved with stakes and empty cartons to decide where should be the major outcrop and its approximate height; where the outlines should be and where the scree or pool.

The old rule of thumb method of setting rocks to form terraces and pockets for plants is to start with the bottom stones and work upwards. In creating a natural

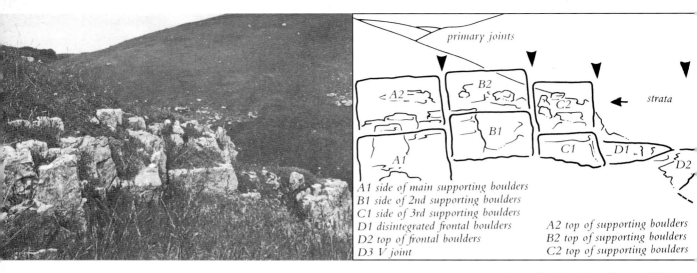

90 A minor outcrop of Purbeck Limestone. It shows in particular a vertically split rock on the far right, from which a triangular lump has fallen creating a V-joint. This is useful when a specially abrupt end is required from all angles.

In the diagram:

*primary joints*

*strata*

*< A2 >* *B2* *C2*

*B1* *C1* *D1*

*A1* *D2*

A1 side of main supporting boulders
B1 side of 2nd supporting boulders
C1 side of 3rd supporting boulders
D1 disintegrated frontal boulders
D2 top of frontal boulders
D3 V joint

A2 top of supporting boulders
B2 top of supporting boulders
C2 top of supporting boulders

In the diagram:

*strata*

*A* *B* *D* *E*

*C1* *B1* *A1* *D1* *E1* *F1* *G*

*B2* *B2* *E2* *F2*

*D2* *E2* *G2*

*E3* *F3*

A, B, C, D, E divided from A1, B1, C1, D1, E1, F1, H
by secondary joint
B2, D2, E2, F2, G2 divided from E3, F3 by secondary joint

91 Vertically tilted strata of Mendip Limestone, built at Chelsea Show by Marcel de Smet, c. 1950.

92 Steeply tilted strata of hard sandstone which has caused the hilltop.

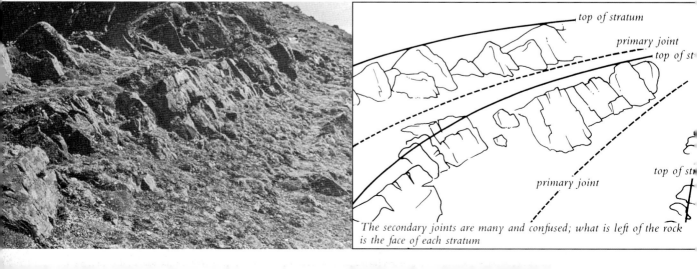

In the diagram:

*top of stratum*

*primary joint*

*top of st*

*primary joint*

*top of st*

The secondary joints are many and confused; what is left of the rock is the face of each stratum

93 Tiny quarry of Sussex sandstone showing sloping strata and primary joints. Near East Grinstead, Sussex.

94 Sussex sandstone set into a bank, to appear as if left after quarrying, soon after completion. Broken stone lies on the soil. For close-up of one of the crevices a year after planting, see Fig. 139.

95 Outcrops of Sussex sandstone on Gravetye Estate, East Grinstead, Sussex, showing stratification slanting into the bank, which it holds up. The upper main layer is obviously of a harder nature than the lower, which it protects. The overgrowth of bushes etc. was cleared from this by William Robinson so that the rocks formed an eye-catcher in the view from his house.

rock garden one should first decide on the sort of picture to be achieved and then place the most important, and usually the largest, rocks on the site. It is these key rocks which will govern the slope of the strata and the positions and slope of outlying rocks at the extreme ends of the whole area. We must imagine that the soil from the hillock, thrust up by the rock outcrop, has been wasted away from the top into the valleys, and that underneath it everywhere is solid rock. This is the fundamental upon which the design of all natural rock gardening rests.

# The Rock

The obvious plot where a rock garden can best be made is where rock of some kind already occurs. Some of the best of rock gardens are of natural, uncovered rock by which I mean that the rock is merely showing through the turf or ground; in places it can be made more conspicuous by scraping away the soil. Wherever it occurs, there are almost certainly tap-rooted weeds and tree seedlings. These must be completely eradicated; where it is impossible to get the roots out, it is best to cut off the plants at ground level and treat the new growth once or twice with weedkiller during the first year. The same applies to invasive grass roots.

Obvious, too, is the fact that if there is a local stone, that will be the best choice for the rock garden. Where there is no stone, and where, even so, it is resolved to have some, the choice is often limited by the cost of cartage. Otherwise the choice has been indicated in chapter 4 and can be made according to whether limestone or sandstone is the most advantageous from all points of view. If the natural soil is very acid, the use of limestone will help rather than hinder, and on a limy soil it matters little whether limy or neutral rock is chosen. If the importation of rock proves too expensive, there are satisfactory substitutes mentioned in chapter 11. In addition tufa should be considered as it is light in weight and cartage will be accordingly less – from Gloucestershire or Derbyshire. Because it has no natural stratification its use for building is easy. It can be laid to suit the owner's taste, who can rest assured that plants will grow well in and around it. At the same time, the purist should bear in mind that it is seldom found 'growing' as an exposed outcrop, but occurs, as explained in chapter 3, underground. Even so, from the purely cultural point of view, and for ease in placing, it is invaluable. It is soft and prone to frost damage when first quarried, but hardens with exposure.

In some districts quarried stone is available; it is, when new, rather unsympathetic and is always hard and angular; thus it has aesthetic disadvantages and it would be best to forget this chapter and pass straight on to chapter 6. In some areas are large rounded river-worn boulders. At first sight they appear to be useless, but I do not find this so; great effect can be made with them if a sandy river-bed type of garden can be attempted. This is a scheme to which the Japanese have brought much art. It is worth noting here that whereas the Japanese are inclined to use rounded or otherwise smoothed and shapely boulders with great effect, giving them each a special aesthetic attribute, the Chinese before them and since prefer fantastic rocks of the most involved shapes – a completely different ideal. In our rock gardens we can surely handle any kind of stone to advantage if enough thought is given to the project.

When I was a schoolboy my first rock garden was composed of flints, bits of sawn building stone, and some arbitrary pieces of alabaster whose pink and white marble-like texture took my fancy! This I should not recommend. But we must remember that we are making an imaginary rocky setting and it is marvellous how one's imagination can colour and disguise even the most untoward of rock or stones.

## The Building

In many books about rock garden construction, including Farrer, it is said that two-thirds of each rock should be buried. This is the plantsman remembering that buried stone is always cool and to the liking of alpine plants which, though perhaps only two to three inches high, may well have roots descending by as many feet. It might be all very well for Farrer to bury two-thirds of each rock; rocks were two a penny to him. But imagine anyone who goes to the expense of carting rock from far afield to his own district thinking of burying so much! The essential is that each rock shall be absolutely firm and in using weathered limestone one cannot guarantee that it can always be laid on its broadest face; it must be laid only as it was in nature. To achieve firmness, a little concrete may be added where necessary but well out of sight, and away from areas where it might obstruct root-run. By all means bury some rock, but let it be small unwanted pieces or even broken brick to retain coolness and moisture in hot weather. Another unfortunate term crops up again and again in rock garden books: the making of 'pockets' for plants. It will be seen from the above paragraph that a pocket of soil would be of little use.

In districts where rock occurs there are frequently pieces lying around where they were left by the glaciers and seas before time. These we know will be hard and last, whereas some freshly quarried stone can crumble in exposure to frost and rain. In any case, unless a dramatic outcrop is attempted, all rock should lie in its original bed, by which is meant that its natural stratification should be preserved. In fact dramatically up-tilted strata should not be attempted unless hard stone is used.

We are at the point, now, of construction. We have our background, our soil, our rock and a path; it remains to decide whether water is to be used to enhance the make-believe of the picture. It will be manifest that in the natural type of rock garden, water must look natural too. A formal design would be as inappropriate as a dead straight path. In these days of plastic pools and electric pumps any scheme may be attempted, but I will leave this until chapter 13.

Probably by now it will be thought that I have raised quite enough details and difficulties to be surmounted, which only goes to prove that much initial thought is necessary. There is no doubt that the larger rock garden is simpler than a miniature scheme. I think miniature schemes are best left to the Japanese and to troughs and sink gardens (chapter 11). If we want to create a piece of natural scenery, we need to use shrubs around it, and to cover most of the ground away from the rocks with either ground-covering plants or a scree. The old exhibition idea of undulating lawns is not practical in the garden, although one might think that with today's 'strimmers' and rotary mowers it might be attempted. There is however always the danger of grasses and weeds with running roots extending from the turf outwards, apart from the labour entailed. The lists at the end of the book call to mind some first-rate, weed-proof ground-covers. And when I advocate a large scheme it is with ground covering in mind. It is the best and only way to make gardening easy today if their choice be right. As detailed in my book *Three Gardens*, for many years I tended satisfactorily an acre on only two days' work per month during the growing season. It is only by means of suitable mulches and ground-cover plants that one can cope with an area where no annual digging and hoeing can be done.

The shingle slides and real screes will be in appearance flowing down from the outcrops and make their own delightful covering. In these more stony places between rocks and on ledges and the old-fashioned 'pockets' and at the edges of the paths are the places for good, small, alpines of flowing growth.

My photographs and diagrams will show, I think, that strata can vary in pitch even in one garden. But what occurs in nature cannot always be copied with equanimity in a garden, and as a general rule the most restful and satisfying effect can usually be achieved by keeping roughly to one plan.

Stone which is mainly in fairly flat pieces can be used at an acute angle, slanting upwards to achieve considerable height. If it is laid more or less flat many layers have to be used to achieve the same height with a corresponding sense of boredom and a tendency towards walling and bricklaying. The most exciting of outcrops are often those with the greatest tilt. It is with violently tilted strata that one often needs a shovelful of concrete at the base to make each rock not only safe in itself but safe enough to carry one's own weight when stepping on them for planting and weeding. It will be obvious, too, that the thin stones put in at an angle on the older parts of the Edinburgh rock garden provide a deep root-run for the plants. In the reverse we may say that the building up of stone upon stone – with a slight tilt – to create height is not satisfactorily achieved when using the north country Carboniferous Limestone which is plucked from the fields. The weatherworn top is quite different from the rough base (which has been protected by turf) and they cannot be superimposed. This fault can be seen at the Cambridge Botanic Garden and also at Polesden Lacey, Surrey.

Different counsel must be given if the only rocks available are rounded boulders from a river bed. It is well-nigh impossible to build these into any sort of outcrop; a line of much lesser significance must be taken using them merely as incidents on a flat or gently sloping terrain. It is surprising how satisfying this can be.

The crown of an outcrop in nature will have been subject to extreme weather-action and the uppermost rocks should accordingly be chosen not for their dramatic top corners, but for broken rounded outlines.

On taking delivery of a few tons of weatherworn rocks it will be obvious that certain pieces have affinity to others. Accordingly it is wise to sort them into related groups, to be used to build together as perhaps they were in nature. Unless one has a really large amount of stone to play with it will usually be found that some of these pieces fit together fairly well but that there is an unfortunate gap here and there. If these gaps cannot be used for planting it is best to fill them in with concrete, tinted to match the stone, and to disguise this liberty by arranging a prostrate evergreen, such as a dwarf cotoneaster, to cover all traces of the subterfuge.

James Pulham made great play with overhanging and receding strata. This is all

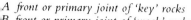

A *front or primary joint of 'key' rocks*
B *front or primary joint of 'weak' rocks*
C *front or primary joint of key rocks of lower stratum*
D, E *outlying finish or primary joints*

96, 97, 98 Three photographs of a demonstration showing how to create an outcrop (using rather characterless river-bed boulders), with sloping strata similar to those in Fig. 92.

E1 *is supported by stones below it and at back, and connected with main outcrop by 2 strata (weak) at F*
E2 *is supported by stones below it and at back, and connected with main outcrop by 2 strata (weak) at G*
H *main strata sloping back to ground level*

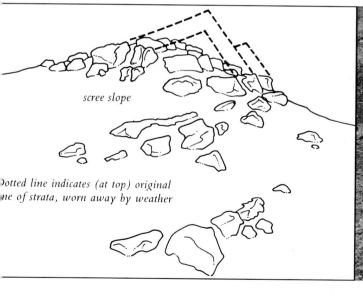

*scree slope*

*Dotted line indicates (at top) original line of strata, worn away by weather*

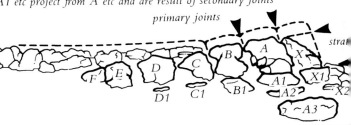

X   disintegrated rock
A   main rock protected by X
B, C, D, E, F same strata as A
A1, B1, C1, D1, X1 lower stratum
A2, A3, and X2 still lower stratum
Y   upper stratum disintegrated on top of main strata
A1 etc project from A etc and are result of secondary joints

99  Outcrop of Mendip Limestone built upon flat ground.

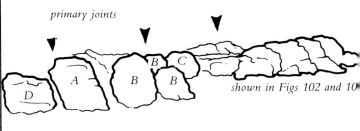

A is the strongest rock, being least worn away
B is the largest rock but has disintegrated into 3 pieces
C & D smaller supporting rocks

100  The outcrop in Fig. 99 photographed from the left, after the soil levels had been adjusted.

101  Small outcrop of Mendip Limestone, showing one thick but much broken stratum. (Right outcrop in Fig. 100)

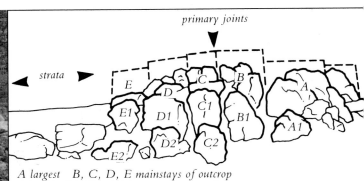

A largest   B, C, D, E mainstays of outcrop
A1, B1, C1, D1, E1 lesser mainstays of outcrop
C2, D2, E2 third lines of outcrop
Secondary joints run behind 2, 1
dotted line indicates original crown of outcrop

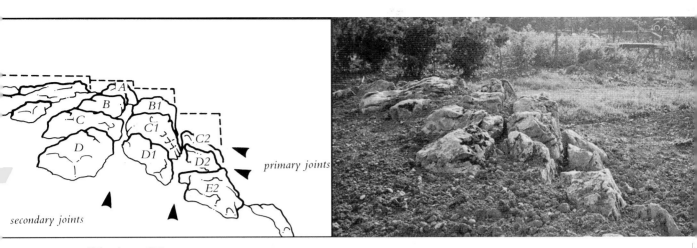

*primary joints*

*secondary joints*

102  Side view of Fig. 101.

103  Lava rock, with river–boulder edging used to contain succulents in the Huntington Botanic Garden, San Marino, California. Like tufa, lava has no stratification.                                                    *Courtesy: W. George Waters*

very well and highly effective when using rock for rock's sake and provides those deep shadows which so help the picture as a whole. But very few plants will grow in a crevice under an overhanging rock except small ferns, and the idea should not be overdone.

Here and there it may be possible to make use of a flat piece of rock to interrupt a path; this I allude to in chapter 13.

The Wisley rock garden benefits from its northern slope; the shadows are dark and on that sharply draining sandy slope excessive drying-out is avoided. This is a pointer to the fact that in hot climates a cool slope may be best for many alpine plants. On the other hand at Wisley constant endeavour has to be made to build out terraces to catch the sun. Seldom does one rule apply to all gardens!

## The Surrounds

It will not do to give my imagination too little rein. While the rock garden of today must, as a rule, be finite because few of us have acres to play with, it is a wonderful thing: it can blend with many types of planting. At Wisley it peters out into a moist piece of meadow which is peopled with tiny daffodils and other bulbs in spring, while below it joins with a stream and woodland planting. At Edinburgh, too, the great rock garden merges with peat beds, ferns and woodland at one end and with a heather garden at the other. It can just as easily be a good neighbour for an assortment of shrubs.

We all like our garden to look as big as possible. It is good to contemplate the infinite. I have already hinted at the way that shrubs can help to soften unpleasant objects in the background. There is also the foreground to be considered. It is an old trick of the painters of landscapes to include in the foreground some plants of large foliage – burdock, foxglove and the like. This is worth a thought in the garden; it helps to increase the perspective. I discussed this fully in my *The Art of Planting*. In sun we have plants such as bergenias and *Viburnum davidii*, and for shade there are many: hostas, *Galax* are but two.

In our rock, heath and woodland we are getting towards that mirage of gardening – the Wild Garden. There is no such thing as wild gardening. To be successful it would take more careful labour than all the rest of the garden put together. The nearest we can sensibly get is what I always term ecological gardening – where plants are grown in such suitable environments that they require little attention. Mostly it applies to that great upsurging effort of twentieth-century gardening, the woodland garden.

## The Art

I hope that what I have written in this and previous chapters will prove that the making and planting of a natural rock garden is as much an art as any other phase of gardening. Even more would I claim that it is a more complex art than other gardening. It is like comparing the music produced by a piano with that from a violin: in the one the notes are there, waiting to be sounded, in the other the notes have to be made by the skill of the player. In planting a conventional garden one usually has the soil and paths ready made; in rock gardening one first has to gather the rocks for the foundation of the picture and then to decorate the scene with a suitable arrangement of plants. Another simile would be that one has first to make the frame and canvas to excellent quality and then to paint the picture. Is it not therefore a great and involved art combining two quite different abilities?

And yet we continue to make 'rockeries' in spite of all that has been written and done in the past! If a small bank is left at the side of a drive into the forecourt of a modest building, it is given – I will not say 'decorated with' – a few pieces of quarried angular stone, with a heather or two, an aubrieta and a juniper popped in to enable the owner to call it a 'rockery'. This perhaps goes with the standard of decoration in and around the dwelling, but when one sees in the midst of London an island roundabout 'decorated' with a few lumps of beautiful Westmorland rock, Man's ignorance cannot be carried much further, and incongruity reigns, with the prostitution of one of nature's greatest beauties. It is as if a Himalayan Blue Poppy were placed in the middle of a rail terminus or junk yard.

## Gathering the Rocks

The creation of a natural rock garden is, as Gavin Jones explained (chapter 4), like bringing a landscape painting to an otherwise dull and conventional room. We can do without it, but why should we? As intimated earlier, it is not in line with conservation which has assumed great significance. But when we consider that mankind has been carting around the world all sorts of natural commodities for hundreds, even thousands, of years we must admit that conservation has few precedents. We decorate our homes with precious timbers from abroad. We bring plants from all over the world to grace our gardens and tropical *Monstera* to give majesty to our bigger rooms; we pave our streets with material from the tropics; we roof our dwellings over much of England with Welsh slate, build our banks and City offices with Scottish granite and give our wives diamonds from South Africa. Some of this is done to clear land for growing crops, such as gathering up loose stones to make a fence around a consequently ploughable field. This is partly why beautiful weathered rock has been available in the Mendips and in Westmorland. It does not, however, answer the question of whether it is right to quarry stone. And yet how picturesque an old abandoned chalk quarry can be! Whether we make rock gardens, mankind will go on digging and delving.

To the ardently conservation-minded would-be rock gardener, I should like to draw attention to the imitation rocks now available. There are some half-dozen shapes available but as each has four or more sides repetition is not obvious. The samples I have seen are of a soft greyish colour, very similar to our native limestones. They have the immense advantage of being of light weight, only a pound or two each. Used with careful thought they might give the impression of being genuine rocks; but, though they may deceive the human eye, they will not deceive the roots of plants. To make them acceptable to the roots they should be cool to the touch, and this is best achieved by filling them with soil, or hypertufa (see chapter 11).

Whatever dodge is adopted, the expense and the hard labour of using genuine stone will be minimised.

If one lives in one of our western counties where rocks abound we might quite well yearn, not for more rock in our gardens but for a patch of rich pasture. It may also be said that rock used well within a rocky county should bring with it the greatest satisfaction. The rock used, whether sparingly or lavishly, should only be used to *suggest* that it is part of the crust of the earth over which our garden is made.

Art deceives the eye; this is its great quality. There is no doubt that a good natural rock garden does the same. I think there are enough photographs of natural outcrops (which I have been collecting for many years) and good examples of styles of rock garden making in this book to show that almost anything can be achieved with rock, subject to its quality and the site concerned.

## *Maintenance*

The question that is sure to be asked by the unenthused and unconvinced is whether a natural rock garden is a practical proposition for today. I think it is. I made my first rock garden when I was a schoolboy and have made many since. I have had the greatest satisfaction from exerting my mind first to think in terms of geology and later in terms of plants in order to beautify a given site. A rock garden is thus highly interesting to make, and long lasting.

The creation and maintenance of a natural rock garden gives no more work than conventional gardening, whether it be shrubs and plants in mixed array or beds of roses on a lawn. When once made, there is no digging nor hoeing. The shingle and plants should cover all soil so that only a little hand-weeding is needed; and when it is needed it is an indication that the choice of ground-cover has not been carefully made or that the shingle is not thick enough. (In any case hoeing and digging, by disturbing the soil, always result in more weeds appearing.) I believe in hand-weeding everywhere, plus the use of dead or growing leaves to suppress germination of weeds. It requires more intelligence than hoeing and digging, that is all. And many of the larger and more forceful rock plants and alpines are now accepted as ground-cover plants. It depends upon the context.

In winter the main work, instead of digging, will be the removal of wet dead leaves which accumulate in nooks and depressions and can ruin certain alpines, and towards spring a general tidying and reduction of too-vigorous plants and some top dressing. I do really believe that rock gardening can be mainly fun throughout the year.

If you are bent on growing a lot of the miniature, non-spreading type of rock plants it would be better not to contemplate a natural rock garden but to expend your energies in the types of cultivation outlined in chapter 11.

With regard to the shingle, it must match as nearly as possible the rock with which the scheme is created. It is to be used to cover the slopes around the outcrops and to look as if over the centuries the chips have broken off the main rocks and fallen to make a scree. If possible it should be debris supplied by the source or quarry local to where the rocks are gathered. On no account should it be uniformly

104  Artificial waterfall in a rock garden of Sussex Sandstone. Giving the effect of having worn away the rock in its passing (see Figs. 50, 65, 69), water should always pour over a low stone in the stratum and never be given an artificial 'lip' to project the fall clear of the main rock.

105  Jonas Ridge, Linville Gorge, the Blue Ridge Mountains, Virginia, United States of America. The big scale of the Ridge is indicated by the flowering bushes of *Kalmia latifolia* in the foreground. The rock formation and slope could prove to be a model for gardens of any size, with ample space for alpine plants in the fissures and in a scree slope below.
*Courtesy: A. D. Schilling*

screened or graded on the surface. While the deep scree itself can be made of crushed and graded quality, like the debris from the outcrop, the surface should be covered with stones from small to large, to give a natural effect. As the shingle slopes descend from the outcrops, that is where the ground-cover plants should begin, small at first – the ground-covering rock plants leading to a close sward of large smothering plants and creeping shrubs, not forgetting the inclusion of small bulbs for autumn and spring.

Having then overcome our conservation scruples, and decided we should like to make a rock garden, we have to consider its suitability and its scale in relationship to the rest of the garden. The suitability and scale of any part of any kind of garden are in the owner's eye, or that of his professional adviser. Successful, no doubt, as are the Japanese miniature gardens, I should feel so out of scale with them myself, like Gulliver, that I would rather devote my circumscribed area to something else. To accommodate a rock garden of the size of those in many of my illustrations it would be almost a necessity to have a garden of at least half an acre. While today's housing estates certainly do not run to much more than an eighth of an acre, there are many gardens about of greater size, in this country and abroad.

So let us bring a breath of the open country into our gardens. It is what the planners are doing in many a new town – planting native bushes and trees instead of pink cherries and cypresses. If they can do it why should not we? Let me indicate to you how, having enjoyed your first exercise in the geology, you can plant your rock garden to give a maximum of beauty with a minimum of work. In the growing months there will be some hand-weeding, which has the advantage of bringing one into close contact with the alpine gems.

# 6

# *The Children of the Hills*

When you try to visualise this flowering society, when you call up
all the flowers you can remember, and their tints and shapes and
scents, the climates they like, the scenery they adorn, the memories
they bring back, your mind begins to riot with flowering, and of
all this colour and perfume and delight there seems no end or order.
Donald Culross Peattie, *Flowering Earth*, 1948

Whatever influence Reginald Farrer may have had on the construction of the rock garden, there is no doubt that his writings on alpine plants – which he called the Children of the Hills – enthralled a vast number of gardeners. In fact when once they started on the cultivation of these little plants this enthusiasm was total. Societies for the advancement of the knowledge about the plants have sprung up in many countries as a result. There are so many kinds of magic in plants that they charm the humblest of gardeners, or, like Peattie – from whose delightsome book I quote above – the ardent botanist.

The interest in alpine plants is comparatively new in the history of gardening, but there is a confusion over the term 'alpines'. The Alps are a range of mountains separating France from Italy, but an 'alpine' has come to mean a plant growing on any mountain, high ground or moorland in either hemisphere. In addition, in certain latitudes they may grow at sea-level. From this it will be seen that the term alpine or rock plant does not necessarily imply that rocks are needed for their well-being. There is yet another point to make: an 'Alp' in Switzerland means a pasture on the hills, and to these alps shepherds drove their animals in the summer for the sake of the lush grasses, returning to the lowlands in autumn. I think there may be some connection between this and the fact that alpine plants were not cultivated as early in history as were the lowland plants, for the simple fact that they had not been observed. By the time the upland meadows were fit for grazing, the earliest dwarf plants would have been out of flower. Moreover, we know that mountains were looked upon with much fear in early times.

We can learn a little from ancient tapestries and paintings. The Unicorn Tapestry, in the Cloisters Museum, New York, is believed to have been worked c. 1500 in Brussels. The *millefleurs* ground-work contains sweet violet, daisy, strawberry, periwinkle, pansy, marigold, wallflowers, primrose, pimpernel and others. Brussels is of course far from mountains: all of the above are lowland flowers. Mountain flowers are scarce, too, in John Gerard's *Herball* of 1596, and even John Parkinson, in his *Paradisus in Sole Paradisus Terrestris* of 1629, includes only *Soldanella* and a few saxifrages, though he figures many foreign plants. There is no doubt that Europeans were familiar with flowers of the open country and thin woodland; the British in particular ventured seldom up precipitous slopes.

## Some Early Books

By 1561 there were over a thousand different plants in cultivation in Germany as recorded by Conrad Gessner in his *Historia Plantarum*. Remarkably for so early in northern Europe, he was deeply moved by the beauty of mountains: 'The soul is strangely rapt by these astonishing heights'. He had written what is considered to be the first treatise on alpine plants, published in 1555. This was the beginning of our modern love for hills and mountains, and was the awakening to untold beauties. In his speech at the opening of the E. H. Lohbrunner Alpine Garden at Victoria, British Columbia, my old friend Professor W. T. Stearn read out Gessner's delight at contemplating mountains: 'I am resolved henceforth ... so long as life is granted me by divine providence, every year to ascend several mountains or at least one, when the plants are in full growth, partly for knowledge of them, partly for noble exercise and gladdening of the mind. How great indeed are the enjoyment and the delights of the spirit as it is affected by contemplating in wonder the vastness of the mountains and raising one's head as it were among the clouds.'

In books on garden and other history one reads a lot about the Grand Tour: the travels abroad, particularly to Italy by the scions of noble families. One such, Sir George Wheeler, as early as 1676 and so young as 25, may well have been the introducer of *Hypericum calycinum*, that engaging and beautiful romper of our gardens. And it is said that he also brought seeds of one of the most reliable shrublets from Greece, *Hypericum olympicum*, of which I much prefer the paler form 'Citrinum'. Both are easy to grow on any rock garden.

In the early eighteenth century J. P. de Tournefort, a French botanist, and his artist companion Claude Aubriet visited many of the islands and countries of the eastern Mediterranean; we can recall *Origanum tournefortii* in memory of the first, a beautiful marjoram for sunny spots, and that universal spring-flowering rock plant, which must surely be on every rock garden in the country, and in many borders and walls besides, *Aubrieta deltoidea*. Long lived and floriferous, it thrives in a limy, harsh soil and far from its original lavender blue is now available from almost crimson to darkest purple.

A serious study of Swiss plants had been the subject of several works by Albrecht von Haller, from 1742 to 1768. It may be said that he really founded the study of this small area of Europe, where so many plants occur, so many of which grace our rock gardens today. Looking through later books we find that in *The Gardener's Dictionary*, that epoch-making work of 1731 by Philip Miller, are listed several alpines including the little white *Androsace lactea*, bold lilac *Aster alpinus* with orange centre, *Geranium argenteum* with its silvery leaves, gorgeous blue *Gentiana acaulis* and the comparatively rare *Phyteuma comosum* (now known as *Physoplexis comosa*), a campanula-relative with the strangest of flowers. They are all European; American species included the Bloodroot *Sanguinaria canadensis*, *Trillium erectum* and *Uvularia sessilifolia*; the last two are woodlanders that cannot be called common even today.

I think we owe considerable thanks, in this cursory look at the introduction of alpine plants to England, to two doctors; Dr John Fothergill and Dr William Pitcairn. They paid for a keen Scottish gardener, Thomas Blaikie, to go to the Alps specifically to collect plants. He succeeded in sending thirty-two new species home. They were real 'high alpines' and included some gems difficult of cultivation and one longs to know how they fared. So far as I can ascertain this little paragraph is a brief record of the first expedition to be made from Britain with the express purpose of seeing and collecting alpine plants; its results and list of plants are recorded in *The Diary of a Scotch Gardener at the French Court*, c. 1775. From his wonder at seeing alpines in their natural conditions his book records some of the treasures he brought home. Among them were *Ranunculus glacialis*, *Pyrola* (*Moneses*) *uniflora*, *Androsace* (*Diapensia*) *helvetica lactea*, *A. villosa* and *Polygala chamaebuxus* 'which overruns their fields like clover'. Of the Mountain Rose or *Rhododendron ferrugineum*:

> In the wild waste remote from human taste
> These Rocks bring forth and desolation smile
> Here blooms the Rose where human face ne'er shone
> And spreads its beautys to the Sun Alone.

It seems that this verse was a true picture of the matter.

A vast compendium appeared in 1778: *The Universal Gardener* by Thomas Mawe and John Abercrombie. It is an encyclopaedia of gardening for general consultation, covering every possible form of gardening, both in the open air and under glass. *Almost* every form of gardening, I should write, because there is no entry for rock gardens nor for alpines, although alpine plants are included. We find the British Bird's Eye Primula, *Primula farinosa*, but not *Gentiana verna* which grows with it in Yorkshire; *Iberis sempervirens*, the very hardy, well-known perennial Candytuft is recommended for the greenhouse with the rather tender *I. semperflorens*; *Gentiana acaulis*, which we are reminded is also called the Gentianella, a name adopted by Reginald Farrer; *Alyssum saxatile* is included but no *Aubrieta*.

It is a big step forward to the founding of the *Botanical Magazine* by William Curtis in 1787; he edited it for seventeen years, during which time the exquisite hand-coloured engravings had among them about three dozen real alpine plants including the winter flowering *Cyclamen coum*; *Gentiana acaulis*; *Rubus arcticus* (a tiny bramble with pink flowers); *Ranunculus gramineus*, a grassy-leafed buttercup; the lovely Gesneriaceous plant for cool positions, *Ramonda myconii* (to which name we have returned after using instead *Ramondia pyrenaica* for about a century!); the superb pink Garland Flower, *Daphne cneorum*; *Polygala chamaebuxus*, box-like but with somewhat pea-shaped flowers; the brilliant blue spring gentian, *Gentiana verna*; *Androsace villosa* and other well known European alpines. Also included are some noteworthy foreigners: three phloxes, *Phlox divaricata*, *P. subulata* and *P. setacea*, popular plants today, and the red–and–yellow *Aquilegia canadensis*, all from North America. From South America came the unique *Calceolaria fothergillii*. *Aristea africana* (as *A. cyanea*) from South Africa, a tender Iridaceous plant with intense blue flowers which grows successfully out of doors at Ilnacullin, County Kerry, and *Chimaphila (Pyrola) umbellata* from various countries round the Northern Hemisphere, including Japan.

John Graefer, who was head gardener to the King of Naples, produced his 'catalogue' of plants in 1794. It is certainly the first 'quick reference' book on alpines that I have come across; he gives full particulars of descriptions and cultivation in a tabulated list. I think he was entitled to claim: 'The Author proposes in the use of his great variety of Herbaceous Plants a more constant and uniform and gay Attraction of Gardens, than has been hitherto pointed out, or adopted.' The work was directed only to plants of floral beauty and included many alpines. Many British species were included and also a nice little handful of best alpines, the diminutive *Petrocallis pyrenaica*, *Teucrium pyrenaicum*, *Antennaria dioica* and *Origanum hybridum*, all plants that would be likely to thrive in a reasonably warm climate.

It was left to a French botanist, André Michaux, to name *Rosa persica* in 1779; it has also been called *Hulthemia persica* and also *Rosa berberifolia*. It is a native of Iran and Afghanistan. It is as near to being classed as an alpine plant as are many other very dwarf shrubs in this book, so I cannot resist calling attention to it here. It might at first sight be taken for a helianthemum with its five bright yellow petals each with a central blotch of scarlet at the base. It is rare in cultivation but might prove a good plant in the drier parts of California. The best plants I ever saw were growing in full sun on a raised bed in lime-free soil at Highdown, the famous chalk-pit garden of Sir Frederick Stern. It is comparatively easy to graft onto briar stock, but is best on its own roots, when raised from seed.

After this little interlude – to help forward a desirable rarity – we may recall that one of the earliest sources of Eastern plants was through the Botanic Garden at St Petersburg, Russia. The vivid blue *Scilla siberica* had been known for a hundred years or more before Count Mussin-Puschkin secured two plants that bear his names: *Nepeta mussinii* and *Puschkinia scilloides*, both from the Caucasus. (But the *Nepeta* is inferior as a garden ornament to the plant that usually bears its name; this is a hybrid, *Nepeta × faassenii*.) With them came *Onosma taurica*, whose tubular flowers nod from hairy stalks above the bristly-hairy leaves, perhaps on some hot, rocky ledge. One does not readily associate the Caucasus with gentians, but two really reliable garden plants are *Gentiana lagodechiana* and *G. septemfida*; the former usually has one flower to each sprawling stem, the latter several. The two are somewhat confused in gardens today owing to hybridisation. Albert Regel of St Petersburg found the former. After his daughter, Julie, is named *Primula juliae*, a diminutive plant with rich mauve-crimson flowers – now seldom seen. It had a profound effect by hybridising with primroses, producing such good garden plants as *PP.* 'Juliana' and 'Wanda'. Regel also collected some excellent, dwarf, early flowering tulip species from neighbouring regions, such as *Tulipa kaufmanniana*, *T. linifolia* and the dazzling *T. praestans*. They are all bright additions to the spring garden. I find *T. praestans* in particular a prolific perennial which is more than can be said for many hybrid garden tulips. Its vivid vermilion seems to warm our

106 *Potentilla fruticosa* — which is a native of most countries in the North Temperate Zone — dwarfed by wind on Hart's Pass, Okanogan Co., Washington, United States of America, at 5,500 ft. This and its related species in their dwarf variants are ideal shrubs for the rock garden. *Courtesy: Brian O. Mulligan*

107 *Clematis tenuiloba* creeping amongst limestone rocks; Medicine Mountain, North Wyoming, about 9,700 ft. *Courtesy: Brian O. Mulligan*

108 *Kalmiopsis leachiana* growing on a spartan diet above North Umpqua River, Douglas Co., Oregon, United States of America. *Courtesy: Brian O. Mulligan*

109 *Lithodora (Lithospermum) gastonii* whose bright blue flowers have white throats. 12–18 inches. Western Pyrenees.

110 White form of *Eritrichium nanum* var. *elongatum* in limestone rocks on Medicine Mountain, North Wyoming, United States of America, at about 9,800 ft. In crevice to right is *Telesonix (Boykinia) jamesii*.
*Courtesy: Brian O. Mulligan*

111 *Erodium brownbowii*. Nearly white flowers with nearly black centres. For well drained sunny sites.

113 'Linda Pope' is a famous large-flowered hybrid of *Primula marginata*.

112 Bright blue tubes of *Moltkia × petraea* – a shrublet of great charm for June.

114 *Moltkia × intermedia*, a low, spreading, dwarf shrub for sunny slopes with bright blue flowers in early summer. A hybrid between *M. petraea* and *M. suffruticosa*

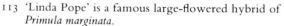

115 An eighteen-year-old *Salix × boydii* growing in a scree. The silvery catkins lighten the grey leaves in spring.

116 *Daphne petraea* 'Grandiflora'. Glistening pink flowers crown this tiny shrub in early summer.

117 Although it only has five petals, each flower of *Dianthus squarrosus* is so fringed that there appear to be many more. In the author's garden.

118 *Campanula* 'John Innes', a rare hybrid of *C. versicolor*. The procumbent stems bear many lilac cups with dark centres. In the author's garden.

119 *Campanula kolenatiana* whose grey leaves and violet blue bells create a satisfactory combination, in full sun. In the author's garden.

120 *Aster yunnanensis* 'Napsbury'. A good showy hybrid for June, whose violet-blue rays are contrasted by orange centres.

prevalent east winds of spring.

By the time we reached 1800 things were really on the move in the West. Charlotte Murray's *The British Garden* mentioned many alpine plants in 1808, and from 1797 to 1807 appeared *The Temple of Flora* by R.J. Thornton, a series of splendid colour plates. They include besides tulips and lilies a wonderful green-edged auricula; *Cyclamen persicum*, the forerunner of our greenhouse strains – which mostly lack the delicate perfume of the species – and the famous picture of *Dodecatheon meadia* with its superb background of a ship at sea. *Dodecatheon* seems to have captured the imagination of many artists, and small wonder, for it is a foreign (i.e. not European) plant of comparatively easy culture; its alternative name, Shooting Stars, conjures up some of its delightful charm. European auriculas, too, were in every book but they were generally grown under glass where their beautifully powdered leaves and flowers could reach perfection, and the mystique of the mixing of their potting composts could be given full indulgence.

Hitherto I have always considered that, though the Chelsea Physic Garden, London, had the oldest established rock garden under glass, the date given by Lady Rockley was the first mention of one in the open. For this Brian Mathew suggested I should look at the *Transactions of the Horticultural Society* (before it became *Royal*) for 1812. Here was described a deliberate attempt to construct a rock-bank in the Jardin de Paris. A bank sixty feet long was built with specially mixed soil and held up by a series of boards against a terrace wall ten feet high, facing south-east. On it were grown such treasures as *Moehringia muscosa*, *Soldanella alpina*, *Primula farinosa*, *Androsace carnea* and *A. lactea* and the tiny arctic willow, *Salix reticulata*. In summer they were given almost hourly watering and in winter a covering of bracken. It is evident that someone had given the growth and existence of alpine plants close attention. It is interesting, in addition, to note that the same sort of construction was used by Sir Charles Isham at Lamport Hall for his dwarf trees and gnomes (see chapter 4).

It is, however, very appropriate that Edinburgh should have produced the first book to be devoted to rock gardens and the growing of alpines. It was James Lothian's *Practical hints on the culture ... of alpine or rock plants*, published in 1845 with a few small illustrations in colour, hand painted: two of them are reproduced in this book because of their delicate charm (see page 146). 'Except in extensive collections and botanical institutes these [plants] are very rarely met with.' Most of our native alpines had not been observed as yet, even in Yorkshire.

Nine years later a book of more international importance appeared: Anton Kerner von Marilaun's *Die Kultur der Alpenpflanzen*, published in 1864. It was he who had seen in 1835 a garden devoted to alpines near Vienna. At last it could be said that the rock garden of the day could become a home for alpines rather than a graveyard. David Wooster's *Alpine Plants* of 1872 contains some excellent paintings, faithfully reproduced; the same plates had appeared in Bernard Verlot's *Les Plantes Alpines*, Paris, 1873, so there was no excuse for ignoring plants on either side of the Channel. These two books, to their dates, were the finest illustrated works on alpine plants for gardeners; the plates, it is worth noting, had been prepared from specimens from the York nursery of James Backhouse. It was at this time that a keen amateur, George Maw of Benthall Hall, Broseley, Staffordshire, made many trips to countries around the Mediterranean and the Middle East, principally to quench his enduring passion for crocuses. His magnificent monograph remains a memorial to his vast energy and industry. We owe to him the introduction of *Crocus etruscus*, *C. corsicus*, *C. minimus*, and fresh introductions of *C. fleischeri* and *C. chrysanthus*. To him from Albert von Regel came *C. korolkowi* from east of the Black Sea. It is well known that Maw introduced the plant we call *Chionodoxa luciliae* which I hear should now be known as *C. siehei*, while *C. luciliae* is transferred to the plant we know as *C. grandiflora* with the few lavender-blue flowers; a most confusing state of affairs. Maw's garden, belonging to the National Trust, contains a number of his bulbs.

Julius Hoffmann, who had given us a well illustrated book on roses in 1905, followed this by an equally good effort, *Alpine flora for tourists and amateur botanists*, 1925. Both were translated into English. And a series of great volumes on the middle European flora were being written by Gustav Hegi which have become standard reference works.

## Some Great Personalities

I should like now to go back to the York nursery of James Backhouse which had such a profound effect on rock gardens and rock plants in this country. It was started in 1816; by 1867 it listed a most varied collection of alpines besides other plants. To peruse one of their catalogues is to realise what great steps forward had been taken. As far as I can judge, two Irish firms approached it closely in the range of stock listed; they were T. Smith of Daisy Hill Nursery, Newry, County Down, and Lissadell in County Sligo, originated by Sir Jocelyn Gore-Booth. The latter nursery has gone but during the 1930s was still listing a remarkable collection of plants. Daisy Hill Nursery is still in existence. On the continent we can recall two famous collections of alpines. F. Sündermann of Lindau-Bodensee, Bavaria, produced incredible collections of European primulas and saxifrages at, to us, incredibly low prices. (I used to import plants for my garden in the late 1920s; it was less ruinous for my pocket!) The other was that of Henri Correvon at Geneva, Switzerland, which also had extensive lists.

Correvon not only sold alpine plants and seeds but established *jardins d'acclimatation* at different altitudes to accommodate his treasures suitably. In one of his gardens, Floraire, occurred that hybrid of *Viola calcarata* which was known as *V. florariensis*; it used to seed, more or less true to type, all over the old sandstone rock garden at Cambridge in the 1920s and '30s and I grew it for years in my Chobham garden. But all of a sudden it died out, which was very sad because it flowered from June to October. It was lilac blue, with darker veins and a yellow eye. I wonder whether it still grows at Floraire. And while on the subject of violas, I am sad that we no longer grow the dark coloured hybrid of *Viola gracilis* in our gardens. In the 1930s this was on every table rock garden at Chelsea Show, delighting us all with its elfin flowers of royal purple, so well depicted in Reginald Farrer's little book *The Rock Garden*. *Viola gracilis* is a native of Yugoslavia, and varies from cream to light lavender. This beautiful hybrid had very narrow, even linear leaves. But to return, Correvon was, moreover, a prolific writer; his books are repetitive but are well illustrated in colour in the *art nouveau* style which gives them a very special, period appeal. His son Aymon, who succeeded him, worked for a while at Wisley and I

121 *Helichrysym lanatum*; the yellow flowers of no account, the broad silver woolly leaves indicate a foreground position. In the author's garden

122 *Globularia cordifolia*; the powder-blue flowers have a background of shining dark green leaves.

123 The dark violet bells of *Campanula pulla*. In the author's garden

124 Few can resist the charm of the pink-and-crimson flowers of *Dianthus* 'Highland Frazer'.

125 *Cypripedium calceolus* growing with *Cystopteris fragilis* in the author's limy bog garden.

126 *Daphne blagayana.* Note that it has had a large rock placed on top of it – which is one of the methods of success with this plant. Further rocks would be placed on the stems as they grow outwards. Creamy white fragrant flowers.

got to know him well. The firm is still in existence. The first quarter of this century saw a great upsurge of interest in European alpine plants; many alluring books were printed, in addition to Correvon's. G. Flemwell produced his own exquisite water colours of flowers and Swiss mountain scenery for his *Alpine Flowers and Gardens*, 1910, and (his best) *The Flower Fields of Alpine Switzerland*, 1911, and also for H. S. Thompson's *Subalpine Plants of the Swiss Woods and Meadows*, 1912. R. A. Malby, a leading horticultural photographer of the time, contributed *The Story of My Rock Garden* in 1912. A book written for the beginner, it is remarkable for the brilliance of its colour plates – I suspect of Swiss origin. In the excellent photographs of plants growing in the wild the colours are unique, in my experience, for having been almost invisibly stippled with opaque tints. As such they have no peer.

Despite their delightful charm, these and other books were overshadowed by the unbridled enthusiasm and effortless prose – well laced with an enormous range of adjectives and adverbs – of Reginald Farrer. He has had good mention in chapter 4. He claimed – and rightly, too – that 'England, alone of European nations, has a rooted personal passion for flowers themselves'. Who could resist the water-colours in his *Among the Hills*, for instance, when accompanied by such a chapter, on one plant only, as 'The Ancient King' (*Saxifraga florulenta*)? Through the kindness of Walter Ingwersen I even possessed a plant of this for a few years; it is seldom seen, being of tricky constitution. Let us linger for a while with a few extracts from Farrer's writings. The masterly description of *Gentiana farreri* I quoted in my book *Three Gardens*. Here are his words for *Meconopsis quintuplinervia*: '[it] now hovers on the fringes of cultivation and ... is going to prove the soundest perennial in the family; and is so beautiful that the senses ache at the multitudinous loveliness of its myriad dancing lavender butterflies over the rolling upper Alps of the Da-Tung chain (Northern Kansu Tibet).' Or *Conandron ramondioides*: 'a most beautiful Japanese rock plant, rambling over the face of stone, and sheeting the cliffs ... in a solid curtain of its ample glossy crinkled foliage, amid which spring so freely on stalks of a few inches those heads of lilac flowers with a bright golden eye, suggesting that a glorified potato had intermarried with *Ramondia Nataliae*.' Or *Saxifraga lingulata bellardii*: 'a treasure of singular and rare magnificence, confined to sunny and shady exposures in the Tenda district of the Maritime Alps, where it forms huge spidery cushions a yard across, and hangs in princely pennons of white from the cliffs of gneiss or limestone here and there on the very highway-side. . . .'

Coupled with good water colours this prose was enough to send alpine plant lovers straight off to the Alps for a holiday, with a tin for collecting plants. With improved rail travel, this is just what they did, amateurs and nurserymen alike. And when nurserymen such as Clarence Elliott issued catalogues of importance from his Six Hills Nursery – where I spent about a year – the cult grew fast. Here is his description for *Oxalis enneaphylla*: 'Choice exquisite rock plant. . . . This plant was so lovely and yet so rare that in 1910 I made a special expedition to collect it in the Falkland Isles, and now hold the finest stock in the country.' Again: *Saxifraga cuneifolia infundibuliformis*: 'In doubt as to their correctness we once dropped these lovely syllables from our catalogue. Now on reassurance from an eminent quarter we gladly restore them. The plant attached to them is a dainty miniature London Pride for shady corners.'

Walter Ingwersen reached very high horticultural and botanical standards when he got into his stride at Birch Farm Nursery. His fully descriptive small monographs on various genera are collectors' pieces today. His kindness, his expertise and his vast knowledge of European and other alpines came to light. He had had a nursery at Croydon before the First World War and later became foreman on the rock garden at Wisley before re-entering the nursery trade with some years at Stevenage and Letchworth before settling on William Robinson's Gravetye estate near East Grinstead. I can see him now, on my first visit to Birch Farm in 1927 or '28, sitting on the edge of a frame and dilating on the beauties and peculiarities of each rare European primula in a nearby trough. I was ready to imbibe, having drunk deeply of the genus from John Macwatt's *Primulas of Europe*, 1923 – I think the first gardener's book on one genus of alpine plants. It is also founded on botany and is well illustrated.

The spirit of collecting alpines abroad had become an infectious enthusiasm, fostered by the great spirits mentioned above, to say nothing of E. A. Bowles and others who had greater interests than alpines alone. In 1932 my friend of Six Hills days, E. K. Balls, went with Dr P. L. Guiseppi to Persia (Iran) looking for new plants from southern mountain ranges. Their greatest find was *Dionysia* – a total of six species was collected. They are tricky, hummock-forming little plants, impatient of winter wet, but in alpine house or frame culture their multitudes of tiny, scented flowers closely spread over the mounds of minute leaves are delightful. *D. curviflora* is pale pink and has remained one of the most tractable species. Two years later he went again to the Middle East, with another old friend, Dr W. Balfour Gourlay, finding the choice *Cyclamen cilicium* var. *intaminatum*, an autumn flowerer with flowers from white to red. Also from Turkey they introduced *Campanula betulifolia*, a monocarpic species which can be grown successfully out of doors. There are not many pink campanulas; this is one of them. Any collector who came back with these and also *Orphanidesia gaultherioides* would be held in great esteem. Now called *Epigaea gaultherioides*, this is a shade-lover of charm with large, scented, kalmia-like flowers among bristly leaves.

## *The Arrival of Bulbous Plants*

From time immemorial what we call economic plants had been cultivated in the cradle of our western civilisation, as well as in China and other more advanced eastern countries. Various grasses were grown for their seeds and gradually developed into wheat and other cereals; fruits were treasured and also herbs of all sorts: those beneficent to health, for flavouring and strewing floors, and many plants which were grown because of their supposed 'virtues'. In these days of almost universal use of drugs in medicine, some of these plants are being re-examined for their values to mankind. It was natural, too, that plants from the countries of Europe and the Middle East were the first to contribute ornamental plants to the gardens of Britain, the Low Countries and France. Some of our earliest imports had come from much farther afield. In Roman times, and probably much before then, trade routes through countries around the Caspian Sea were known to have reached

China, to and fro, across the inhospitable and barely colonised vast areas of Central Asia. In this way, long before the Portuguese found their way to China by sea in 1516, the peach and the apricot reached Europe and also *Hibiscus syriacus*. Named from its cultivation in Syria, this highly ornamental shrub has apparently no economic value and thus is a very early example of a plant being imported to western countries purely as an ornamental, thousands of miles from its eastern countries of origin, India and China.

In early days the monasteries were the chief homes for plants of all kinds, ornamental or economic, and only field crops were grown by the rest of the populace. Because of the contact between religious houses – in particular the Cistercians – plants gradually spread to the more settled countries.

The great influx of eastern plants started in the late sixteenth and early seventeenth centuries, the time of the rapid expansion of the Turkish or Ottoman Empire. The Empire advanced into Europe by way of Belgrade, as far as Vienna. It so happens that much of the Middle East experiences brief wet springs, hot summers and cold winters – ideal for many bulbous and tuberous plants, and these were of course just the kind of plants which were easy to transport in a dormant stage, and would as likely as not astonish the recipients with unbelievable beauty in the first season of flowering. Some of this surprise and wonderment is apparent to John Parkinson, writing his great book in 1629:

> To satisfie therefore their desires that are lovers of such Delights, I took upon me this labour and charge, and have here selected and set forth a Garden of all the chiefest for choice, and fairest for shew, from among all the several Tribes and Kindreds of Natures beauty, and have ranked them . . . in affinity one unto another.

Something of the same sort happened with bulbous plants from early conquest in South America by the Spaniards in the sixteenth century; only those that became dormant and thus could be lifted and stored away from frost for the winter became valued garden plants – other than seed-raised annuals.

Apart from mentioning George Maw's connection with the introduction of bulbs, my notes have been confined to other types of plants, but with the enthusiastic E. A. Bowles always avid for bulbs of all kinds and crocuses and snowdrops in particular, their use on rock gardens became more common.

Peter Barr, founder of a famous bulb firm in 1862, introduced or re-introduced several small species of *Narcissus* from Portugal, Spain and the Maritime Alps. They include the nodding *N. asturiensis* (*N. minimus*), a tiny flower of true daffodil shape, and usually the first species to greet the spring in our gardens. As for *N. bulbocodium*, this has long been one of the great sights of spring in the moist alpine meadow at Wisley; there it is in its bright yellow form, while at the Savill Garden there are several acres devoted to the pale yellow form 'Citrinus'. The easiest way of establishing them in damp acid soil is to gather and broadcast the seeds – if you have seven years' patience to await their flowers! *N. cyclamineus*, the bright yellow species with swept-back perianth segments that have influenced many hybrids, also prefers a damp spot. Among others, Parkinson described his 'strawe coloured bastard daffodil' which Barr re-introduced; it is known as *N. pallidiflorus*, and is a delightful tone of pale yellow, and flowers early, with *N. pseudonarcissus*, to which it is related.

Several firms have introduced bulbous plants from the Middle East, but none has been more famous than C. G. Van Tubergen Ltd of the Zwanenburg Nurseries, Haarlem. I am glad to find that Michael Hoog, the son of the proprietor, is carrying on the tradition from a separate address in the same town. One of their autumn flowering crocuses,*Crocus goulimyi*, bids fair to settle down in British gardens. At first sight, from its colour it might be thought a form of *C. tomasinianus*, but its rounded flower on a tall stalk marks it apart. *C. etruscus* 'Zwanenburg' is a particularly good very early flowering form of the deep lilac species. For sheltered spots or the alpine house there is *Cyclamen pseudibericum*, close to *C. coum*, but larger and of richer colouring. I wish 'Guinea Gold', a magnificent January-flowering aconite, would spread as quickly as *Eranthus hiemalis*; it is a selected form of *E. tubergeniana*. The spring is ushered in by the precocious flowering of *Scilla tubergeniana*, now to be called *S. mischtschenkoana*, which has perhaps the longest display of any spring bulb, in palest blue. It increases freely. *Muscari tubergeniana* is two toned, dark blue at the bottom of the spike and pale blue above. Two little early irises are of Tubergen's introduction also, *Iris histrio* var. *aintabensis* and *I. histrioides* 'Major', both of light blue. The latter is a hearty good garden plant, defying snow and wind. One of the snowdrops with green tips to the outer segments, *Galanthus nivalis* 'Viridapicis', is likewise good of increase. Tulips are not perhaps quite suited to the rock garden, but dwarf, early species such as *Tulipa violacea* (a form of *T. humilis*), the yellow form of the Lady tulip, *T. clusiana chrysantha* and the vivid vermilion of *T. praestans* are all welcome in the early year. Tubergen's firm was also the introducer of a superior form of *Iris danfordiae* which had been introduced at the end of the nineteenth century.

## The Far East

But it is time we turned East. While Japan was closed to adventurers, a few ports in China were open to trade in the late eighteenth century. Special treasures began to reach Europe but they were not really rock plants; the Chinese had scarcely explored their immense mountainous territories to the west, being content in the populous coastal regions with treasured camellias, irises, *Viburnum farreri* and Tree Peonies.

Meanwhile travellers had gone to Nepal. Nathaniel Wallich, Director of the Calcutta Botanic Garden, discovered *Gentiana ornata* and *Podophyllum hexandrum* (*P. emodi*) and introduced *Geranium wallichianum*. The gentian I found amenable to Surrey cultivation; when introduced later it astonished, among its relatives from Western China, by not only its dark blue colour but by its wide bells. *Geranium wallichianum* is a good easily grown garden plant, thriving in sun or shade; the original form introduced, and repeated from time to time, was a rich lilac colour. However, for some reason or other in the garden of E. C. Buxton, in North Wales, a form with nemophila-blue flowers appeared, and has, under its name 'Buxton's Variety', proved a lode-star ever since. It is just as easy to grow and is illustrated in my two books – *Perennial Garden Plants* and *Three Gardens*. Dr J. H. Royle followed Wallich in those parts of the world and two of his introductions, appraised so much in these days, were the 'drumstick' primula, *Primula denticulata*, and *Polygonum vaccinifolium*. The latter is a first rate carpeter with small spikes of pink flowers in September and autumn, generally finishing the alpine display of the year.

Dr J. Thomson travelled around these southern parts of the Himalaya also; he is best remembered by his *Rhododendron thomsonii*, but *Primula sikkimensis* and *P. capitata* also fall to his credit. I find they need frequent renewal from seed but otherwise are not difficult in cool spots. The former has lemon yellow bells with a delicious scent which is found again in *P. alpicola* and *P. florindae*; the second is rather like a dark version of *P. denticulata*. As with many other primulas, the farina which is dusted over stem and calyx – and sometimes elsewhere – gives these eastern species as great a charm as it does to the auriculas from Europe.

Let us return to the Far East for a few plants introduced during the second half of the nineteenth century. *Primula japonica* has become naturalised in moist cool gardens in the British Isles. In fact in one garden, Penrhyn Castle in North Wales, seeds remained dormant for something like thirty years under a welter of bamboos, and germinated freely on exposure to light. John Gould Veitch of the famous nursery firm introduced it in 1892, along with *P. amoena*. This is a soft purplish 'polyanthus' type from the Middle East which hybridises easily with our native primrose.

I have already called attention to Maximowicz's activities; in 1864 he found the popular little rock-garden shrub *Spiraea japonica* 'Bullata' with crimson flower heads, having previously given us *Epigaea asiatica*. Lovely and easily grown though the latter is, its tinted flowers have not the fragrance of the more tricky *E. repens* already noted. *Daphne genkwa*, *Platycodon grandiflorum* 'Mariesii' and *Conandron ramondioides* were found by Charles Maries in 1877. The Abbé Delavay discovered *Omphalogramma* (*Primula*) *vinciflora*, *Meconopsis betonicifolia* and *Primula flaccida*, better known as *P. nutans*, but they were left to later collectors to introduce. He did collect the wine-purple *Primula poissonii*, a good and hearty bog garden plant. We struggle with *P. flaccida*'s (*P. nutans* of gardens) violet beauty in the south of England but in the north it is a superb success, in common with all the blue poppies, species of *Meconopsis*. But high on the northern slopes of Box Hill, Surrey, in lime-free soil my old friend Edmund F. Warburg used to grow the delectable *Omphalogramma vinciflora* to perfection. It was helped, I think by the cool nights on the hill. It is one of several species originally included in the genus *Primula*, with flowers shaped rather like those of a *Pinguicula*; Farrer raved about it in some of his most purple prose: '... a regular, small, flat star of deepest violet velvet, and then swells and expands and retorts and protrudes until it has developed the full pouting eccentricity of its clear purple maturity'. It dies down to a hard round bud in winter to burst forth again in spring.

Prince Henri d'Orléans discovered that most dainty of all the poppies, the yellow flowered *Meconopsis chelidonifolia* of which a drawing occurs in my *Perennial Garden Plants*; he also found *Primula vittata*, which is a well-powdered wine-crimson version of *P. sikkimensis* with the same delicious odour. A favourite dwarf daphne, *D. retusa*, and the vivid red *Primula cockburniana* recall A. E. Pratt's travels in 1888. The daphne is one of the more tractable species in our gardens, producing good seeds after the sweetly scented flowers have faded.

## *Japan*

While the Chinese ports had been open to trade, Japan was closed for two hundred years from 1614. Gradually foreigners were allowed in, particularly those employed by the Dutch East India Company. Once again it was not alpines but trees, shrubs and herbaceous plants which reached Europe first. Robert Fortune secured *Euonymus fortunei* and *Saxifraga fortunei*. The latter flowers late, is susceptible to frost but carries the flag in the rock garden into autumn with *Polygonum vaccinifolium*. As to the *Euonymus*, it has proved a hardy dwarf or climbing shrub prone to 'sport' in many ways, its smallest being *E. fortunei* 'Kewensis', which has evergreen leaves the size of a lentil, and is a charmer for miniature gardens, troughs etc. This in turn sported to a stronger but completely prostrate form in Sir Frederick Stern's garden in Sussex, and as a consequence is named 'Highdown'. It bids fair to be a first rate ground-cover and so far has not reverted to its parent nor to the original type. Will Ingwersen gave me the Japanese *Davallia mariesii*, introduced as long ago as 1879 by Charles Maries. It is one of the Hare's-foot-ferns and I suppose it was always grown in greenhouses for it has not been grown out of doors until recently, due to persuasion from Will. It appears to be perfectly hardy; its rhizomes like cool soil or moist rock to creep over and give rise to delicately cut fronds. It is a real gem.

## *Professional Collectors in the Far East*

As will have been realised, the collecting of plants from foreign countries was becoming a business in England as the nineteenth century advanced. It was not left to tradesmen, adventurers and missionaries to discover and send home the odd plants they came across. Syndicates subscribed to cover the travelling expenses of trained gardeners and botanists to search for certain plants of which news, but not material, had been received. I have already mentioned one of the first, Robert Fortune. He was followed by Augustine Henry from Ireland, E. H. Wilson (of *Lilium regale* fame), George Forrest, William Purdom, Frank Kingdon Ward, Reginald Farrer and Joseph Rock. All of these collected in the hinterland of China and the Himalaya, but their objectives were mainly trees and shrubs. This was because the syndicates which sent them were often composed of great garden owners, specially interested in rhododendrons. However, Farrer in particular went for alpines but became enthused by rhododendrons and shrubs in general as well, and Wilson, Forrest and Kingdon Ward could none of them pass a beautiful plant without collecting it or at least recording it. And what a list it makes, this mainly twentieth-century series of expeditions. Many of our most prized garden plants are found among them. Take for instance Wilson, sent out specifically to get *Davidia involucrata* seeds, to whom we owe *Meconopsis integrifolia* of which a magnificent full scale coloured plate occurs in William Robinson's *Flora and Sylva*; and the short-growing form of *Lilium philippinense, formosanum*. And Forrest who collected partly for E. K. Bulley whose garden at Ness on the Wirral forms now the garden of the Ness Botanic Garden — and whose initial B gave rise to his nursery of Bees, Chester; the buff yellow *Primula bulleyana* and the cool lilac *P. beesiana* come to mind. Forrest gave us the prostrate, scarlet-belled *Rhododendron forrestii* (*R. repens*), and the tiny *R. radicans* with its pansy-flowers of vinous purple, both perfect rock garden shrublets; and also the much prized *Arisaema candidissimum*, illustrated in my *Perennial Garden Plants*. Those two stately members of the Ginger Family spring to memory, *Roscoea cautleoides* (of which there is a 'Bees' Variety') and *R. humeana*. Their broad lance-shaped leaves are just what is required to show off their hooded flowers of lemon yellow and rich purple respectively. They need cool moist positions like many primulas. *Allium beesianum* in true blue and *Codonopsis meleagris* (which used to be called *C. ovata* – a different species), whose nodding bells of pale blue are so exquisitely marked with violet and orange inside, are both of high quality but among true alpines none stands so high as the sapphire blue *Gentiana sino-ornata* of which countless thousands have been propagated and sold since its introduction. Among the many shrubs displaying autumn colour at the National Trust garden at Sheffield Park in Sussex, two long beds add their rich and contrasting colour in autumn. How lovely it might appear if we could trust around it the Silver Weed, *Potentilla anserina*, a British native but also almost circumpolar; it appears in Forrest's photograph of the gentian in Yunnan.

William Purdom joined with Farrer for a year at least. The prostrate gentian *Gentiana gracilipes* (formerly known as *G. purdomii*) is a good garden plant for any open situation and *Trollius pumilus* is an excellent dwarf Globe Flower of bright yellow; we owe both of them to him. My first effort at growing *Meconopsis quintuplinervia*, Farrer's Harebell Poppy as he called it, was in the early 1930s; it had wide flowers borne on sinuous stalks, palest lavender with a dark base to each petal. Perhaps this was the form introduced by N. M. Przewalski in the late 1880s from his expeditions from Russia. At any rate all other plants of this species that I have seen, and which I now grow, are of a type with darker flowers of narrower outline borne on erect stems, as they appear in the photograph, taken about 1939 at Wisley, which is in my *Perennial Garden Plants*. This form I believe to be Farrer's. Przewalski also introduced the little blue *Allium cyaneum*, which can be so pretty in trough gardens.

Farrer's *Allium cyathophorum* var. *farreri* is a soft purple; *Geranium farreri* – which may be a form or synonym of *G. napuligerum* – is a lovely little alpine of palest pink enhanced by black anthers; his *Aster farreri* – the Great Bear – is rather a straggler in violet with orange centre, one of the group united with *A. yunnanensis*, *A. subcaeruleus* and *A. tongolensis*. *Rhododendron calostrotum* is close to *R. radicans* but larger, of intense rose-crimson in the form which goes under the name of 'Gigha' but which was raised at Sunningdale Nurseries by Harry White, and which when I was manager of that nursery we used to call 'Cherry Red'. We also had a paler form from Farrer's seed. *Nomocharis farreri* is one of the most elegant and beautiful of plants for semi-woodland gardens in cool districts, its pink, spotted, lily-flowers nodding with unnecessary modesty, and we should not forget the lemon-scented Edelweiss *Leontopodium haplophylloides*, formerly named (and more sensibly) *L. aloysiodorum*, bringing to mind the fresh fragrance of the so-called Lemon Verbena. I have quoted elsewhere (*Three Gardens*) Farrer's description of his own *Gentiana farreri* and its picture appears in this book (page 202); today, it is seldom if ever seen in its original form having become much hybridised with *G. sino-ornata*

127 *Primula sieboldii*. A hardy Japanese species delighting in cool leafy soil in part shade. Flowers white, pink, lilac etc.

128 *Roscoea cautleoides* 'Bees' Dwarf'. Light lemon yellow. 8 ins.

129 *Cypripedium reginae*, white with lilac-pink pouch. For acid bog. Behind are flowers of *Roscoea cautleoides*. In the author's garden.

and others. The painting was done from original stock in 1928. *Primula agleniana* is one of the supreme glories of the race even among the aristocrats of the Nivalis Section and one can only hope it will be introduced again and may settle down in our northern gardens now that the requirements of such plants are better understood. In its honour, and in hope, I include in this book Farrer's original painting of this plant in the wild, through the kindness of Mrs J. Farrer.

A visit to Edinburgh Botanic Garden or other northern garden in early summer will reveal the beauty of *Primula alpicola*. It does not thrive for long in the south. Another of the Sikkimensis group, it has the same lovely powdering of stalk, calyx and bell, and the same lovely fragrance. The form *luna* indicates its moony pale yellow; at one time I did a lot to select good colour forms of the form *violacea*, but their strange habit of turning grey after pollination defeated me. This primula brings us to Kingdon Ward's additions to our rock gardens; another is *P. burmanica*, which is of similar colouring to Forrest's *P. beesiana* but lacks the powdery stems and calyces. *P. chungensis* is a vivid orange-red flowered species of the same Candelabra group. But personally I remember Ward best by contemplating *P. florindae*. In this we have a hearty grower for boggy soil, so prolific of its large foliage that it makes its own ground cover by seeding itself and, long after all the other primulas are over in the sultry days of July and August, keeps up a succession of big powdered heads of bright lemon-yellow bells, with the same fragrance as all others of the Sikkimensis group. Sometimes it throws orange-coloured flowers, possibly hybrids with *P. waltonii*. But nothing is more beautiful than the original lemon-yellow nor more telling in the garden, and the orange forms should be ruthlessly exterminated immediately on revealing their colour in bud so that further crossing may be avoided. It is superb through July and August around the snake pool at Sezincote, Gloucestershire. So many of these Chinese upland plants benefit from cool and moist air that I fear most of my selection from the many treasures that have reached us are only suitable for cooler districts in the southern counties. The same may be said of one more of Ward's gems, *Cyananthus lobatus* var. *insignis*, whose stems flop around from a central rootstock and each produces one or more violet-blue flowers like a most sumptuous periwinkle, in late summer.

This recital of plants from China, Burma and the Himalaya is long, but it is believed that the area is that from which so many genera originally occurred, in the history of the world; even so, what I have mentioned from this great region, and indeed all others, is a mere tithe of the riches that have been brought to these islands by dauntless travellers. And my few paragraphs are only concerned with plants that might be grown on rock gardens, peat beds, woodland gardens etc. and are all of a modest height.

For us gardeners some of the most important expeditions to the Himalayan ranges were undertaken by Frank Ludlow and Major George Sherriff from 1904 onwards. They were joined by others including George (now Sir George) Taylor. Many primulas were found including several new species: *Primula sherriffiae*, *P. ioessa* and *P. ludlowii*. Notable poppyworts also came from their enterprise. *Meconopsis superba* in rich colouring, the pink *M. sherriffiae* and the renowned deep blue *M. grandis G.S. 600*. These are not really plants for the south of England, except the last, but have done well in Scotland, while *Corydalis cashmiriana*, previously only known in a form which did not take kindly to cultivation in this country, has been superseded by a new collection of theirs which is much more amenable. Its clear blue flowers are a wonderful sight in the spring.

# North America

In the mid-seventeenth century, European ships were making ever longer voyages. Plants began to reach our shores from the eastern seaboard of North America. They were mainly herbaceous plants, shrubs and trees. It was some time before the colonists penetrated to where they would find their first alpine plants, on the Appalachian Mountains. But I like to recall two of my favourite garden plants reaching our shores so early: *Smilacina racemosa*, that fragrant relative of Solomon's Seal, for cool moist parts of the garden, and *Aster tradescantii*. This was named after John Tradescant, gardener to Charles I, and introduced in 1633. The plant I have known all my life under this name – a valuable, wiry, self-reliant autumn-flowering pure white daisy of some four feet – is apparently wrongly named. Our lovely garden plant, according to latest botanical advice, is *A. pilosus* var. *demotus*, and *A. tradescantii*, the first Michaelmas Daisy to be introduced, is much inferior from a garden point of view. The pure yellow, long-spurred *Aquilegia chrysantha* is a great joy, but these plants hybridise so freely that one seldom sees the true plant unless grown from wild-source seeds. It is a parent of the many large-flowered strains of long-spurred Columbines. That beautiful small fern *Adiantum pedatum* reached us from North America about 1656. It and its dwarf and also tinted-leafed forms are much treasured on shady rock gardens.

From the eastern states of North America we find some old favourites reached us in the early eighteenth century, such as the Virginian Cowslip, *Mertensia virginica*, whose greyish leaves and cool lavender-blue bells delight us in spring, and *Dodecatheon meadia*. *Epigaea repens* arrived over here by 1766 but has remained very rare and intractable ever since, though I do remember one great mat of it, yards across, thriving between rhododendrons in moist peaty soil at Knap Hill Nursery, near Woking, between the two world wars. It is intensely fragrant. This was one of the plants from the rising ground west of the seaboard, which John Bartram introduced. Others, more approaching alpine plants, were *Galax urceolata* (*G. aphylla*), *Iris cristata*, *Phlox divaricata* and *Phlox subulata*. Here we have a prolific rock plant, now available in other tints than just pink, and a worthy rival to *Aubrieta*. The names of choice plants begin to crowd upon us: *Oenothera tetragona*, *Allium cernuum*, *Uvularia grandiflora*, *Jeffersonia diphylla*, *Dicentra eximia* and *Iris fulva*. But we still cannot record such early eighteenth-century introduction of real alpine plants. The settlers had enough to do without climbing mountains, but we get a little nearer with *Mimulus luteus*, which has become naturalised in our mountain becks as well as lowland streams; diminutive *Saxifraga sibthorpii*, which grows almost as a weed on cool rock gardens and elsewhere; the exquisite *Erythronium grandiflorum*, a Dog-tooth 'violet' from the western States; *Oenothera missouriensis* and *Penstemon glaber*.

From what is now Canada came the beauteous *Trillium grandiflorum*. Though I shall never see it in its native habitat, I make an annual pilgrimage to a wet, peaty part of the Savill Garden in Windsor Great Park where its flowers can be numbered almost in their thousands. The pure white blooms have a quality apart from everything else.

The close of the nineteenth century and the early years of the present one saw a mass of new plants arriving from western North America; plants from higher altitudes were found, including *Phlox hoodii* as far north as Calgary in Canada. David Douglas was one of the earlier collectors in those parts and noted in his journal in April 1826 seeing *Erythronium grandiflorum* in flower: 'this exceedingly beautiful plant came under my notice fifteen or sixteen days ago, but being not then in blossom I took it for a *Fritillaria*; abundant over all the undulating country, under the shade of solitary pines in light dry soils; it has a most splendid effect in conjunction with *Dodecatheon* and a small species of *Pulmonaria*; omit not to procure seed and roots of such a desirable plant'. Douglas was a professional plant collector, sent over by the Horticultural Society (later Royal) of London. Douglas has one of the loveliest of small alpines named after him, *Phlox douglasii*, which in cultivation has yielded many colour forms and hybrids. Some twenty years later John Jeffrey was sent out to what became the Western States and succeeded in finding the glowing *Penstemon newberryi*, *Dodecatheon jeffreyi* and *Silene hookeri*. Later again, William Lobb, of conifer fame, found one of the yellow-flowered dicentras, *Dicentra chrysantha*, which has been grown successfully at Kew in the open air.

But I want to go back to erythroniums. One of my most treasured old nursery catalogues of 1931–1932 was from Carl Purdy, of Ukiah, California. In it are two colour plates – extremely rare in plant catalogues of that time – one of *Calochortus* hybrids, quite enough to make one's mouth water, but of course scarcely amenable to cultivation in this country, and the other of Dog-tooth violets or erythroniums, reproduced in this book. One can understand the dog-tooth part of the name from the shape of the corms, but how they could ever become confused or even associated with violets is past my comprehension. They bear the most exquisite nodding turk's cap flowers of all the Lily Family. If one can once get fresh corms, or seeds, most species seem quite easy to please, I think, in the cooler part of the rock or woodland garden. *Erythronium revolutum* is almost a weed in the Savill Garden and in my small way I have established several species. Nodding flowers always delight me. No doubt Purdy propagated some in his nursery, otherwise how could he have offered one called 'Purdy's White', but one cannot help suspecting that the bulk of his stock came from the wild; conservation was an unknown word (see page 195).

From the Western States come the species of *Lewisia*, named after Captain Meriwether Lewis of the Lewis and Clark expedition across North America. These are some of the gems of suitable rock gardens, but particularly of the alpine house, where they are usually grown in England. I have failed with them in the open air but they grow well in west-facing walls at Bodnant, North Wales. One of the first to be introduced in 1898 was *L. tweedyi*; it is also the largest in flower, but the several species with branching flower heads are perhaps more amenable; they are headed by *L. cotyledon*. Several species are much mixed by hybridisation but have resulted in some superlative colours in the hands of Jack Drake of Aviemore, Inverness; his Sunset Strain is derived from *L. cotyledon* and is outstanding. Likewise, at Chelsea Show in most years the Ingwersen table rock garden displays a magnificent range of colours.

130 *Trollius pumilus.* A bright yellow flower for moist positions. *Celmisia spectabilis* (above) grows among rocks in good drainage. At Edinburgh.

131 Seed-raised mixed auriculas in a variety of colours. They are best in a stiff loam, here covered with shingle to prevent weeds.

132 *Primula forrestii*
growing among
north-facing
sandstone rocks in
Sussex. Clear
yellow flowers.

133 A single rosette of
*Saxifraga longifolia*
which may take
six or more years
reaching 8–10 ins
across before
flowering. From
*Alpine Flowers* by
William
Robinson, 1870.
*Courtesy: Royal*
*Horticultural*
*Society*

134 A charming onion
in rosy mauve,
*Allium*
*narcissiflorum* and
*Calceolaria* 'Halls'
Variety' in clear
yellow.

Another great North American genus is *Penstemon*; Captain Lewis also found *P. fruticosus*, which is closely allied to *P. menziesii*. *P. rupicola* is to my mind the gem of the genus, a dwarf plant with surprisingly large deep rose flowers, introduced about 1910. These are delightful dwarf shrubs for warm sunny ledges.

# South America

South America, where the Andes ascend to great heights, has likewise yielded many good plants for our rock gardens. One charming little creeping plant *Nierembergia repens* (*N. rivularis*) with white, nearly stemless, fragrant convolvulus-shaped flowers thrives in some sheltered gardens; it was introduced as long ago as 1860 or thereabouts by Richard Pearce, collecting for James Veitch & Son. More truly alpine plants will be mentioned in a later paragraph, but I must recount the amusing set of coincidences of the strawberry. A Frenchman, A. F. Frezier, went to South America in 1712 and brought back from Chile a large-fruited strawberry which was *Fragaria chiloensis*. When it was hybridised with a species already introduced from Virginia, the results were our modern garden strawberries. In her book *The Quest for Plants*, Alice M. Coats records: 'Frezier may have taken a special interest in these 'fraises' [French name for strawberries] as he was descended from Scottish ancestors whose name was originally Frazer and whose blazon was three strawberry flowers (*Frazirs* in Scottish heraldry) on a blue field'.

Perhaps because I worked at the Six Hills Nursery shortly after Clarence Elliott had been to the Falkland Isles, I have a special *penchant* for plants from that region. One of the first plants he gave me to pot was the dainty *Sisyrinchium filifolium*. The narrow grassy leaves are overtopped by dainty creamy bells, veined with purple. And other plants from the same expedition in the mid 1920s were *Oxalis enneaphylla* and its pink variety. They both grow well in cool peaty positions, their wide silky flowers spread over the grey folded leaves. *Oxalis* species are fairly common in South America also; Chile gives us two: the pink *O. adenophylla*, resembling *O. enneaphylla* but more robust, clump forming, and preferring full sun, and the intriguing bright dark yellow *O. lobata*. I say intriguing because it goes to the trouble of producing two sets of leaves each year, but neither set coincides with the flowers; these appear in autumn from apparently empty ground. And there is tiny, creeping, white-flowered *O. magellanica*, suitable for hot sun or shade. A great treasure from Patagonia is *O. laciniata*, in the same class as the first two above with flowers from palest pink to rich purple. A hybrid with *O. enneaphylla* which I find quite tractable in a cool position is 'Ione Hecker'; its flowers are of soft purplish tones delicately veined. I have this plant growing next to a minute Patagonian fern, *Asplenium dareoides*, received from Jack Drake. It is an invasive plant but is only an inch or two high and is no trouble. And while on the subject of little ferns, I find *Adiantum venustum* a perfectly hardy dwarf Maidenhair of rapid increase. It hails from the Himalaya.

A charming little, prostrate, fragrant, evergreen creeping shrublet is *Myrtus nummularia*, also from the Falklands and Argentina. Though this is not totally hardy, it used to thrive in North Wales in A. T. Johnson's garden and produced its dark

*Gentiana excisa (G. kochiana).* European plant, grown in gardens as *G. acaulis*; for scree or normal soil in sun. Water colour by Simon Verelst (1644–1721). Enlarged by about $33\frac{1}{3}\%$.

*Courtesy: Royal Botanic Gardens, Kew.*

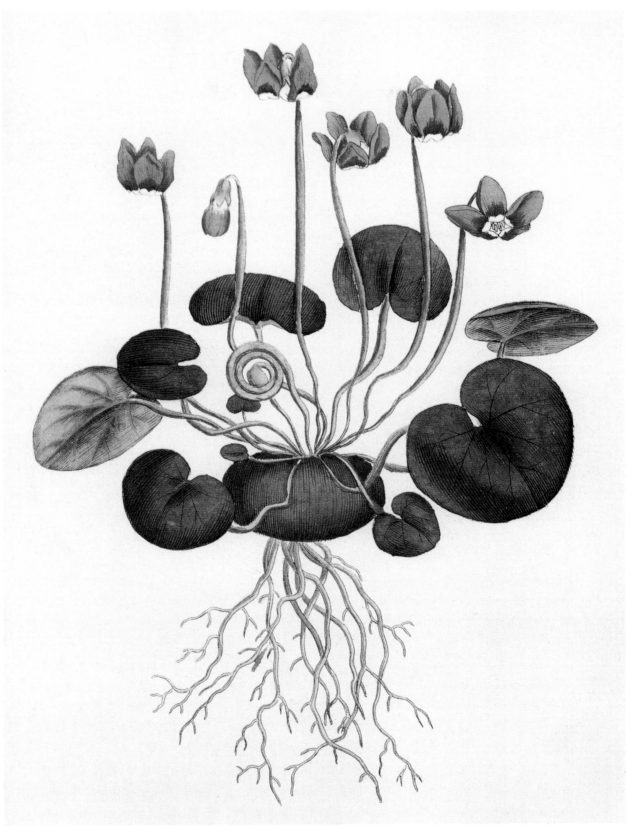

*Cyclamen coum.* For winter and spring flowers, from white to crimson. Leaves plain green to mottled. Eastern Europe, Asia Minor etc. From *The Botanical Magazine*, t.4, 1787. Enlarged by about $33\frac{1}{3}$%.

*Courtesy: Royal Botanic Gardens, Kew.*

pink berries freely after the crop of tiny white flowers.

Judging from a lecture I heard by Mrs J. D. C. Anderson, many Patagonian plants may before long find their way into our gardens from collections by her and her husband; they will include some real surprises.

## South Africa

Many bulbous plants reached British gardens from South Africa in early days. This was for two main reasons. Before the Suez Canal shortened journeys to the east, the Cape was a useful port of call for revictualling ships, and those with an interest in such things would explore the immediate country. More or less dormant bulbs would survive the journey back to Europe better than other plants. Most bulbs soon adapted themselves to the changed seasons. However, such beauties as nerines, amaryllises, montbretias and crinums do not come within the scope of this book, but it is inevitable that so large a continent, covering some five thousand miles from north to south and with so varied a terrain, should contain at least a few plants suitable for British rock gardens. Most demand protection from our oft-recurring rains and a consequent lack of resting period.

Apart from discoveries hundreds of years ago, the first real awakening to Africa's riches from an alpine point of view was, to me, the expeditions made by Mrs Milford during the 1930s. She was a little lady with a nursery at Chedworth, Gloucestershire, and was therefore known affectionately among a few of us as 'the Chedlet'. *Helichrysum milfordiae*, whose silvery tufts produce white daisies from crimson buds in a sunny scree or alpine house, was one of her finds.

I cannot write with any enthusiasm about *Rhodohypoxis baurii*; they have long flowering periods and can be quite successful of increase in peaty soils, not wet in winter, but moist during the summer months, and freely produce their little flowers of white through pink to crimson for weeks on end. But their central parts, stamens and all, are covered up with a strange folding of the floral segments, and thus lose, to me, much charm.

Thanks to Mr B. L. Burtt, of Edinburgh Botanic Garden, we have several species of *Diascia* to play with. *D. barberae* (annual), *D. cordata* and their hybrid 'Ruby Field' were the first to appear in our gardens and have proved reasonably hardy in warm gardens. *D. rigescens* is more spectacular but rather large for rock gardens and it has not proved reliable with me. I hear better reports about the smaller *D. fetcaniensis*. Their great character, apart from their long flowering period, is their peculiar soft tone of pink, verging towards copper or terracotta.

Probably the most famous African 'alpine' plant is *Euryops acraeus*, a silvery, almost white bushlet with brilliant yellow daisy-flowers in summer. It is proving hardy in well drained, sunny positions in warm gardens – and under shelter – but is not long lived in mine; it may need moister, cooler conditions.

## The Antipodes

It was not until the early years of the nineteenth century that Australia and New Zealand were seriously botanised, by such adventurous men as the Cunningham brothers, Alan and Richard, also William Colenso and J. C. Bidwill, whose names are known by their plant discoveries. But I think it would be right to say that it is Antipodean trees and shrubs which have become best known in our gardens, rather than rock plants. Many plants, particularly from northern parts of both countries, would not be hardy in Britain. Tasmania also provides a good selection of all classes of plants for our gardens. New Zealand, remarkable though it may seem in view of the distance involved, has given rise to nurseries whose plants are exported in quantity to our shores. On the whole – but with some exceptions – plants from the antipodes need all the warmth we can give them, and thrive best in frames and alpine houses. One firm, County Park Nurseries owned by Graham Hutchins, frequently exhibits at the shows of the Royal Horticultural Society, stocking their stands with a ravishing array of alpine plants, tiny shrubs and the like.

J. C. Bidwill travelled in New Zealand and Australia in the first half of the nineteenth century. One of his finds was the carpeter *Acaena microphylla*, so arresting when freely decorated with its bright crimson, spiny seed-heads. But I think most of us would associate Bidwill with what we have long known as *Veronica bidwillii*, a little evergreen of miniature charm which, like the larger and more colourful *V. catarractae* and *V. lyallii*, had a spell under the name of *Hebe* but which is now known as a species of *Parahebe*. Not so *Hebe epacridea* and *H. buchananii* 'Minor', which, with *H. macrantha*, remains in the genus. With its bold leafage and large snow-white flowers this species never fails to draw attention.

At about the same time we received from Richard Cunningham in New Zealand the diminutive almost prostrate *Fuchsia procumbens*; it is usually seen in an alpine house or frame, its tiny, but exquisite flowers outclassed by its large pink fruits. Two particularly useful and beautiful summer-flowering gentians are *Gentiana saxosa* and *G. bellidifolia*. They are amenable plants for scree or trough and have pure white flowers. The thick-leafed *Saponaria caespitosa* with huddled pink flowers could join them. The well-known raoulias from New Zealand are no longer known by their old names; silvery *Raoulia australis* is now considered to be a hybrid and what we knew as *R. lutescens* (*R. subsericea*) may be the correct *R. australis*. But the botanists are still busy with them and we had better leave it at that and await the final outcome. If you can get the rosy *Douglasia laevigata* to flower next to these silvery carpets, the senses will be delighted with New Zealanders hobnobbing with a North American in any well-made scree.

Species of *Celmisia*, mostly natives of New Zealand, seem to be more at home in Ireland and the north of England and Scotland than they do in the south. The most magnificent of all that I know is *C. spectabilis*, which I have mentioned elsewhere, but there is no lack of smaller species, all with daisies of pure white in varying sizes over clumps of greyish tongue-like, leathery leaves. A plant that I have admired many times at Edinburgh is the Liliaceous *Milligania densiflora* from Tasmania. Again with clumps of similar leaves, the plants are topped with branching heads of cream starry flowers. It enjoys a sandy, peaty soil and a cool spot and thus brings us to the prostrate *Pernettya tasmanica*, a mat-forming diminutive evergreen with conspicuous red berries. For cool peat beds the ourisias are much treasured, though in mild gardens they need little encouragement, colonising freely. Two notable species from New Zealand are *Ourisia macrocarpa* and *O. macrophylla*, both with good flowers of pure white. Hybridised with a South American red-flowered

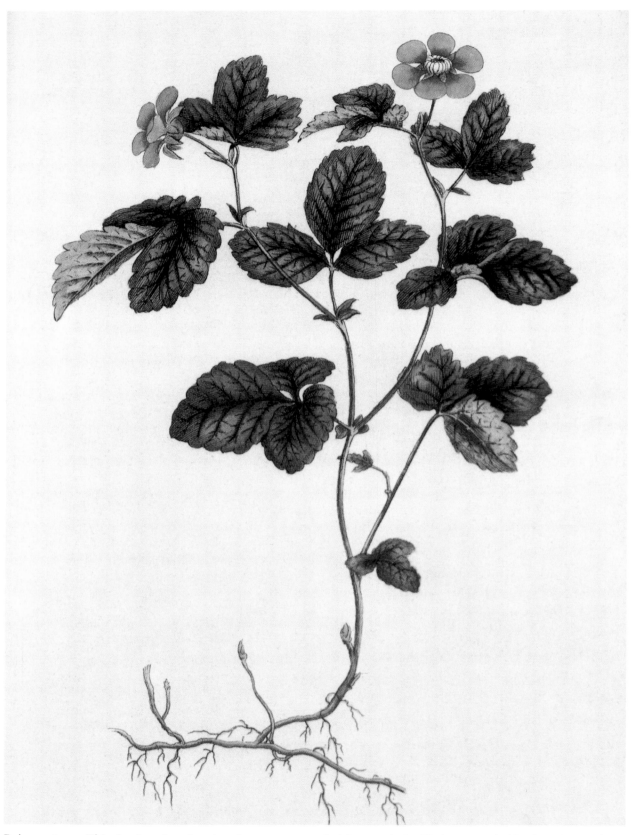

*Rubus arcticus.* This tiny invasive plant is at home on a peat bed in part shade. Native to arctic Northern Hemisphere. From *The Botanical Magazine*, t.132, 1790. Enlarged by about $33\frac{1}{3}$%.

*Courtesy: Royal Botanic Gardens, Kew.*

*Sedum populifolium.*   Neglected Siberian species for August flower. Good ground-cover. From *The Botanical Magazine,* t.211, 1792.

*Courtesy: Royal Botanic Gardens, Kew.*

species, *O. coccinea*, the latter has produced 'Inverewe' in a rich pink, which occurred in the garden of that name in north-western Scotland where all species do so well.

The species of *Pratia* also like cool, moist conditions. The lawn in Seven Acres at Wisley, as well as my own and that at Nymans, is starred with white in summer from *P. angulata*'s thread-like shoots, weaving their way through the turf. Of late years I have been captivated by the lavender blooms of *P. pedunculata*, an equally good carpeter, but probably not so hardy.

These somewhat geographical notes could well be closed with a reference to the magnificent but rather intractable *Ranunculus lyallii*, one of New Zealand's glories. It is possible to grow it in a moist sunny position in some of our more amenable counties and enjoy its splendid, rich green, almost circular leaves. And when, and if, it flowers you will be entranced by its wide white buttercups and realise that, as with *Myosotideum hortensia* (*M. nobile*), the antipodes can well hold their own in flowers of spectacular beauty, though these two may be rather large for all but the most extensive of rock gardens.

## Post-War Introductions

The story of alpine plant introduction since the Second World War becomes considerably involved. Ever since countries began to settle down again to the hoped-for peace, from about 1955 onwards there have been numerous expeditions in search of plants, some of a week or two, some for much longer, and comprising two seekers or four or more. Partly because of the expense of more distant journeys, and because of the ease of getting to Asia Minor and neighbouring countries, many of the expeditions have centred upon what we broadly term the Middle East; for our purpose we can include countries from North Africa through to Afghanistan. Bulb fanciers have been very much to the fore, and looking at the record of these and other plants largely, we must admit that most of the plants, seeds and bulbs collected are more for cultivation in frames and alpine houses, where the dry periods can be best controlled and unwelcome rain warded off. Some of those most concerned with bulb exploration and introduction are Brian Mathew, Paul Furse, James Archibald, W. K. Aslet, Peter Davis. Oleg Polunin is an important name, too, and apart from whatever contributions others may have made to horticultural literature, he, Brian Mathew and later Martyn Rix have produced valuable books. J. M. Watson, C. Grey-Wilson, J. Marr, M. Cheese and many others have contributed to our knowledge of these regions; A. W. A. Baker has penetrated to Spain and the USSR, also J. Marr and Peter Davis.

The countries farther east, so much covered by earlier expeditions, received many explorers: Ludlow and Sherriff, Peter Cox, R. McBeath, T. Lowndes, A. D. Schilling, Roy Lancaster, and the Stainton, Sykes and Williams venture, also the Alpine Garden Society's journey to Sikkim. Of late years there have been several trips to China by Alan Leslie, James Russell and C. D. Brickell; to the last I owe much help with these paragraphs. He has also been many times to the Middle East, as well as to the United States of America and Canada, a huge slice of the world where Brian Mulligan has done much work.

The Andes have attracted several explorers, notably Mr and Mrs J. D. C. Anderson, Kenneth Beckett, Martyn Cheese and J. M. Watson, while Graham Hutchins has introduced us to many plants of New Zealand where Brian Halliwell has also been active – and in Tasmania and Japan as well. In all probably over a hundred expeditions.

But it seemed to me that among the many plants introduced there were few which could take their places with the older stalwarts of our rock gardens. So many of them seem to need the protection of an alpine house or frame, mainly to combat unwanted rain at certain times of the year. Thinking that there should be several dozen good new hardy species among them, I sought assistance from several old friends in the alpine plant world, asking them to list for me proved perennials among new plants. This I did because my walk of life has led me rather away from rock gardens and their plants of late years. To my gradually growing amazement it became obvious that my suspicions were correct. It may well be that we are beginning to come to an end of the alpine plants of the wide world which are prepared to put up with our weather, though they might approve of our climate.

Like many other spheres of horticulture, it seems that we may have to resort to hybrids and specialised forms for novelty to keep our appetites whetted. In these pages I have already mentioned some hybrids of excellence. We could add *Campanula* 'Joe Elliott', *Dianthus* 'Joan's Blood' and *D.* 'Inshriach Dazzler'; *Geranium* 'Ballerina', *Phlox* 'Chattahoochee', *Saponaria* 'Bressingham Hybrid', *Saxifraga* 'Southside Seedling' and the little bright yellow-leafed *Thymus* 'Bertram Anderson'. Among them are gems to be treasured for all time. The purists may consider them vulgar, but nobody could complain that passers by would not be arrested by their vivid effects.

*Calceolaria fothergillii* from Patagonia and the Falkland Isles. Introduced in 1777. Cool, peaty soil in garden or alpine house. From *The Botanical Magazine*, t.348, 1795. Enlarged by about $33\frac{1}{3}$%.

*Courtesy: Royal Botanic Gardens, Kew.*

*Aristea africana* (*A. cyanea*).   For greenhouse except in very warm districts. South Africa. Full sun. From *The Botanical Magazine*, t.458, 1799. Enlarged by about 25%.

*Courtesy: Royal Botanic Gardens, Kew.*

# 7
# *Planting the rock garden*

I have said that you should not use yellow for a dominant large patch close to the rocks.... I feel that, as the earthquake caused the mountain, and storm has weathered it so that kindly Nature could soften it in places with life, storm and the colours of storm should run through the garden – purples, reds, bronzes, and deep blues, relieved by lighter tones, with occasionally a spot or thin streak (not a square patch) of yellow, like a fitful gleam of sun. These are the colours of the mountains. All other colours can be used restrainedly, but the predominant tones to use are the tones of the hills.

B. H. B. Symons-Jeune, *Natural Rock Gardening*, 1932

My book *Plants for Ground Cover*, first published in 1970, has sold many thousands in its first and second editions and reprints; enough to make me feel perhaps that this chapter might not be necessary. But that book sought to cover all types of ground-cover plants, whereas now we are concerned entirely with plants for rock gardens and their environs. And I repeat that the best way of managing a rock garden is to ensure that all its open spaces are covered either with plants or shingle.

As suggested earlier in this book, the rock garden should have a green background of shrubs, or blend into a heath garden or woodland. Whatever size the rock garden may be, it will still represent a small piece of natural scenery, and we should make our art extend to the surrounding planting. The first decision to make is that there shall be no large-leafed plants except in the foreground. There they will increase the sense of perspective. Likewise all bright colours, white, red, orange and yellow shall be in the foreground and give way to the soft and pale tones in the distance. This has the same effect. Where the rocks occur is the place for the saxatile plants, obviously: the rosette type and the really compact dwarfs. It might be thought that they will require hand-weeding, but not if, as is correct, they be given an inch depth of stone chippings around them. The stone chippings should lie around all the rocky areas and appear to have fallen off the outcrop, down the sloping ground, creating in some places merely a surface covering, and in other places developing into a real, deep scree. This is where exhibition rock gardens so often have their first errors in natural presentation; the mown grass should not ascend to the foot of the rocks. I like to see the greater and smaller rocks in contrast to the fallen debris as well as the green of plants. None of the plants I am about to recommend will give a close-mown effect; I do not feel this is achievable nor is it desirable. I only intend recommending evergreen plants, but a few others are bound to creep in! I feel that the grey or other tint of the stone needs greenery as a contrast. This does not mean that among the saxatile plants no deciduous species can be allowed.

The sort of outcrops we shall build in our gardens will be on the top of the soil. Even were we to build with the two-thirds of the rock beneath ground level – advised by earlier writers – the rocks would still be arranged with soil beneath them, whereas in nature the bigger the outcrop the more it would be supported by firm strata beneath it. This means that, if we imagine our outcrop is merely the uppermost representation of a massive lot of stone, the surface should only be given dwarf saxatile species of plants. Anything of a luxurious nature would not grow on a spartan hillside, but would congregate on the depressions of the soil nearby. This applies also to free growing shrubs, i.e. they should only be placed where no rock is imagined immediately beneath the soil surface. On the other hand, tiny creeping shrubs can well occur on the outcrops and upper ledges.

Certain rules seem to me to govern the choice and siting of plants on a natural rock garden. We are going to look at a picture composed of not more than three elements: the colour of the stone (the rocks themselves, their smaller pieces surfacing the scree and paths), the colour of the plants' foliage and flowers, and perhaps water. Because we are aiming at a true representation of nature, any plants with variegated foliage should, in my opinion, be utterly eschewed. Yellow or white variegated conifers and shrubs and yellow and orange tinted leaves of heathers would be completely out of place. 'Coloured' foliage would 'upset the nightingales', as A. T. Johnson used to say. His entire garden was composed in shades of green. There is enough variety to be enjoyed in the light and shade on the rocks, and the plants whose foliage may be green or greyish, or burnished in winter, to satisfy if a proper selection be made. But shrubs of some kinds are needed to link with the background and to give a sense of solidity and darkness. They should only be placed where we – in our imagination – visualise a deep root-run between outcrops. Dwarf conifers come instantly to mind. Their foliage gives at once the dark dense effect needed so much to balance the rocks' solidity. These are given chapter 12 to themselves.

So let us see with what plants we can achieve these ideals. In ascending mountains in search of alpines one first traverses the lower alps, through lush meadows, to where what trees there are start to peter out, the rocky escarpments begin, plants get smaller until one reaches those tiny inhabitants of rock fissures and windswept moraines and screes. If we want to imitate nature in the garden we should do the same.

In the immediate foreground, therefore, to accentuate the perspective of what is at best but a microcosm of an alp and a mountain, we should choose a few plants of bold foliage. As likely as not our low, moist ground will be there, with perhaps a pool. Here would be the flat leaves of miniature waterlilies, the tinies such as *Nymphaea tetragona*, *N. pygmaea* and their hybrids (their nomenclature and parentage is confused) and *N.* × *laydekeri* forms for larger pools. The tinies will thrive in only

*Chimaphila umbellata.*    A peat-lover for cool positions; related to *Pyrola*. Northern Hemisphere, including Central Europe, 1762. From *The Botanical Magazine*, t.778, 1804. Enlarged by about 25%.

*Courtesy: Royal Botanic Gardens, Kew.*

*Dodecatheon meadia.*  The Shooting Stars of Eastern North America, 1744. Cool moist positions. From *Temple of Flora* by R.J. Thornton, 1812.

*Courtesy: The Royal Horticultural Society.*

135 Only the largest of rock gardens could give space for *Viburnum davidii*, here seen at Edinburgh. Plants with broad leaves in the foreground increase the perspective in more distant planting.

137 The right and wrong methods of making crevices for deep-rooting alpine plants. From *Alpine Flowers* by William Robinson, 1870. The diagram on the left shows wide mouths for planting and free root-run among the small stones. On the right the mouths are too narrow and there are insufficient small pieces of stone in the root-run, which the piece of stone marked 'N' obstructs.
*Courtesy: Royal Horticultural Society*

136 The rosy tubes of *Penstemon rupicola* flowing down from a well drained rock ledge.

138 A sunny shingle slope decorated with *Androsace lanuginosa*; pink flower-heads over silvery foliage.

139 Joints in a rock garden of Sussex sandstone effectively filled with *Campanula garganica* 'W.H. Paine' and encrusted saxifrages, while *Parahebe catarractae* covers the space between the strata. (cf. Fig. 95)

140 *Pterocephalus parnassi (P. perennis)* subsisting in the sharpest of drainage on a sunny ledge, such as it would inhabit in Greece.

141 Another lover of a sunny slope, *Hutchinsia alpina.*

(*Left*) *Dryas octopetala*, Northern and Central Europe, and *Loiseleuria* (*Azalea*) *procumbens*, alpine and arctic regions of the Northern Hemisphere. From *Practical hints on the culture of rock plants*, by James Lothian, 1845.

*Courtesy:*
*The Royal Horticultural Society.*

(*Below*) *Acaena microphylla.* The colourful seedheads in summer of this dense carpeter for sunny places, from New Zealand. From *Alpine Plants* by David Wooster, 1872–4. Slightly enlarged.

*Courtesy:*
*The Royal Horticultural Society.*

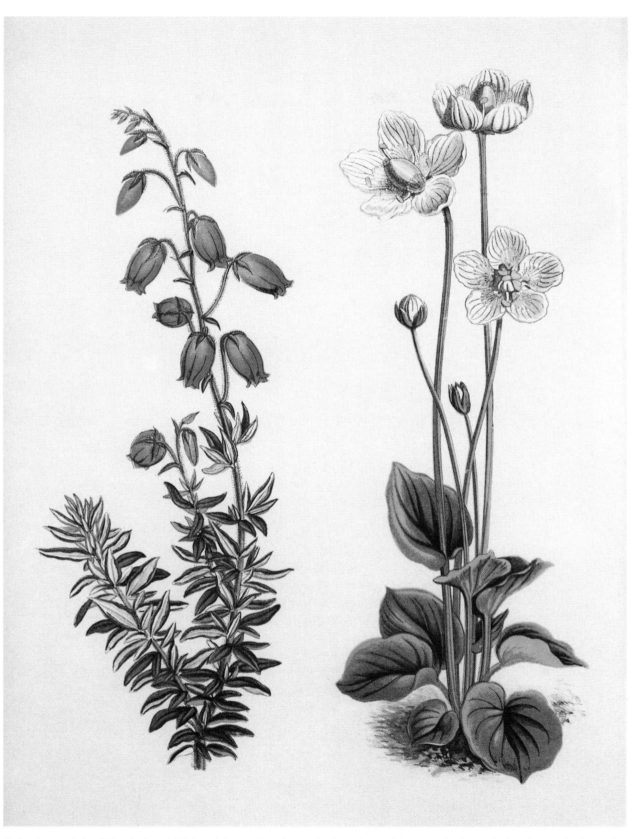

*Daboecia cantabrica (Menziesia polifolia)* and *Parnassia palustris*, both natives of the British Isles and elsewhere. The latter for bog, the former for sandy soils, both lime free. Summer flowering. From *Alpine Plants* by David Wooster, 1872–4.

*Courtesy: The Royal Horticultural Society.*

a few inches of water and may even be grown in troughs in a sheltered place. The margin of the pool could take Marsh Marigolds or Kingcups (*Caltha*), *Peltandra*, *Sagittaria* and perhaps *Primula florindae*. For covering the verges of the concrete, ajugas and *Rubus calycinoides* are admirable, also the little mat-forming creeping evergreen fern, *Blechnum penna-marina*. Equally mat-forming is *Astilbe chinensis* 'Pumila', whose fluffy pale magenta spikes are so effective after midsummer; another plant of similar creeping habit is the little *Gunnera magellanica*; it is somewhat tender and has no beauty of flower. In a sopping wet spot, with sphagnum moss mixed with the peaty soil one could toy with *Pinguicula grandiflora* whose violet flowers are as big as large violets themselves; it grows wild in southern Ireland, and alongside it would be appropriate to have *Parnassia palustris*, in whose beautiful white, green veined flowers the stamens ripen and shed their pollen on the stigma and then move out of the way! The North American *P. fimbriata* is even more beautiful and with them in permanently moist peat might be the place to try *Gentiana pyrenaica*.

As a bold frontal shrub *Viburnum davidii* would be useful. It slowly achieves some six feet across but can be kept to whatever size is required by pruning. The smallest *Bergenia*, *B. stracheyi*, in white or pink, makes a dense mat of rounded evergreen leaves in sun or shade. *Pachyphragma macrophyllum* produces its white flowers very early in the year and possesses handsome, almost orbicular leaves for the rest of the growing season; of comparable growth and size of foliage, *Galax urceolata* is an evergreen of great quality; both thrive in shade. I should not like to be without the crisp dark green rosettes of the London Pride group of saxifrages, *Saxifraga × urbium* and all the forms and hybrids of allied species of the Robertsonia section. Undoubtedly the most colourful of the London Prides that have come my way is a hybrid of rich colouring and dark foliage, known as 'Chambers' Pink'.

As a complete contrast there are the black-green fingered leaves of our native *Helleborus foetidus*, for sun or shade, while *Hosta minor* in plain green is valuable for its graceful August flowers in shades of violet.

These few plants give an indication of bold foreground planting. We will leave saxatile plants for the neighbouring outcrop over the pool until later, and next consider all the main slopes which in nature would be covered with herbage or scree. Among short carpeters, still with comparatively bold foliage there is that absolute winner, the dense carpeting, evergreen *Waldsteinia ternata*, whose yellow strawberry-flowers are quickly over in spring, leaving for the rest of the year its lovely glossy dark green leaves. It is weed-proof. A carpeting shrub of similar value and quality is the evergreen *Cotoneaster dammeri*; larger, up to a foot in height, there are the two dwarf mahonias *Mahonia nervosa* with glossy foliage and *M. repens* with dull, bluish green leaves. Both spread freely by suckering when suited in half shade. One of the very best crisp, glossy, slow carpeters is *Asarum europaeum*. For hot dry slopes we could hardly choose anything better than *Sedum spurium*, especially in its dense non-flowering form 'Green Mantle'. It is a vivid light green.

Away on the outskirts of the slopes, approaching the larger shrubby background, we could use the glittering green of *Lonicera pileata*, *Cotoneaster* 'Gnom', dwarf ivies such as *Hedera helix* 'Feastii', and dwarf rhododendrons. The latter are for lime-free soil, of course, and with them would be blended that dense, vigorous carpeter *Arctostaphylos uva-ursi* – also the related plant known as *A. nevadensis* – and clumps of irises of the Louisiana hybrid strains for variety of texture. And continuing on lime-free ground there are the hosts of heathers from short-carpeters such as the incomparable *Erica herbacea* (*E. carnea*) 'Springwood White' to much taller callunas and *E.* × *darleyensis* forms, with their close relatives *Cyathodes colensoi*, *Empetrum nigrum*, *Leiophyllum buxifolium*, vacciniums, particularly *Vaccinium vitis idaea* 'Nana', and also *Betula nana*. The heath with the longest flowering period – from June onwards – is the Irish species, *Daboecia cantabrica*, available in lilac, white, crimson and particoloured. The comparatively large bell-flowers are a sumptuous joy, and it is a big vigorous grower. Away in the shade under larger shrubs ferns will thrive and that rich blue of spring *Omphalodes cappadocica*, which should be given Narcissus 'Hawera' as a companion, and the sweet woodruff *Asperula odorata*, so prettily dotted with tiny white flowers in May.

I must give a passing word to the merits of *Luzula sylvatica*, the common woodrush, for shady and preferably lime-free soils. A friend once rudely said to me he wouldn't give it garden room. But it has many redeeming features for a natural piece of landscape such as we are attempting. It will cover even difficult steep banks in a creeping mass of grassy leaves, overtopped by brownish grass-like flowers, is completely weed-proof, and ideal where a background of no maintenance is required, perhaps in those difficult places under prickly shrubs. I am not going to recommend many grasses, though grass-like foliage is necessary for relief; one species that has no rivals is *Festuca eskia*, in the dark green form that used to be called *F. crinum-ursi*. It is a pity that the name had to be changed, because *crinum-ursi* means the hair of a bear and a yard-square wad of it looks like nothing so much as a bearskin rug in darkest green (see Fig. 158). It is flat and tussocky, remains as a dense rug and does not keep to isolated tufts as does the blue-grey *F. glauca*. And, as Clarence Elliott wrote about grasses for the rock garden, they are 'a corrective to the temptation to have flowers, flowers, flowers, and colour, over every inch of the rock garden'.

The hot dry slopes can be given some brooms: *Genista sagittalis* and *G. procumbens* and the flat growing form of our common broom *Sarothamnus* (*Cytisus*) *scoparius prostratus*. Also yellow-flowered and closely related is *Anthyllis hermanniae*. A complete contrast would be found in the very dark green of *Cotoneaster microphyllus cochleatus* with surprisingly large red berries in autumn, while even flatter are forms of *Juniperus horizontalis*, some of which like 'Douglasii' turn to violet-blue in winter. *Eriogonum umbellatum* and the old perennial candytuft *Iberis sempervirens* would complete this little collection, with a few helianthemums for warm dry gardens. If you like 'flowers, flowers, flowers', choose the double-flowered cultivars, whose petals do not fall so early in the day as the singles.

I have always wanted to see a bank covered with cascades of the yellow winter jasmine, *Jasminum nudiflorum*, intermingled with the red berries of *Cotoneaster horizontalis*, but this would be a bit out of scale for all but the largest rock garden outskirts. The red borders at Hidcote demonstrate the value of the dusky dark green of *Pinus mugo*, the bushy mountain pine. Nothing else gives just that touch of the mountain tops nor is anything so appropriate for *Clematis alpina* to weave its stems through; the large pale blue flowers of 'Frances Rivis' are superb against the dark green in spring.

*Gentiana andrewsii* from N.E. United States and Canada, 1776. The flowers are showy in summer but do not open. Damp woodland soil. From *Alpine Plants* by David Wooster, 1872–4.

*Courtesy: The Royal Horticultural Society.*

*Ramonda myconii* 'Alba'.    For cool peaty positions, on the flat or in walls. Early summer. From *The Garden*, 1890.
Enlarged by about 10%.                                                    *Courtesy: The Royal Horticultural Society.*

*Saxifraga × boydii*.    Hybrid raised in 1890, probably between *S. aretioides* and *S. marginata*. Alpine house. From
*The Garden*, 1890. Enlarged by about 10%.

*Courtesy: The Royal Horticultural Society.*

Over sunny rocks *Cytisus* × *kewensis* will tumble its creamy primrose colouring in spring; if you can arrange to have some purple aubrietas nearby the combination will be highly satisfying. We do not often see *Jasminum parkeri* in the south of England; it is more to the fore in the softer climate of Ireland. Tiny yellow starry flowers are made the more apparent by the dark green leaves and stems, over the entire hummock. Where there is room for them, *Daphne cneorum* and *D. blagayana* are well worth growing. Between the wars the former put in regular appearances on every rock garden at Chelsea Show, but then it petered out everywhere. However, A. T. Johnson raised 'Eximia' from seed and now we have this joy – I find it spreads freely in ordinary garden soil in full sun. Not so *D. blagayana*, which so far has withstood my blandishments in spite of heaping stones over it and giving it humus. *D. tangutica* and *D. retusa* are compact little bushes while *D. napolitana* will achieve three feet. *D. jasminea*, a lovely little spring flowerer, with white stars emerging from pink buds among greyish leaves, is one of the smaller species. A curiosity, but a very beautiful one, is *D. jezoensis*, often confused with the greenish *D. kamtchatica*. The bright yellow stars appear in late winter and spring on plants of varying size. The leaves are produced in autumn and die in spring. It seems to prefer an acid or neutral soil, with humus. All have delicious fragrance. For carpeting the ground in good open sunny spots one can hardly beat *Dryas octopetala*, the Mountain Avens whose white flowers are followed by elegant fluffy seedheads. The American species *D. drummondii* is yellow in flower; some forms open well, others are apt to remain almost closed. In any case I should choose *D.* × *suendermannii* which is bigger and stronger in every way than either with cream flowers. It commemorates Franz Sündermann, the great Bavarian alpine gardener, who first raised and listed it in 1910. For a minute evergreen carpeter for sun or shade there is *Euonymus fortunei* 'Kewensis'.

I am tempted to include some of the dwarf hebes, but apart from a few variants of *Hebe pinguifolia* – and we don't want grey-leafed plants, I think – they tend to make rather formal rounded hummocks unless planted extravagantly closely. In this case they will soon become starved and unsightly.

We now get to the areas around the outlying rocks, where less vigorous plants are more suitable. Here would occur aubrietas, arabises, armerias or thrifts, and the tufts of the small Lady's Mantle, *Alchemilla conjuncta*, the silvery silky undersurfaces of whose leaves are such a joy to touch and see. There are many alpine phloxes, natives of North America which have enriched our gardens so much in spring. They flower at the same time as aubrietas, but are choicer and to me more beautiful in flower, though they last less long. I should give best marks to 'Bonito', a pale lavender-blue, remarkably vigorous and free-flowering and a complete ground-cover into the bargain, mounding up to about six inches. But there are many more garden hybrids from *Phlox subulata* and *P. setacea*, while lesser, but equally beautiful are the hybrids and forms of *P. douglasii*. These should be used higher up, among the rocks, for we are still on the general slopes. *Gypsophila repens*, in white or pink, will make a great carpet in full sun, while *G. fratensis* is, like *Phlox douglasii*, a lesser but even more charming plant for higher ledges, troughs and sinks. Here and there for contrast we could include the invaluable *Potentilla alba* whose soft green tuffets are bespangled with white flowers in spring and autumn, and *Pulsatilla vulgaris* and its hybrids and forms – the Pasque flowers or *Anemone pulsatilla* – make good incidents, likewise that useful late-flowering, purple *Hyssopus aristatus* which does not flower before August when colour on the rock garden is getting scarce.

By August two excellent knotweeds will start flowering to carry on until the frosts put a stop to such efforts. My first is *Polygonum affine*, which perhaps should have been included in an earlier paragraph: it is a vigorous carpeter, and both it and the next prefer a soil that does not become dry. One of the great attractions of *P. affine* is its rich brown winter colouring, for it is not an evergreen but retains its leaves. Spikes of pink appear from July onwards. There are several forms: the original pink, 'Darjeeling Red', which is a darker pink, and 'Superbum', which I chose from a German catalogue and which has proved well up to its name. (In some nurseries it has been re-christened 'Dimity'.) It has flowers of palest pink gradually turning as they age to rich crimson; the two colours make a delightful mixture through the season. 'Donald Lowndes', with pink flowers of a slightly salmon tint, I have not found a reliable plant, but none of these withstands long dry periods of east wind in spring. The other knotweed is *P. vaccinifolium*, equally free flowering, from early September. It is a free grower, covering rock and ground alike with tiny leaves and dainty spires of pink only a few inches high. The glossy dark leaves and good white flowers of *Fragaria chiloensis* are an asset anywhere and when it grows strongly in not too hot a place, it is a good cover.

We could next consider a few completely prostrate runners to show up the sudden foundations of the rocks. *Cotula squalida* is to me a rather squalid plant, but its more feathery relative *C. acaenifolia* is a good carpeter which does not so quickly become thin and bare if starved, thereby letting in the weeds. Although *Thymus drucei* (*T. serpyllum* of gardens) is an admirable carpeter while young, it tends to become bare after a few years; its form *lanuginosus* is the most prolific and reliable, and little *minus*, small though it may be, is dense and permanent. *T. nummularius* is not often seen but is worth a place and is a good dark green and dense. Acaenas, again, are rampant spreaders but I like particularly *A. buchananii* with foliage of pale jade-green, prettily lobed and divided as are the others. *Acaena inermis* is a much darker bronze-green, much the same as that of *A. microphylla*. This is, however, even more dwarf; whereas the other species have no particular floral or seed-head attractions, the seedheads of *A. microphylla* are of a bright crimson, highly conspicuous in late summer.

It is rather pleasant to let a little geranium thread its way through these true carpeters, *Geranium pylzovianum*; it does no harm and produces single pink flowers at midsummer. Another wanderer which behaves likewise is *Campanula cochlearifolia* in pale blue or white. It will come through all but the most dense carpeters. For some heads of silvery bracts, plant *Paronychia argentea*, and against dark brown rock two silvery carpeters can be chosen: *Antennaria dioica* and *Raoulia australis*. The antennaria has white flowers normally, but there is a pink form *A. d.* 'Hyperborea Rosea'. As for the *Raoulia*, in well drained or scree positions it will make dense carpets of minute silvery leaves; while I have walked on it – luxuriantly – in favoured Irish gardens, I have never seen it mounded up into hummocks, as happens in New Zealand, where it has earned for itself the name of 'vegetable sheep' from its appearance on the hillsides. There is also the more vigorous green-leafed

*Oxalis enneaphylla.*    Falkland Isles, 1876. Peaty rocky soil in cool positions. From *The Garden*, 1897. Enlarged by about 25%.

*Courtesy: The Royal Horticultural Society.*

*Pulsatilla (Anemone) alpina*, subspecies *sulphurea* and *Gentiana acaulis* of gardens.  Water colour painted in May in the Alps
by G. Flemwell. From *The Flower Fields of Alpine Switzerland* by the artist, 1911.

Courtesy: The Royal Horticultural Society.

*R. glabra*; both become studded with tiny flower heads in June, yellow and white respectively. Turning back to antennarias, there is a little-known, but highly serviceable species with much larger leaves, *A. plantaginifolia* which I find a good contrast in its leaden green with almost any plant.

It is unfortunate that *Sagina glabra* is not fully hardy in parts of this country. One never loses it altogether, but frost often damages the tops of hummocks. It is such a dense, dark green, moss-like growth that it should certainly be used in mild climates. The little white 'everlasting' flowers over the grey-green mat of tiny leaves from *Helichrysum bellidioides* are ideal for a sunny slope.

It is among all these carpeting plants on sunny or shady slopes that some of the best places are found for many spring bulbs. I have allowed myself the luxury of indicating a few autumn-flowering bulbs in chapter 6, but I feel I cannot embark wholly on recommendations for the spring. They would need a complete chapter to themselves. There are several dozen species and good garden hybrids of *Crocus*, *Galanthus* (Snowdrop), *Iris*; a few each of *Eranthis*, *Scilla*, *Chionodoxa* and *Muscari*. Spring is not complete without their welcome flowers and all survive untoward weather except the crocuses. Tucked away in a special corner I should put the unique *Iris* 'Katharine Hodgkin' in green and blue and cream, a fascinating blend – and the clear yellow *I. winogradowii* and early *I. danfordiae*. To contrast with and accentuate their delicate colourings I recommend the nearly black leaves of *Ophiopogon planiscapus nigrescens*. I like particularly the lavender of *Crocus tomasinianus* with the blue of *Scilla bifolia* and the white of snowdrops. But the catalogues will give you a full range of all of these and also of the smallest daffodils.

We are now coming to the slopes up to the main rocky outcrops. Here may be accommodated many of the best, easily grown plants. If you are lucky, *Gentiana acaulis* may grow and flower well. Of all rock plants this is perhaps the first which comes to mind when we think of rock gardens, and yet it can be contrary and exasperating – sometimes it will grow and flower without any care, as at Bodnant, Mount Stewart and Sizergh Castle. With me it will do neither, but with its close relative *G. angustifolia*, raised from seeds, I have had better luck, lining it out in rows in an open field where it has thriven mightily. Of the group headed by *G. kurroo* and *G. gracilipes* I have had occasional success for a few years. It is perhaps with these non-invasive, later flowering plants that the early spring species of *Corydalis* may be planted. They are also non-invasive, and die away soon after their intriguing clusters of pretty foliage and small, lipped flowers are produced. *C. caucasica* and *C. cava* are found in a variety of pale tints. And to contrast with the flat-growing gentians later in the year there are several species of *Sisyrinchium*, the small blue *S. angustifolia* and large-flowered bright yellow *S. macrocarpum*, all with tufts of grassy leaves.

For early spring the tight hummocks of white from *Iberis sempervirens* 'Little Gem' are unsurpassed, lasting for weeks, and a startling contrast to some of the dwarf, scarlet species of *Tulipa*. Another good little dark green hummock is *Thymus micans*, also with white flowers; it makes a good effect in paving, away from footfalls. I have no difficulty with that exquisite *Jeffersonia dubia* in sun or part shade, so long as it is given some humus. Though its flowers look like pale lavender poppies, it belongs to the *Berberis* Family. A superb colour contrast may be made by planting the rich blue *Linum narbonense* with hypericums of the *Hypericum olympicum* persuasion, of which I prefer the form known as 'Citrinum'. Another good group for blue – always a rare and much-sought colour – is found among the Boraginaceae genera, *Lithospermum* (now *Lithodora*) and *Moltkia*. *M. petraea* is a good shrublet up to some twelve inches; *Lithodora intermedia* a lovely rug-like carpeter; both have blue tubular flowers and grow well in all but the coldest gardens. And nearby may be placed the prostrate *Globularia cordifolia*, with powder-blue, rounded heads of blooms. The spreading scabious *Pterocephalum parnassi* is most at home flowing down between two rocks; its lavender-pink rounded flowers assort well with the downy foliage. Something of the same sort of growth is found in *Teucrium pyrenaicum*; it will thrive on dry slopes and presents its rosettes of violet and cream flowers in summer.

Of the alpine phloxes I have already written, but we are besieged with new American forms, such as the splendid 'Millstream', 'Blue Ridge' and 'Pink Ridge' which seem amenable to cultivation, but with the superb 'Chattahoochee' I can do nothing. Even if my cultivation pleases it for a year or so, the slugs polish it off in one night. More's the pity, for a lovelier combination of lavender blue with purple eyes would be hard to envisage. It appears to like humus and coolth, so I must try it again and not give up.

Geraniums have long been favourites of mine; one of the best of rock garden size is the form known as *lancastriense* of our native Bloody Cranesbill, *Geranium sanguineum*. *G.s. lancastriense* only grows on one tiny island off the coast of Lancashire, and is, in choice forms, almost prostrate, presenting its round pale pink flowers enlivened by crimson veins to perfection. In the hands of Jack Drake many brilliant seedlings have been raised, such as 'Shepherd's Warning'. *G. dalmaticum* is one of the best dwarfs, and has hybridised with *G. macrorrhizum* to give us a first class small carpeter named by Dr Peter Yeo *G.* × *cantabrigiensis*. It has rather muddy pink flowers, but its more compact white counterpart 'Biokovo' is highly pleasing. This was found in the wild; the pink one was raised at Cambridge Botanic Garden. This brings us to one of the very best: 'Ballerina', a hybrid between *G. cinereum* and *G.c.* var. *subcaulescens*. The lilac-pink flowers, darkly veined, are produced from early summer onwards.

Most rock gardens are floriferous up to and including June, and I want now to call attention to a good plant which prolongs the display, for ordinary sunny sites. For some unaccountable reason *Dianthus* 'Hidcote' has never become widely known in spite of the fact that it is infinitely superior to the little tufted 'Mars', which created quite a lot of interest in the 1930s. 'Mars' remains a tight dwarf; 'Hidcote' makes a goodly sward covered in June and intermittently thereafter has flowers. Both are double, rich crimson: 'Hidcote' is depicted in colour in my *Gardens of the National Trust*. A more easily satisfied perennial dwarf pink cannot yet be found. I often wonder about its origin: was it a chance seedling of that wonderful old garden plant 'Bat's Double Red' of the eighteenth century? It has similar foliage.

But I ought to have continued, after the geraniums, with the closely related erodiums. Of all the long-flowering rock plants these are about the best. The woody trunks support feathery foliage; *Erodium macradenum* is pink with black blotches, *E. trichomanifolium* pure pink; *E. supracanum* equally beautiful but more compact and

*Primula farinosa, Gentiana verna,* Micheli's Daisy, *Polygala alpina, Pinguicula alpina* and *P. vulgaris.* Water colour painted in May in the Alps by G. Flemwell. From *The Flower Fields of Alpine Switzerland* by the artist, 1911.

*Courtesy: The Royal Horticultural Society.*

*Dryas octopetala*, Mountain Avens. Creeping woody evergreen native to the Western Northern Hemisphere. Long cultivated, with ease. The pictures on this page are enlarged by about $33\frac{1}{3}$%.

*Geum reptans*. European Alps, usually lime-free. Long cultivated, best in scree with leafmould. Two water colours in Art Nouveau style by Philippe Robert. From *The Alpine Flora* by Henry Correvon, 1912.

*Courtesy: The Royal Horticultural Society.*

*E. guttatum* white with black blotches. At least that is how I have always labelled them; botanists may differ, but none will disappoint you on a sunny well-drained slope. *E. castellanum* is somewhat coarser than the above, and may be described as a more compact *E. manescavii*. Toning in with all these soft colours, *Osteospermum barberiae* 'Compactum' will produce lilac-pink daisies from summer until autumn.

Two other good pink late-flowering tufted plants are *Tunica saxifraga* 'Rosette', which honoured me by germinating, by chance, from the usual single type, and *Silene schafta*; its pink campion-flowers appear in August. Pink seems popular with these late-flowering rock plants; there are several lovely sedums, *Sedum ewersii, S. cauticola* 'Lidakense' and the uncommon, shrubby, *S. populifolium*, which like so many of its genus is beloved by butterflies. *S. middendorfianum*, on the contrary, has dusky foliage and red and yellow flowers, toning with the clear yellow *Oenothera linearis* – and *O. missouriensis* if its flowers are not too big for you. Spreading around annually from a central rootstock, *Potentilla* × *tonguei* has soft yellow flowers with red eyes for weeks on end. With it can be grown the dwarf yellow species with an equally long flowering period, *P. cuneata*, which used to be called *P. ambigua*. With these warm-coloured flowers I would group *Sedum spurium* 'Purpureum' for the sake of its beetroot-coloured leaves and also Joe Elliott's *S.* 'Vera Jameson', another good plant with dusky foliage.

The latest flowering rock plants – if we may call them such – are the Californian Fuchsias – species and forms of *Zauschneria*. In good sunny spots *Z. microphylla* (*Z. cana*) will put up a spectacular autumn display of scarlet flowers over silver foliage. (If you can place it near *Ceratostigma plumbaginoides* it will startle anyone.) A pink form of *Z. californica* has reached me from California, called 'Solidarity Pink'; I hope it will thrive in Surrey. But we will leave other late-flowering plants to the appropriate chapter. The zauschnerias are now grouped with *Epilobium*.

Whatever effect we are aiming at, there is, I feel, one rule that should always be observed. It is that the tops of outcrops, and the raised portions of the rock garden, are the places for the true 'Children of the Hills'. This is their place, where they will best thrive. Their only other place is the scree. In both places the drainage is of the sharpest and will keep them dwarf. I call to mind how at Cemmaes Bay, on Anglesey, the blue squills, *Scilla verna*, in early June cover the limy hummocks all along the coast, but do not grow in the hollows. Their soft grey-blue melts away into the distance. The greater plants, the coarser ground-cover and the short growing shrubs are in the open spaces where the soil is richer and deeper. Thus for the topmost rock crevices the plants in the following paragraphs all qualify.

First and foremost the Silver saxifrages – 'Silver' because their leaves are encrusted with lime deposit, even when growing in lime-free soil. Saxifrages seem to have gone out of favour during the last quarter-century; between the wars they formed the dominant genus among alpines. I defy anyone to produce a more scintillating display than an outcrop – or trough or lump of tufa – planted exclusively with these graceful floriferous plants, and even when they are out of flower their foliage is highly attractive. *Saxifraga paniculata*, as we must now call our old favourite *S. aizoon*, is easily satisfied; as a first choice I recommend *S.p.* 'Lutea' and the hybrid 'Esther'; *S.p.* 'Rosea' and the hybrid 'Kathleen Pinsent'; the spotted 'Canis Dalmatica' and miniature *minutifolia (baldensis)*.

But that is only one species; even more beautiful in pure white are forms and hybrids of *S. cochlearis* – 'Major', 'Minor' and the hybrid *S. × burnatii*. And then, perhaps for cooler positions, where I think they flower more freely, are the forms of *S. callosa*, which used to be called *S. lingulata*. *S.c. bellardii* is very beautiful, with graceful sprays; *S.c. albertii* and *S.c. lantoscana* are more upright. The queen of all the tribe is of course *S. longifolia* from the Pyrenees. In a crevice in full sun and good gritty soil it will make an ever-increasing neat rosette, eventually some eight inches across, when it produces a conical plume of white flowers at least eighteen inches tall. It then dies, and unfortunately hybridises freely, so you never know what the next generation may produce. If you can obtain seeds from its native haunts all is well. But there is no need to go to all this trouble; its hybrid 'Tumbling Waters' raised by Captain B. H. B. Symons-Jeune, of rock garden fame, produces offsets. These should be taken off as they appear, and given a fresh start on their own, otherwise the danger is that they may all flower together. The main rosette dies after flowering. It is one of the most spectacular of all alpines and gives a wonderful effect when growing sideways out of a crevice.

I hardly dare embark on assessing houseleeks or sempervivums; there are so many species and also hybrids. There are, however, a few very distinct kinds and without hesitation I give pride of place to *Sempervivum arachnoideum*, the Cobweb Houseleek. Its tight rosettes are covered in white webbing and its flowers are rosy red stars – a delightful colour-scheme. The common *S. tectorum* has some good forms or close relatives in *S. calcaratum*, sometimes known as *S. comollii*, with very large leaves of purplish mahogany and *S.t.* 'Giganteum' with very large green rosettes. 'Malby's Hybrid' I regard as the richest dark mahogany red, with 'Commander Hay' and *S. marmoreum* also of dark glowing colours. The last has quite a handful of synonyms into which I will not go, but the richest coloured form is often grown as *S. ornatum*. These all contrast well with the pale green of *S. tectorum* var. *calcareum* and var. *glaucum*. Unfortunately none of the above, which are brownish in colour, has the lovely floral colouring of the Cobweb species. I usually pull out the rosettes which are about to flower when growing them purely as ornaments in pots and containers. On the other hand there is a pale yellow-flowered form of *S. heuffelii* which should be sought; it used to be called *S. reginae-amaliae* and sometimes *Jovibarba heuffelii*. This species has the strange habit of increasing itself by means of dividing its rosettes, whereas all the others produce stalked runners. All of these plants can be given the driest, hottest positions.

In fact there are several excellent plants for the high-up crevices; *Onosma cinerea* (*O. alboroseum*) produces annually its nodding white tubular flowers – pink after pollination – from the top of a dry brick wall at Sissinghurst Castle, Kent, with apparently no other nourishment than old mortar. And species of *Acantholimon*, *A. glumaceum* in particular, love a hot sunny ledge and will develop old woody drooping trunks, given time; the spiny hummocks are covered in short clusters of pink flowers in June. *A. venustum* is hardy, and by far the most beautiful of the genus, but its rarity and beauty deserve culture in the alpine house or frame. Alpine pinks have this same habit, with age, of making woody trunks and hanging down the rock faces; our own Cheddar pink, for instance, once conveniently known as *Dianthus caesius*, now *D. gratianopolitanus*, and its smaller relative *D. arvernensis*, are

(*Left*) *Saxifraga paniculata* (*S. aizoon*).   Widespread European species, 1731, for any sunny well drained spot, or tufa. White, cream, pink.
(*Right*) *Saxifraga cuneifolia*.   From the Alps, 1768. A dwarf London Pride. Prefers part shade. Two water colours in Art Nouveau style by Philippe Robert. From *The Alpine Flora* by Henry Correvon, 1912. Both pictures are enlarged by about $33\frac{1}{3}$%.

*Courtesy: The Royal Horticultural Society.*

*Gentiana purpurea*, *G. purpurea* var. *flavida*, *G. acaulis* of gardens (blue and white) and *G. campestris* (mauve and white). Water colour by G. Flemwell. From *Sub-alpine Plants* by H. Stuart Thompson, 1912. Enlarged by about $33\frac{1}{3}$%.

two of clear soft pink, while *D. pavonius* (*D. neglectus*) – more of a clump-former – is of brilliant pink with buff reverse. In the 1930s we all grew a specially large and brilliant pink form or hybrid called 'Roysii', but this, sadly, seems to be extinct, and we must put up with *D. boydii* instead. Alternatively we can turn to the richness of Jack Drake's 'Inshriach Dazzler', another *D. neglectus* hybrid. Very sweetly scented, the white *D. petraeus*, tiny-flowered, and *D. squarrosus*, larger and deeply fringed, both have delightful doubles. Another excellent plant for hanging down is *Androsace lanuginosa* with silvery leaves and pink flowers; its variety 'Leichtlinii' is longer in flower but the flowers are white with pink eyes. If they are planted near to those rich carmine-pink, dwarf shrubby penstemons from North America, *Penstemon rupicola*, *P. davidsonii* 'Six Hills' and other hybrids, the contrast is all that one can desire.

For the sunniest hot spot choose *Erinacea anthyllis* (*E. pungens*) whose prickly little bushes are well set in June with lavender-blue pea-flowers; it makes a good companion for the plant, indeterminate botanically, which has long been known as *Micromeria corsica*. The little pinkish flowers grace the bushlets of tiny grey leaves which, to use Clarence Elliott's description, have 'the smell of an oyster bar, with the lemon predominant, and the whole keyed-up to a nose twisting pungency'. No better description could be given, and the plant to me is only beaten in its fragrance by another Elliott plant, the seed-cake thyme, *Thymus herba-barona*. I should not like to be without *Thymus nitidus* (*T. richardii nitidus*), whatever garden I made; it doesn't have to have a rock garden, but is admirably suited to any sunny well drained spot. Neat little grey bushes become smothered in rosy lilac flowers in June. For the topmost ledges we could choose *Dryas octopetala minor*, the tiniest pinks such as *Dianthus alpinus*, *D. freynii* and *D. simulans*, *Potentilla nitida* (in a scree mixture) and *Silene acaulis*. The last two should be obtained in free-flowering forms. *Polygala calcarea* 'Lillet' or 'Bulley's form' in true blue, the smallest sempervivums, *Genista delphinensis* and *Cytisus hirsutus demissus* in bright yellow can join them. Here too the long-flowering *Scutellaria indica* and its variety *japonica* would produce their violet tubes over grey leaves.

Down among the rocks in full sun with a good root-run we may expect to grow both *Omphalodes luciliae* and *Lithospermum oleifolium*; both have greyish leaves and pale blue flowers, the first all summer through, and the latter only in spring. I find the *Omphalodes* grows best in a strong loam with old mortar rubble mixed in it. We seem to be mostly concerned with blue and lavender tinted flowers in these paragraphs. There is the whole race of the trailing campanulas of the *Campanula garganica* persuasion, *C. garganica* itself, its variety *hirsuta* and others such as *C. fenestrellata* or *C. erinus*, *C. elatines*, and the old hybrid 'W. H. Paine'. The last is violet-blue with white eye, the others pale lavender-blue; all have starry flowers in June and are prone to sending out a few suckers but are less prolific in this way than *C. portenschlagiana* of which a good violet-blue form has been named 'Bavarica'.

Now we will look at a few gems among campanulas. These next four make compact woody rootstocks, very slowly increasing, from which spring erect tufts of wiry stems each supporting a few dark violet-blue starry cups, apart from *C. tommasiniana* whose flowers are narrow tubes. The others are *C. waldsteiniana*, *C.* 'Wockii', 'Puck', and 'Stansfieldii'. It would be difficult to find more easily grown, compact little plants for late summer flowering in crevice, terrace or trough than this little group. I give them full marks.

Totally different is one of America's choicest species, *C. piperi*. It may succeed as a crevice plant, but is safer in the alpine house. The violet-blue almost stemless flowers are contrasted by red anthers.

In writing these paragraphs one's store of adjectives often runs out; what better refreshment, then, to turn to Farrer? Here is his description for *Campanula tommasiniana*: 'This lovely treasure is confined to the district above Istria, and even there is local. But in cultivation it is the delight of any open soil, in a select corner, sending up sheaves and bushes from its increasing tuft, of fine single stems, often six to nine inches high, set with thick and narrowish saw-edged foliage, and then in summer and on into August hanging out a little steepleful of long pale blue bells beneath which the elastic leafy shoots must bend and sway and decline.' There is not a superfluous word here, but of course his two-volume work, *The English Rock Garden*, contained over 500 pages!

All of the plants in the above paragraphs, from the pinks onwards, are best displayed against brown rock. But if you want a dark green dense hummock, scattered with minute yellow flowers in late spring, you cannot do better than *Bolax glebaria*; it is magnificent on grey limestone.

I think we might now look at a few shade-lovers, or at least plants that prefer a northern slope, so we will ascend gradually to the cooler heights from the shrubby area below. In the cool are ferns, Solomon's Seal in several species and forms, the broad shining blades and white, scented stars of *Speirantha gardenii*, *Uvularia*, *Vancouveria*, *Viola cornuta*, particularly its *lilacina* variety and the pure white *alba*, in flower from June onwards. To tower above it we could plant the intriguing *Paris polyphylla*, whose extraordinary cart-wheel like flowers of green and cream and violet are followed by red berries (if you can obtain both male and female); the carpeting *Tiarella cordifolia*, the Foam Flower, and all the choicer aquilegias. *Aquilegia glandulosa* is the queen of all in blue and white, but a tricky plant and best raised and planted when young from seed. The seeds are, I believe, unlike those of all other columbines; they are dull instead of shiny. *A. alpina* is an amiable plant of blue, generally, which has given rise to the 'Hensol Harebell' strain. Dainty little *Semiaquilegia ecalcarata*, in chocolate-mauve, and the 'viri peculiar' *A. viridiflora* can join them; their quiet tones will be awakened by the red and yellow of *A. canadensis* – and, as like as not, they will all interhybridise.

Up the stems of some small shrub will ascend the twining shoots of *Codonopsis vinciflora*. Few flowers have more charm than its semi-nodding, lavender, starry bells. And I must say the same about *Thalictrum diffusiflorum*. Its dainty leaves and airy sprays of pale lilac are entrancing to say the least. *Gentiana asclepiadea*, a thirsty plant, produces sheaves of blue trumpet flowers in September, from hearty, easy plants up to three feet in height. The beautiful white forms, and 'Knightshayes' – bright blue with white throat – should be grown with it. Farrer raised and cooed over a pale blue form which he called 'Phaeina' but this has long since died out, if it was ever propagated. At Sizergh Castle, Cumbria, are many pale blue forms, all very charming, and I have found that seeds from them germinate well, producing about 60% of the same colour. As a substantial good ground-cover among these

*Geranium sylvaticum* (mauve and white), *Paradisia liliastrum* (St Bruno's Lily) and *Anthericum liliago* (St Bernard's Lily). Plants for the open meadow. Water colour by G. Flemwell. From *Sub-alpine Plants* by H. Stuart Thompson, 1912.

*Courtesy: The Royal Horticultural Society.*

*Primula* 'Mrs J. H. Wilson'.    Impressive hybrid plant for good soil, in not too hot a position. From *The Garden*, 1909.
*Courtesy: The Royal Horticultural Society.*

larger plants, one could hardly do better than *Oxalis oregana* whose large clover-leaves are well decorated with large pink flowers in spring. It is invasive, but is only a surface-creeper. Lastly we have one Sedum, *Sedum pulchellum*, which goes against family tradition and prefers a cool, moist position. It has heads of pink stars and should not be passed over without due regard.

As we approach the higher shady ledges and crevices our plants get less lush and more compact. There are all the mossy saxifrages, for instance, harbingers of spring, from deep crimson through pink to the most magnificent white 'James Bremner'. The London Pride group would join them, especially *Saxifraga cuneifolia* of elfin charm. A unique species *S. brunoniana*, has yellow flowers from bright green rosettes, each connected with the next by a scarlet thread. With it we might put *Delphinium brunonii* in dark or light purple, thus growing both of Mr Brown's Himalayan plants together.

Usually one makes up the soil on the cool side of a hillock with more humus, reserving the grit more for the sunny side. This therefore makes desirable homes, in the less rocky parts, for those superb autumnal gentians, the famous *Gentiana sino-ornata*, in royal blue, its beautiful white form, and its hybrids, but these I have treated in chapter 10.

Some broader ledges can be given still more humus, to make congenial homes in lime-free soil for some tiny Ericaceae, such as *Rhododendron radicans* and the July flowering brick-red *R. nakaharai*; species and hybrids of *Cassiope*, specially 'Muirhead' and 'Edinburgh'; the dainty little *Arcterica nana* and *Phyllodoce nipponica*, blue-berried *Gaultheria trichophylla*, trailing *Hypericum reptans*, in flower from July onwards; soldanellas, particularly *S. villosa*, so like *S. alpina* but an easier plant to grow and with the same exquisite spring flowers, and the fairy charm of *Linnaea borealis*, the Twin-flower. 'The most conspicuous ground cover ... is the dainty twin flower – the favourite plant of the great Linnaeus. This woody vine is an evergreen that sends up slender stems a couple of inches high from which two tiny pink bells are suspended. Their fragrance is haunting; they are delicate creations to find in forests of towering trees and huge granite boulders sitting on lava rock' (William O. Douglas, *My Wilderness*). The American variant is more accommodating than our own native, in peaty soil. For late summer and autumn there are various species of *Cyananthus* among which, in spite of the larger flowers of several, my favourite is *C. microphyllus* (*C. integer*).

Two irises should join the above: *Iris gracilipes* and its white form from Japan, and *I. cristata* from North America. They resent moving except immediately after flowering. Nearby the little pale blue starry flowers of *Houstonia caerulea* – especially 'Millard's Variety' – will appear from June onwards. Pleiones I have never grown – small orchids which are seen looking so healthy and easy at shows. *Pleione limprichtii* with rich pink flowers is generally considered a good one to try, but they are all on the borderline of hardiness.

With a cool limestone rock just behind them is the place for *Hepatica*. There are several species and colour forms, but none in my estimation surpasses *H. × media* 'Ballardii', a hybrid raised years ago by the 'Wizard of Colwall', between *H. nobilis* (*H. triloba*) and *H. transsilvanica* (*H. angulosa*). It is unfortunately seldom seen, but the other species have the same Spode-blue flowers, though not the size. The most beautiful, perhaps, of all American dwarf phloxes, *Phlox adsurgens*, is generally considered to like the cooler slopes, but in Surrey I have not been able to make it content for more than a season or two. The flowers are of clear pink, almost salmon, and very alluring.

As we climb higher among the shady rocks, the conditions get drier and this is just the place for some of the smallest ferns, *Asplenium trichomanes*, *Ceterach officinarum*, *Cystopteris* species, the invasive *Adiantum venustum* and even *Cheilanthes gracillima*. With them I should want *Onychium japonicum*, perhaps the daintiest of all dwarf ferns, which, despite its name, was raised from spores collected on Mount Omei in Sichuan, by my friend Alan Leslie. Its beauty would conquer even the most inveterate of fern-haters. *Cyclamen* species for most seasons of the year will be content as a rule. A touch of dark purple would come from the hybrid *Viola gracilis* if one could obtain it; meanwhile we must comfort ourselves with 'Huntercombe Purple' and Joe Elliott's 'Martin', named after his non-gardening son, and the fascinating almost black flowers of 'Molly Sanderson', which replaces the old smaller 'Black Knight'. Now let me whisper it: in a bed of pure leafmould I once had a patch (for six or seven years) of *Gentiana pumila*, the relative of *G. verna* from the limestones of S.E. Europe, at least eight inches across, which flowered annually but failed to set seeds. Perhaps if I had given it some really old cow-manure with the leafmould – as is recommended for *G. verna* – I might have fared better. The sight of the blue stars of *G. verna* on the limestone of The Burren, County Clare, makes me long to grow it again. And its pale blue forms too, which were picked out at a distance by Charles Nelson's eagle eye.

One can imagine the blue carpet of *Lithodora* (*Lithospermum*) *diffusum* tumbling down from the upper rocks. The old form, 'Heavenly Blue', has been superseded by the more vigorous 'Grace Ward'. It needs lime-free soil and good soil into the bargain, and in the milder climates is a great beauty.

It is often said that a rock garden should be in a sunny position. With this I do not disagree, but it is not always possible to site it thus, and in any case many rock plants thrive on the shady side of a rock though not under trees. There is, too, the thought that in building our rock outcrop the uppermost ledges may suffer frequently from drought. Watering is considered in chapter 13. A visit to Wisley rock garden, which faces north, will speedily prove what a lot of plants thrive with this exposure. In fact if the soil has been suitably prepared, many rock plants thrive just as well on a northern slope as on one facing south.

Those gems the European primulas, from the exquisite *Primula marginata* to tiny *P. minima*, are very happy in north-facing declivities. They are an entrancing study on their own; I would stress the value of strong loam and stone chips rather than peat for them. *Saxifraga oppositifolia* and its forms, *Anemone flaccida*, the tiny pink *Rubus articus*, *Rhodothamnus chamaecistus*, *Tanakaea radicans* all come to mind and, of course, ramondas and haberleas. These alone would make a shady rock garden worth having. To see those beautiful lilac flowers projecting from the furry green rosettes of *Ramonda myconii*, set in a vertical crevice, is one of the great spring joys to me. One can prolong the display with *R. nathaliae* and *R. serbica* and increase the colour range with white and pink forms. All are highly desirable, likewise *Haberlea rhodopensis* and its white form. In this genus the flowers are more or less

*Primula edgeworthii* (*P. winteri*).   From the Himalaya in 1932; best in cool peaty positions. From *The Garden*, 1912. Enlarged by about 25%.

*Courtesy: The Royal Horticultural Society.*

SOME LITTLE-KNOWN PLANTS

1. Roscoea sikkimensis.
2.   ,,    purpurea.
3.   ,,    cautloides.

*Roscoea auriculata, R. purpurea* (1820) and *R. cautleoides* (1912). From Western China and the Himalaya, these all prefer cool moist soil. From *The Garden*, 1914.

*Courtesy: The Royal Horticultural Society.*

tubular, and the leaves do not form such attractive rosettes. *H. ferdinandii-coburgii* is a similar species or form with slightly larger flowers. I do not feel that the planting of a rock garden is complete without some of these plants, and, contrary to oft-repeated rules, both ramondas and haberleas will grow perfectly well on flat ground, well enriched with humus.

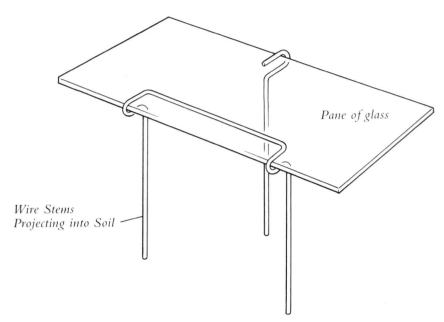

*Pane of glass*

*Wire Stems*
*Projecting into Soil*

142  Method of protecting alpines from excessive rain in winter.

# 8

# The scree garden and the alpine lawn

Screes support a few highly specialised plants, which exhibit morphological peculiarities deserving of mention. Their root-systems, which are of immense length, are often strengthened with T-shaped bracing pieces, while their stems have scarcely-developed internodes. Their leaves too are either succulent or hairy or red.

F. Kingdon Ward, *The Land of the Blue Poppy*, 1913

Having given us two books describing his garden and plants, as well as *Among the Hills*, Reginald Farrer produced a small book called *The Rock Garden*. It was published at a moderate price in the Present Day Gardening series, and was obviously aimed at popularising all that was concerned with alpine plants and rock gardens at the time. Apart from a brief mention in Meredith's book *Rock Gardens* of 1910, Farrer's little book contained the first real description of and reason for the moraine in the English language, though the famous Bavarian nurseryman Franz Sündermann had given information about it in 1889.

In his wanderings in the Alps, Farrer had noticed how the more saxatile and 'high' alpines grew well in shingle slopes, very often in blazing sun but watered from below by the melting snow from the heights above. He gave explicit instructions how to achieve moraine conditions in our gardens. But before long, alpine gardeners had changed the name to scree; it means much the same thing but there is less stress on the underground water. There must be hundreds of scree beds in these islands and all are successful if they have been made where water can drain away. One of the oldest was at Cambridge Botanic Garden (chapter 4); a very fine one is at Edinburgh Botanic Garden which was made on a slope facing north; others are at Kew and Wisley. There is no doubt that, especially on a retentive soil, some sort of scree is beneficial to the majority of sun-loving alpines.

The idea has been extended to the growing of all sorts of larger plants, witness the successful demonstrations at Ampfield House in Hampshire, laid out by the late Sir Harold Hillier, and what is known as the 'dry garden' in the Savill Garden, Windsor, a brain-child of John Bond. Besides being so good for plants, this type of garden – where gravel is dug into the soil in quantity and then topped with about three inches of washed shingle – has the result that few weeds

*Primula agleniana.* Tibet, Yunnan, Upper Burma. Water colour in Upper Burma, 1920, by Reginald Farrer. From *The Plant Introductions of Reginald Farrer*, edited by E. H. M. Cox, 1930. Lost to cultivation.

*Courtesy: Mrs J. A. Farrer.*

*Androsace alpina.*   From the Alps, in 1775. The Glacier Rock Jasmine needs lime-free scree but is only likely to be a (short-lived) success in the alpine house.

*Eritrichium nanum.*   From high mountains of the Northern Hemisphere, 1869. Best in alpine house or frame. From *Alpine Flowers* by Paul A. Robert, 1938. Enlarged by about $33\frac{1}{3}\%$.

*Courtesy: The Royal Horticultural Society.*

appear and one can walk about on it without leaving footmarks. The same thing applies to woodland gardens where a covering of shredded bark or pine needles is applied.

A scree is the natural product of rocks, weather and slopes. An extreme form is the almost precipitous slope of 'the screes' above Wastwater in the Lake District. Because the shingle is so constantly sliding down, little grows in it. But it only requires a gentle slope between a few rocks, as in the illustration (Fig. 143), to produce a garden scree. It should always be narrower at the top than at the bottom, where its largest pebbles and pieces of stone should appear to have rolled. To simulate the idea still further the rocks above and around the scree should show broken and irregular faces as if the shingle had been split from them by frost and accumulated in the valley.

In the garden the scree is one of the most successful methods of growing the gems of the higher regions; a few flat stones here and there add interest and make work easy on it, but of course it has one disadvantage: the tiny plants are far from the eye.

In making a moraine or scree, the soil should be excavated to about two feet and this hole must not form a sump for water. Whether on clay or gravel, chalk or sand, water must have an easy exit to lower ground. It is therefore not a suitable prescription for growing special plants on flat, heavy land. In such conditions it is necessary to raise the site to ensure free drainage and it may well be that the raised bed, described in chapter 11, would be the best answer.

Provided that drainage is satisfactory, the hole can be filled with washed shingle or road-metal – from pea to walnut size – to which soil should be added at the rate of one-fifth. The soil should be the standard mixture for almost all alpine plants: one-third each of loam (or the topsoil of the site), sharp, washed sand, and leafmould or peat. On top of this scree mixture a covering of about two inches of the self-same stone of the rock garden should be applied for the sake of congruence.

It may well be asked what is the point of all this excavation and shingle. In the first place it gives perfect drainage for the deep-questing roots of tiny alpines which find moisture down below, and secondly it provides the little plants of the high mountains with as dry a surface for their 'necks' and foliage as is possible in the open garden. Many small alpines have woolly grey leaves which collect moisture in our fluctuating winter climate, whereas they would be dry and warm under snow on the mountains. I have found it helpful, even on a scree, to protect the most woolly with a pane of glass about six inches above their foliage, suspended on galvanised wire stems as in the illustration on page 172. For larger clumps, a barn cloche is most suitable. Then it can be said we are doing all we can to make their lives enjoyable. If we do not, they will depart this life. In my experience in trying to grow alpines in the open garden, I find that far more losses occur annually with them than with shrubs and perennials. The higher upon the mountains they grow, as a general rule, the more fussy they are. In periods of drought it will be found that a canful of water does far more good on a scree than on the garden soil; it speedily reaches the lower roots.

143 The suggestion of a natural scree, showing Westmorland limestone with large and small shingle having apparently fallen from the rocky bluff. The possibilities for planting are endless, in crevices and in the actual scree.

144 The scree bed at the National Botanic Garden, Glasnevin, Dublin. A free and open site with sharp natural drainage, filled with scree mixture.

145 The great scree bed at Edinburgh, facing north. Homes for a vast number of otherwise tricky plants.

# Planting the Scree

Like most other garden schemes, the planting of a scree needs forethought. It is ineffective if little plants are dotted about singly but it is equally disappointing if it is overcrowded with plants so that no shingle shows. To take a page out of Hidcote's book, all rock garden planting should be done with as natural an effect as possible: to have different-sized groups, for instance, and, having planted a group, to pop in another plant or two of the same kind, singly, some distance away. I explained this fully in my book *The Art of Planting*. I can feel my readers nudging my elbow, so to say, and gently (or forcefully) reminding me that screes today are measured in feet rather than in yards or poles. Even so, in small screes one should use small plants so that all is in scale, including the pattern of planting.

To show up against the shingle, dark green is best though so many of the suitable plants are grey-leafed. The tight green hummocks of *Armeria juniperifolia* (*A. caespitosa*) 'Bevan's Variety' are completely obscured by bright pink flower heads in April. Following it are several asperulas. There are dark green tuffets of *Asperula gussonii*, looser tuffets of *A. lilaciflora caespitosa* and silvery tuffets of *A. suberosa*, all surmounted by tiny pink tubular flowers, the last two with very long flowering periods. They resemble in great part our native Squinancywort, *A. cynanchica*. Related to the thrifts are several species of *Acantholimon*, all with dark spiny foliage and pink flowers. *A. glumaceum* is the best known but the most beautiful is *A. venustum*, which is sometimes labelled *A. olivieri*, but it is very difficult to propagate and so remains scarce and expensive. The airy, arching sprays of pink, trumpet-shaped flowers are scarcely more beautiful than the autumn trumpet-shaped buff-coloured calyces.

*Veronica canescens* decorates its silvery tufts with light blue flowers and *Edraianthus pumilio*, also greyish, with lavender-blue bells; these are two gems for the scree. To tone with them I would add *Campanula allionii* and its close relatives *C. bellidifolia*, *C. saxifraga*, *C. tridentata* and *C. aucheri*, all resplendent with almost stemless large bells of shades of violet. With them I should want to grow Joe Elliott's hybrid (named after himself – deservedly!) between *Campanula morettiana* and *C. raineri*. With such distinguished and lovely parents 'Joe Elliott' could hardly avoid being beautiful himself. Open bell-shaped flowers of rich lavender-blue are produced for several weeks. Even if you forget the plant one week, the slugs will not, but these creatures do not like crawling on rough shingle.

As a complete contrast there is *Dianthus alpinus* with rich green foliage and startling large flowers of glowing pink. It is not particularly long lived but is easily raised from seeds. Here again Joe Elliott produced a noted form called (after his wife) 'Joan's Blood'. It is an exceptionally gorgeous crimson-red offset by black centres and blue pollen, and will keep reasonably true to form when raised from seeds. By planting nearby *Campanula excisa*, a plant of delicate charm and wayward, travelling habit, we can have an interweaving of great delight. For late flowering, *Trachelium rumelianum* (*Diosphaera rumeliana*) makes a sort of rosette of prostrate stems from a central rootstock, with upturned heads of small misty blue flowers soon after *Teucrium pyrenaicum* has flowered, flat on the ground likewise. Of course, many of the Kabschia and the Encrusted (or Silver) saxifrages are quite at home on

146 Two choice campanulas in a Somerset scree. *Campanula betu-laefolia* pale pink (left), *C. hypopolia*, lavender-blue.

147 *Celmisia coriacea* – a New Zealand species of great beauty for a well nourished scree in our cooler western counties. The white daisies are held above silvery grey leaves.

148 *Lithodora (Lithospermum) oleifolia* in a warm sunny corner of a scree. The pale blue flowers assort well with the greyish leaves. Pyrenees.

149 *Erinacea anthyllis (E. pungens)*, a prickly, tiny shrub with lavender-blue pea-flowers.

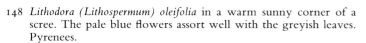

150 *Thymus membranaceus*. Unusual white flowers; for a sheltered corner. Spain.

151 Light lilac trumpets of *Edraianthus pumilio* over grey foliage.

152 Its label seems too large for the dwarf, dark lilac trumpets of *Campanula alpestris*. (*C. allionii*).

153 (*Middle left*) *Armeria juniperifolia* (*A. caespitosa*), a vivid pink hummock in early spring.

154 (*Middle right*) A taller denizen of the scree – *Hypericum hyssopifolium*. Lemon yellow flowers in June. 15 ins.

155 *Lewisia tweedyi* flowering well in a scree, after winter protection from a pane of glass. Native of Washington, United States of America.

the scree and produce their yellow or white flowers profusely. I really prefer them when raised from the flat, except for the only tall pink one, *Saxifraga* × *kolenatiana*, which achieves eighteen inches. For very early flowering the Kabschia saxifrages are unrivalled, in white, yellow and pink, while with them flower white and yellow species of *Draba*.

Elizabeth Strangman's delightful pink marjoram 'Kent Beauty' is a hybrid between *Origanum rotundifolium* – with large pale green bracts – and *O. scabrum*, richly coloured but small of flower. 'Kent Beauty' has combined the assets of both and will seed itself, but so far I have seen nothing to equal the original. It is another good late-flowering plant, likewise the exquisite *O. amanum* whose long pink tubular flowers project in abundance from the close growths. Many, in fact all, androsaces prefer scree or alpine house treatment; some of the easiest are forms of *Androsace sarmentosa* and *A. lanuginosa*. *A.l.* 'Leichtlinii' is repeat-flowering until early autumn. Their trailing shoots bear rosettes of small, pink flowers, or white with pink eyes in 'Leichtlinii'. Of *A. sarmentosa*, vars. *yunnanensis* and *chumbyi* are good geographical forms: in wet districts the closely related *A. sempervivoides* should be chosen on account of its nearly glabrous leaf rosettes. Few could resist the charms of *Saponaria* 'Olivana', a hybrid between *S. pumilis* and *S. caespitosa*. The comparatively large pink flowers are arranged neatly round a tuft of small leaves.

Silvery leaves do not show up well against grey shingle until late summer when their foliage is at its best; plants I should not like to be without are *Tanacetum densum amani* and *Artemisia glacialis* (*A. pedemontana*). They are both wide spreaders. As a perfect contrast is *Stachys lavandulifolia*; few gardeners could remain unimpressed by the dense tuft of leaves surrounded by a circle of lilac-pink flowers. In the same class is *Salvia caespitosa*, in clear pink. Again silvery leafed is *Veronica bombycina* with clear light blue flowers, and the dark grey-green of *Lithospermum oleifolium* (*Lithodora oleifolia*) is a good setting for its pale blue flowers produced for many weeks in spring. And for a specially sunny spot against a rock *Pelargonium endlicherianum* from Asia Minor should thrive and produce its deep pink, perky flowers.

I never see or make a scree without calling to mind a conspicuous success with the North American *Lupinus ornatus*, whose silver leaves and seventy spikes of blue flowers, eighteen inches high, covered over a yard square. Its portrait is in my *Perennial Garden Plants*. This was before the war; the plant then died but produced plenty of seeds. I have not seen it since, to my sorrow. This is an example of a big plant for which one must be prepared to give good space; it is worth it and is not likely to grow anywhere else. I used to grow also a plant called *Hypericum hyssopifolium lythrifolium*, which came from Dr Fritz Lemperg through A. T. Johnson; from a carpet of tiny leaves ascended ten inch stems of small flowers of warm yellow. This is another regretted loss.

I could go on for long on this ploy, but I think I have said enough to indicate the rich array of plants available for screes. It will, I hope, be seen from this chapter that I regard the planting of a rock garden to be just as much an art as any other part of the garden. The colours are much more interesting if graded from bright to cool, and the size of the plants from large to small the farther we go from the path or up the outcrop. It all makes a surprising difference from those rock gardens which are looked upon merely as places to grow an assortment of alpines. If one considers the making of a rock garden a form of art, the art *must* extend to the planting. To have a few square yards devoted to a proper scree in an isolated position for the benefit of 'tricky' alpine plants would militate against our idea of a natural rock garden. I have intimated that every portion of the rock garden should be covered with ground-cover in the form of colonising plants or dense growth of a dwarf kind, or with broken stone. Thus the scree can blend into the sward of the alpine lawn where the soil may be deeper (in imagination).

## The Alpine Lawn

I have explained at the beginning of chapter 6 the difference between a mountain and an Alp. Screes roll down the sides of mountains until they reach more level land where the Alp begins. It is these lovely rich flowery slopes that gardeners have been trying to imitate, without much success. G. Flemwell, in his exquisite book, *The Flower-Fields of Alpine Switzerland*, published in 1911, was, I think, the first author to draw our attention to the beauty of the flowery Swiss meadows, even going so far as to suggest they be copied in England. 'Moreover', he wrote, 'an Alpine rock garden shorn of its meadow-setting is less than a picture devoid of its frame'. Once again this stresses the importance of the right surround for a rock garden. I think it was Clarence Elliott who made the first real attempt, at the Six Hills Nursery. William Robinson was another guide and prophet along these lines; he was ever for the natural effect.

On the other hand, it is of course quite a simple matter to sow the ground with fine-quality dwarf grass seed, and interplant with bulbs and a few tussock-forming plants such as geraniums, aquilegias and *Gentiana lutea*. It will need mowing in July and again in September but is only suitable as an adjunct to a large rock garden.

I am never sure whether to be a whole-hearted advocate for this scheme, or whether it is a form of wishful thinking. There is no doubt about its beauty if it is successfully achieved. Imagine an undulating expanse of creeping plants broken here and there by tufts of grassy foliage and dwarf bushes and an odd piece of rock or two (mainly to provide stepping stones); thus some patches are cooler than others, providing for the need of different species. To prepare for this galaxy of beauty the soil must be specially dug, all weeds eliminated, and well-laced (I am always amused at this phrase – it sounds like Mrs Beeton!) with grit and leafmould or peat to give it an absorbent, spongy texture, valuable for retaining necessary moisture and getting rid of any surplus.

Over the whole area you plant low creeping plants: thymes of all colours, acaenas, cotulas, alpine phloxes of the more vigorous kinds, mat-forming pinks and achilleas, antennarias, all running together to form a kind of turf or mat. In this anti-splash mixture, in select places and groups, you plant small scillas and crocuses, miniature daffodils and again crocuses for autumn. For relief in height are *Fritillaria pyrenaica* and *F. meleagris* (our own native Snake's Head Fritillary if the soil be inclined to heaviness) can be joined by *Allium cernuum*, *A. senescens*, *A. glaucum*, *A. narcissiflorum* and *A. ostrowskianum* – but above all avoid that beguiling siren the white *A. triquetrum*, which would soon be everywhere, so prolific of seed and increase it is. In warm sheltered gardens I should expect the blue flowered grass-like plant

159 (*Top left*) The sort of picture in nature that we should all like to own. *Scilla verna* in powder blue on the north coast of Anglesey, North Wales, at Cemmaes Bay. June.

157 (*Lower left*) Ground-covering tussocks of *Iris innominata* hybrids. They make ideal 'lawn' plants.

158 (*Above right*) The coarser rock plants used as ground-cover in sunny well drained soil, including *Thymus serpyllum*, *T. micans*, *Festuca eskia*, *Achillea argentea*, helianthemums, *Artemisia*.

156 (*Below right*) The flower fields of Somerset bogland, near Shapwick, Sedgemoor. It was a surprise finding cowslips and Bee Orchids growing in the acid sedge-peat. Also present are *Dactylorchis maculata*, *D. latifolia*, *Habenaria viridis* and *H. conopsea*, *Listera ovata*, *Briza media*, *Linum catharticum*, *Crepis biennis*, *Cirsium brittanicum*, *Ajuga reptans* and many others. Together they made a 'lawn' of great beauty which could be mown in August.

*Aphyllanthes monspeliensis* to thrive, and of course several sisyrinchiums, such as *Sisyrinchium bermudianum*, *S. angustifolium*, both blue, and *S. douglasii*, *S. californicum* and *S. filifolium* in yellows and whites, will all add to the grassy effect; the perennial Quaking Grass *Briza media* could be allowed to seed here and there, likewise little *Erinus alpinus*, *Papaver alpinum* and *Campanula barbata* would soon make themselves at home. It would be a good opportunity to grow snowdrops in the parts perhaps partially shaded by rock or shrub, with *Crocus tomasinianus* accompanied by the quaint little yellow heads of *Hacquetia epipactis*. This is a slow, imperturbable, clump-forming plant whereas the crocus, which seeds itself everywhere, has been called the prettiest weed in the garden. Other good seeders are the blue Flax, *Linum perenne*, and *Dianthus deltoides*, the Maiden Pink, which is available in many tints from white and pink to strong crimson.

It would be the right place to grow clumps of the very dark green grassy *Liriope muscari*, not forgetting its spikes of violet flowers in autumn. And as a good companion we could choose the variegated Moor Grass, *Molinia caerulea* 'Variegata', which has dainty sprays of white stalks in autumn, hung with purple stamens. Among these taller plants – for the larger areas – forms of the orchids *Dactylorhiza elata* and *foliosa* would be appropriate, their rich purple spikes so freely produced in not-too-dry positions. St Bruno's and St Bernard's lilies, *Paradisea liliastrum* and *Anthericum liliago*, so much part of the alpine meadows, and the relatives *A.l. major* and tiny-flowered *A. ramosum*, are all lovely in June, while earlier the little mat-forming violet-purple *Iris ruthenica* is just the right sort of dwarf plant for our carpet. To the carpeting plants we must return, having indulged ourselves in the above taller plants for the larger garden.

The turf-forming plants such as most eriogonums, *Waldsteinia geoides* and *Arnica montana*, *Potentilla alba* and *P. aurea* can be given the September-flowering pink, creeping, *Sedum anacampseros*. The very early flowering *Corydalis cava* and *C. solida* will flower and die down and soon be covered over by the growth of thymes. In cooler corners *Saxifraga granulata* 'Plena' – the 'Pretty Maids' of the nursery rhyme – will do the same. Creeping Bugles, *Ajuga reptans* forms, are rather invasive, but their blue spikes in spring are echoed by *A. genevensis* 'Brockbankii' which is much more compact. For cool spots are those two small irises, *Iris cristata* and *I. lacustris*, both in lavender-blue, and the dainty *I. gracilipes* in violet or white. As the first two are North American it might be good to establish with them the strange *Gentiana andrewsii* from the same country whose rich blue trumpet flowers never open, thereby proving a puzzle to bees, who have however learnt a trick or two in regard to tubular flowers. Then I think you should introduce a few clumpy plants for further relief: *Adenophora bulleyana*, *Campanula sarmatica*, *Codonopsis meleagris*, *Delphinium tatsienense*, *Phyteuma scheuchzeri* and various thrifts or *Armeria*. A few small shrubs help to give the views some shape and we might include, if there is plenty of space, that most compact of the forms of *Rosa pimpinellifolia* (*R. spinosissima*) 'William III' in plum colour and also *Rosa pendulina pyrenaica*.

Is it not a lovely idea? It is possible, but will require as much or more attention as any other part of the garden. If dead heads are removed promptly and the bare patches that occur are speedily replanted or top dressed, your visitors may go away entranced, and imagine you give it no care at all.

# 9
# *The peat garden*

What is it then, that makes some gardeners want to construct a peat garden, however small? Why, too, if they want to grow small plants, are they not satisfied with the traditional rock garden (if there is such a thing), and why, once they have built it, does it become a thing on which they focus a great deal of interest?

Alfred Evans, *The Peat Garden and its Plants*, 1974

The first American plants to reach Europe and England in particular came obviously from the eastern coastal areas which were named Virginia after Queen Elizabeth, Carolina after Charles I and II, and Pennsylvania, granted to William Penn, the famous Quaker, by Charles II, all before 1682. They all run from the coast westwards into and over the Appalachian Mountains – the Alleghenies and the Blue Ridge, with, farther north, the Catskill and Adirondack Mountains. Apart from a large area of Pennsylvania, the land and mountains are lime-free. Many of our most treasured shrubs come from these regions, such as *Kalmia latifolia*, *Rhododendron carolinianum* and other species including azaleas, *Comptonia asplenifolia*, *Hamamelis virginiana*, *Magnolia virginiana*, *Vaccinium pensylvanicum* (now known as *V. angustifolium* var. *laevifolium*), *Halesia carolina*, *Leucothoë fontanesiana* and *Gaultheria procumbens*. At the time of the earliest introductions it was found that their preference was for lime-free soil. To them in due course were added calcifuge perennials, clintonias, *Gentiana andrewsii*, *Smilacina racemosa*, *Galax*, certain lilies, *Asarum virginiana*, *Collinsonia*, some trilliums, *Iris verna*, *Houstonia caerulea*, *Epigaea repens*, *Shortia galacifolia* and *Chimaphila maculata*. The gentian is a comparatively easily grown plant and is quite showy, though its flowers seldom open fully. Apart from this long recital of calcifuge plants, it might be added that it would be unusual to visit a British garden today without finding an American species in it; many of the plants from the eastern seaboard and the north-western take kindly to our gardens.

There had been a trickle of plants arriving from the early colonies from Queen Elizabeth's time, but in 1675 Henry Compton (*Comptonia*) became Bishop of London; it was he who first made any concerted attempt at introducing plants from the other side of the Atlantic. He was followed in the early eighteenth century by the Duchess of Beaufort, who attempted to grow new shrubs and trees at Badminton, Gloucestershire. But during the 1720s and onwards a merchant of London, Peter Collinson (*Collinsonia*), gardened at both Peckham and Mill Hill and endeavoured to import plants and seeds. Things were not easy until he got in touch with a farmer of Philadelphia, John Bartram, who was deeply interested in the native flora, being a keen amateur botanist. Before many years had passed Bartram was sending numerous consignments of plants and seeds to Collinson, who not only grew many species but also acted as intermediary, sending collections to great landowners, the Dukes of Bedford, Richmond and Norfolk, the Earl of Bute, who was concerned with the future Kew Gardens, and the Chelsea Physic Garden.

The species received were by no means all calcifuge, witness *Acer pensylvanicum* and *Magnolia acuminata*, but an impact had been made on British gardens and we find that Humphry Repton, who started on his career as a landscape designer on 'Capability' Brown's death in 1786, felt that they warranted special attention and respect. He recommended beds of bog earth for American plants. Before then few plants from Europe and the Middle East had proved intractable in our soils but here, now, was a whole new collection of plants needing special treatment. It was pretty obvious that the area given to these plants should be called an American Garden. This name was accepted everywhere, particularly with the nurserymen who congregated around Fulham and Chelsea. As the land around London grew in value the centre for nurseries moved out to the Woking district of Surrey, where the soil was easily worked and lime-free and peat off the commons was easily obtained. Certain nurserymen continued to list the plants in a special section of their catalogues as American plants until after the Second World War, despite the fact that by then they had been joined by other calcifuge plants from other parts of the world.

'Bog earth' could be obtained from many upland areas of Scotland, Wales and Ireland; also Sedgemoor in Somerset, and from the Fens of north Cambridgeshire. The digging of peat for fuel for countless years and over wide areas had caused the formation of the Broads in Norfolk; solid blocks were needed for this. Above layers where such could be cut there was always a top layer of loose peat of more recent growth. Peat in Britain is formed from roots and debris of sedge or from sphagnum moss; both grow in or near acid water and have been built up to great thickness over the centuries, the acid water preventing decomposition. In fact in the photograph (Fig. 160) the peat cutter dug up some of the debris from *below* the solidified peat, and leaves of many plants and seeds of birches could be distinguished easily. And according to the reckoning the area had been under water a thousand years ago, in King Alfred's time, and the peat had never been dug from that field before. It seems unbelievable, but I think it is true. The Fen peat is much more recent and has not solidified but was used by nurserymen in the 1930s in Cambridgeshire and neighbouring counties, being much cheaper than fuel peat from far away. In the Woking area loose blocks of peat were dug from woods in which bracken grew freely, but the most nutritious for young rhododendrons was the top of heather-clad commons. The top three inches or so were sliced off, reversed and stacked and used a year or two later. This is all by the way, I know, but we gardeners must not take it for granted that all peat is moss-peat from Ireland, nor that there is an inexhaustible supply, when all needs are taken into consideration. One often sees it scattered prodigally around freshly planted shrubs; this is to no purpose because it has so little nutrition in it; its main virtue is its moisture-holding capacity and it should be around the roots.

160 (*Above*) Sedge-peat cutting by hand on Shapwick, Somerset, in 1938. The top 18 ins. is loose and would have been sold for garden use. The four feet of close black material was cut into blocks, stacked to become dry and sold for fuel. Below the water table were many feet of undecomposed material composed of tree leaves, twigs, catkins etc. This area had not been cut before and was under water in King Alfred's time.

161 Method of building peat walls in readiness for planting, at Wisley. *Courtesy: Royal Horticultural Society*

For the last fifty years or more what was known originally as the American garden has gradually become known as the peat garden. This arose, according to Lady O'Neill, writing in *Country Life* in August 1979, through an American, Wilhelm Miller, being surprised by the term American garden, which as years went by contained more and more plants from other countries than America. My friends at the Edinburgh Botanic Garden tell me that the first time in horticulture that fuel peat was used to build walls on sloping ground for the cultivation of plants was at Logan, on the Mull of Galloway in the extreme south western tip of Scotland – only some 35 miles as the crow flies from Mount Stewart in Northern Ireland. Here the brothers McDouall created a garden in the early part of this century; it is still famous and is now under the aegis of the Royal Botanic Garden at Edinburgh. In 1938, after a visit to Logan, senior staff at the Botanic Garden decided to treat an area west of the great rock garden as a peat garden. The first peat walls were built by W. G. MacKenzie, commemorated in *Clematis orientalis* 'Bill MacKenzie' and an old friend of mine. He tells me that they ascended to a height of some three feet but during renovations since they were made lower. There are not many areas in these islands where more choice alpine and woodland plants are grown than on this north-facing slope at Edinburgh. The air is cool which helps the 'coolth' loving plants considerably.

Excellent use of peat walls is made at the Northern Horticultural Society's garden at Harrogate, Yorkshire, in the Ness Botanic Garden on the Wirral, Cheshire; also in the Royal Botanic Gardens, Kew, and the Royal Horticultural Society's garden at Wisley and in the Savill Garden, all three in Surrey. In every case it is at once obvious that the plants chosen are growing well; in fact many of them, such as primulas of the Petiolarid section, could scarcely be made to thrive in Surrey without the peat walls.

In making a peat garden the same preparation is necessary as for rock gardens: attention to drainage, thorough and complete eradication of all perennial weeds and avoidance, if alpines are to be grown, of overhead tree-shade and the dryness that their roots would cause. There are, however, numerous lovely woodland plants and ferns which will be successful in areas of light woodland. Likewise the laying of the peat blocks follows the same rules as for the building of retaining walls, the batter and the overlapping of joints, but no soil is needed between the blocks. Many people put up with fuel-peat which is usually in thin brick-shaped pieces. The ideal is much larger cubic pieces – if arrangements can be made to have them cut to this shape. It is necessary to build with damp or even wet blocks; fuel peat is usually delivered dry – fortunately for the owner's pocket – and it needs to be thoroughly soaked before use. It is well nigh impossible to wet it after building, nor can planting be done until it is moist. Further, it is necessary in a garden of any size to have overhead irrigation, preferably in the form of mist, to ensure that the walls do not become dry. Because there will be no digging and hoeing, it is important to arrange stepping stones at convenient places. These should be large and firm, to cope with the peaty, spongy ground. If the peat blocks are to be built up to more than two feet it is wise to place here and there, along the bottom course, some substantial blocks of sandstone to give the walls stability.

There is no doubt that many of the choicest primulas and other rosette-type plants thrive in these cool north-facing walls, for a north-facing position is essential. The surrounding soil should be liberally mixed with peat, too, so that the whole area becomes a habitat for all those classes of plants – mostly from the mist-laden mountain ranges of the world – to 'feel at home'. I refer to such genera as *Trillium*, *Meconopsis* and *Gentiana*, to say nothing of dwarf rhododendrons and their relatives in Ericaceae – *Cassiope*, *Phyllodoce*, *Gaultheria*, and *Epigaea* – but heaths and heathers themselves prefer more open conditions. Plants such as these will all be compact and will be a joy at all times. But beware of species with fast-running rootstocks: *Convallaria*, *Houttuynia*, *Smilacina bifolia*, *Uvularia sessilifolia*, *Chamaepericlymenum* (*Cornus*) *canadensis*, *Gaultheria procumbens*, *Maianthemum bifolium* and certain small ferns of invasive habit; species of *Gymnocarpium*, *Hypolepis*, *Dennstaedtia* and *Thelypteris palustris*. It is virtually impossible to extract their underground roots from peat blocks or, indeed, from other plants. An eagle eye must be constantly on the watch.

Much the same must be said for weeds, whether they be our native weeds or self-sown rhododendrons and other trees, shrubs and plants, all of which will find the peat an excellent germinating ground. Unless they can be extracted while quite small – to avoid breaking or loosening the peat – it is best to destroy them with a touch of systemic weedkiller.

Peat gardens are not difficult to maintain if the points I have raised are followed. In addition, it is important not to allow the autumn's wet leaves to lie in corners and in the middle of rosette-type plants. It is helpful to the plants to firm them in spring; some of them will be partially out of the ground after severe frost. Likewise a topdressing of peat is beneficial at the same time.

It should be borne in mind that leafmould from many native and other trees contains a percentage of lime, and is best used elsewhere than on peat beds. There is, however, more nutrition in leafmould than in peat; peat is very acid and often needs a dressing of slow-acting general fertiliser containing superphosphate of lime. I should recall here a strange fact: I had under my care at Sunningdale Nursery many rhododendrons. On one patch of soil, despite all care, they were sickly and did not grow. We gave them a dressing of nitro chalk, whereupon they grew strongly and even 'Britannia', which normally has leaves of a yellowish green, became rich green. It goes to prove that some soils and peats, when their pH is lower than, say 5.0, benefit from raising it to 6.5 or thereabouts.

Some garden owners having to live in limy districts feel terribly frustrated through not being able to grow calcifuge plants. It is no use digging out a large bed and filling it with a neutral or acid mixture of soil and peat, because moisture will rise, bringing the native lime with it, sooner or later. The best method is to build beds a foot or two above ground level. Even on his chalk, Sir Frederic Stern at Highdown, Sussex, made large square raised beds with timber (old railway sleepers are excellent if available) and after some forty years the rhododendrons are growing reasonably well even in that hot garden. The beds of rotted sawdust at Hidcote are still effective after a longer span.

I shall extol the virtues and beauty of the Himalayan gentians in chapter 10. Many of the primulas from the Himalaya may also be expected to thrive – the violet spikes, red-topped, of *Primula vialii*, the white powdered delicacy of *P. chionantha* and its close relative in lilac, *P. sinopurpurea*, equally powdered; dainty

162 *Trillium sessile* in a carpet of *Anemone nemorosa* in a peat bed.

163 *Meconopsis quintuplinervia* in Andrew Harley's garden, Perth, 1946.

164 The soft lilac flowers of *Roscoea purpurea* var. *pallida* at Wisley.

165 *Gentiana pumila* is a close relative of *G. verna*, with the same lovely blue colouring. This clump grew for many years in the author's care in a peat bed in full sun, but shaded in summer.

166 *Cyananthus lobatus* 'Albus', a white form of a normally blue genus useful for flowering in late summer and autumn.

167 (*Left*) *Gentiana sino-ornato* in September splendour.

168 (*Right*) *Gentiana* 'Macaulayi', a hybrid between *G. sino-ornato* and *G. farreri*; exceptionally clear blue large flowers.

169 (*Left*) *Cyananthus delavayi*. A choice autumn-flowerer in violet blue.

170 (*Right*) *Linnaea borealis*, the Twin-flower, a frail carpeter for peat banks.

171 *Epigaea repens*. Life size reproduction of the pearly white flowers which are deliciously fragrant.

172 The tiny shrub, *Arterica nana*, in white flower in early spring. (*Pieris nana*).

173 *Rhododendron hanceanum* 'Nanum'. A six-year-old plant 6 ins. high and wide. Pale yellow.

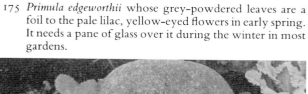

175 *Primula edgeworthii* whose grey-powdered leaves are a foil to the pale lilac, yellow-eyed flowers in early spring. It needs a pane of glass over it during the winter in most gardens.

174 *Pulsatilla alpina* var *sulphurea* (*Anemone sulphurea*) in a bed of peat, 18 ins. high.

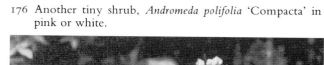

176 Another tiny shrub, *Andromeda polifolia* 'Compacta' in pink or white.

*P. reidii* and its variety *williamsii* in creamy lilac; all of the tricky species of the Petiolaris section, *Primula edgeworthii*, *P. scapigera*, *P. boothii* and its white form and all the rest; the best thing to do is to get a good book or catalogues to study this vast genus. Many are difficult and short-lived, but worth a lot of trouble; when thriving they will even seed themselves. We need no seeds, however, for the lovely mauve-pink *P. kisoana* and its white variety which have stoloniferous roots and soon form a wide colony. They would be ideal for growing under rhododendrons in cool conditions and should not perhaps be trusted in the peat garden.

Dainty white *Pteridophyllum racemosum* is a rarity from Japan; the pinnate leaves and tiny white flowers are charming and will defy all but an expert botanist to place in the Family of Papaveraceae.

The peat beds, if large enough, could be the best place for species of *Nomocharis*, the biennial smaller species of *Meconopsis* and of course trilliums. These North American plants exert a great fascination on gardeners. We can go to the Savill Garden in Windsor Great Park to see *Trillium grandiflorum* luxuriating in quantity – great pure white three-segmented blooms over three leaves (hence their generic name), the rare double white and the still rarer single pink; sumptuous *T. chloropetalum* and *T. sessile* in a variety of shades (see pencil drawing in my *Gardens of the National Trust*), the pure white form of *T. erectum*, and the exquisite pink *T. catesbaei* (*T. nervosum*). These are all over one foot in height; smaller is the pale yellow *T. luteum*, and still smaller are *T. nivale* and *T. rivale*, the former white and the latter with a rosy mark in the centre; a richly coloured form has been named 'Purple Heart'. Many of these have prettily mottled leaves to add to their undoubted aristocratic beauty.

This is the place, too, to try any species of *Omphalogramma*. *O. vinciflorum* is the species most likely to be available and I referred to this in chapter 6. *Cyananthus* species, *Clintonia*, *Chimaphila*; *Shortia galacifolia* and *S. uniflora* and all their forms will give undoubted joy in foliage and flower; the Shooting Stars, *Dodecatheon* of all kinds, the blue *Corydalis cashmiriana*; the dainty yellow poppy *Hylomecon japonicum*; ourisias; *Tanakaea radicans* and the little lily-relative *Luzuriaga radicans*; these and many more will make you wish your peat garden had more beds and ledges in it. Some tiny shrubs, too, such as all species and hybrids of *Cassiope*; *Gaultheria trichophylla* with its blue berries; *Arcterica nana* and the very smallest of rhododendrons – *R. radicans*, for instance, only an inch or two high, and the late-flowering *R. nakaharai*.

*Phyllodoce nipponica*, *P. aleutica* and other species are also for this select company, all minute evergreens with tiny bell-flowers in white, pink and creamy tints. Various cassiopes delight in spring with their small white bells; two reliable plants are *Cassiope* 'Edinburgh' and 'Muirhead', both hybrids of vigour. To them I would add *Pernettya tasmanica*, whose large red berries in autumn astonish, lying on the mat of tiny leaves.

Threading their way through these little bushes would be any and all of the species of *Pyrola*, in white or pink. And for great spring delight there are the North American species of Dog Tooth Violets – *Erythronium*, whose marbled leaves have given rise to the name of Trout Lilies. Of all spring joys these to my eyes have the greatest charm; they all follow the same pattern – a pair or so of broad leaves and

*Sempervivum arachnoideum*, the Cobweb Houseleek, 1699. Europe, from the Pyrenees to the Carpathians. For hot sunny crevices, scree, pots. From *Alpine Flowers* by Paul A. Robert, 1938. Slightly enlarged

*Courtesy: The Royal Horticultural Society.*

*Erythronium giganteum, E. grandiflorum* 'Robustum', *E. citrinum, E. hendersonii, E. revolutum, E. califoricum* 'White Beauty' and *E. revolutum* 'Johnsonii'. For leafy, moist soil in cool conditions. From a hand-coloured monochrome photograph in a printed catalogue of Carl Purdy, Ukiah, California, 1931–2.

*Courtesy: The Royal Horticultural Society.*

*Cyclamen libanoticum*. A slightly tender species discovered in the Lebanon in 1895. From a watercolour by H. G. Moon, published in *The Flora and Sylva*, 1903.

*Courtesy: The Royal Horticultural Society.*

a swan-necked stem bearing one or more nodding lily-flowers, in yellow, cream, pink or violet. The bulbs should never be allowed to become dry and should be planted in early autumn. In many gardens *E. revolutum* seeds itself with abandon, but it dies down by July and is so beautiful that we can forgive its conquering spirit. It would be best not to plant it on a peat bed but to refer it to the shrub or woodland garden – or anywhere where it is moist and cool. Another that colonises freely is *E. californicum*. In *My Wilderness* William O. Douglas refers to this species: 'This delicate white flower with an orange centre thrives at the very edge of melting snowbanks. It makes one who sees it more reverent and humble. For it creates exquisite beauty out of extreme adversity. The finest displays are probably on the lower slopes of Mount Rainier.' One very small surface-runner may be allowed to colonise the blocks of peat (it is easy to remove): it is *Linnaea borealis*, the Twin Flower, whose tiny bells are held above tiny-leafed stems in May and June.

With the present craze so rife for hostas, it is not surprising to find some quite small hybrids cropping up, such as 'Thumbnail'. There are several new, spreading ones with yellowish leaves, too. But I should go at once to the refinement of *Hosta minor*, whose dusky violet flowers do not appear until late summer. Of all the comparatively new plants that have come my way, *Silene keiskei akaisialpinum* inspired me specially to make a painting of it. Its cool colour is so much more acceptable than the usual darker pink form for the hot days of August.

Both *Helonias bullata* and *Heloniopsis* species – pink-flowered Liliaceous plants – delight the eye in early spring, and little white *Anemone flaccida* is an unusual charmer for the same period. For later in the year I would give a similar spot to the beautifully veined lilac flowers of *Oxalis laciniata* and its hybrid 'Ione Hecker', though sometimes it is recommended for sunny, stony positions. The yellow spikes of *Bulbinella hookeri* will be produced freely, and it will seed itself even to be a nuisance unless the seedheads are removed.

Epimediums are easily satisfied in any soil in partly or fully shaded positions, but I should reserve for the select positions in the peat garden the smallest, hybrids of *Epimedium diphyllum* and *E. grandiflorum*, known as *E.* × *youngianum* 'Niveum' and 'Roseum'. Their elfin charm is only appreciated when distant from their more vigrous relatives.

Lastly the peat garden is the place for dwarf ferns, though they will grow perfectly well in cool places on the rock garden. I have already warned against entertaining the species with running rootstocks, but little gems such as our native *Asplenium trichomanes* and *Adiantum pedatum* in its smaller forms are eminently permissible. *Adiantum venustum* would speedily become a nuisance.

# 10

# *The rock garden in autumn*

Have you ever known the mists and mystery that soften the great and gorgeous carnival with which Nature celebrates the closing round of her live seasons? . . . . Have you ever stayed for autumn in the Alps? Have you seen the Bilberry glowing among the stolid Rhododendron; the Eglantine and Berberis bowing beneath the weight of their fiery fruit? . . . . If you have, then you will, I know, bear witness with me to the fullness of this season's allure.
　　　　　　G. Flemwell, *The Flower-Fields of Alpine Switzerland*, 1911

The rock garden is bright with expectation when winter recedes. April and May are thrilling months, but June eclipses them with the wealth of good hardy alpines. After the middle of July flowers become scarce and by August we begin to ask ourselves what we can do about it. I am not one to sit down and say all is over. There are many autumn flowering alpines, besides which September and October are the months when many of the grey-leafed plants, both glaucous and silvery, are at their best. As a contrast there is the dark green of dwarf evergreens, and certain plants begin to take on autumn tints. There is a wealth of dwarf conifers to choose from and also the many heathers. In fact when well cultivated, many of these plants continue in beauty through the winter, though they may become dull and tawdry in and after periods of sharp frost and icy winds.

Let us first look at a few late-flowering plants. Some of these have been mentioned in chapter 6. Few would quarrel with the statement that certain species of *Erodium* have the longest flowering period of all late-flowering rock plants, starting as they do by mid June and carrying on until autumn. Their woody stems bear abundant feathery foliage, green or silvery, and the flowers are white or pink – with or without more or less black central blotches – or pale yellow. The last denotes *E. chrysanthum*; for the others a choice can be made from such species as *E. absinthoides, E. petraeum, E. brownbowii, E. kolbianum, E. daucoides, E. macradenum, E. trichomanifolium* and *E. guttatum*. They do not disappoint in full sun.

Apart from the yellow *Sedum kamtschaticum* and its variegated form, there is *S. middendorfianum*, whose yellow flowers contrast with reddish leaves. Several pink-flowered species are useful: *S. ewersii, S. cauticola, S. sieboldii* (a little tender,

SHORTIA GALACIFOLIA

*Shortia galacifolia* from North Carolina, 1881. From a watercolour by H. G. Moon, published in *The Flora and Sylva*, 1905.
*Courtesy: The Royal Horticultural Society.*

*Trillium catesbaei.* South-east United States, c.1823. For cool woodland positions. Watercolour by the author, 1986. Slightly reduced.

particularly its beautiful variegated form), all of which are clump-forming as opposed to the trailing *S. anacampseros*. There are a few good hybrids, too, such as 'Ruby Glow' and the dusky 'Sunset Cloud' and 'Vera Jameson'. In October we may generally expect the white daisies of *Chrysanthemum nipponicum*. For trailing over rocks and walls is the charming pink *Polygonum vaccinifolium*; much larger and only for the outskirts of the rock garden we may include *P. affine* in its best form 'Superbum' ('Dimity'). All the forms of this species excel also in the dark russet of their winter foliage. One of Tony Schilling's introductions from Nepal, *Aster indamellus*, is a small grey-lilac daisy about nine inches high, useful for late summer and early autumn.

Beautiful small bulbs for the early autumn months are many. *Galanthus nivalis reginae olgae* is a normal snowdrop for a sunny, well-drained position, regularly flowering after the tiny snowflake *Leucojum autumnale* is over. *Crocus speciosus* and its forms are exquisitely veined, their violet tints contrasting with their bright orange stigmata. The most richly coloured is 'Oxonian'. *C. kotschyanus*, which used to be known as *C. zonatus*, is similar but usually paler. A most distinct and beautiful species for autumn is *C. banaticus* (*C. byzantinus, C. iridiflorus*) with a shape of flower unlike those of any other species: the inner three segments are shorter than the outer ones and remain erect, all of them usually of a rich purple. This will thrive and increase in shady positions. I grow a pretty little white form of *C. cancellatus* in a warm sunny position. Those who love the myriad blooms in early spring of *C. tomasinianus* should try its prolific counterpart *C. goulimyi* for October. *C. laevigatus* is usually in flower at Christmas; it has a long season from late autumn, its lilac-tinted flowers beautifully striped with dark violet on a creamy-grey exterior. For a warm spot I should choose *C. medius*, whose stigmata are scarlet, shouting at the flowers in tones of lilac; *C. nudiflorus* is equally richly contrasted and prolific. Another prolific species is *C. tournefortii*; it is fine in good weather but the flowers remain open (unlike those of most other species) in rain and thus are particularly prone to damage. I have left till last the Meadow Saffron, *C. sativus*, of which a form of rapid increase has been in cultivation in many countries for centuries, on account of its large orange style which contrasts satisfyingly with the usually dark violet flower. It is satisfying too in that it is grown for the collection of these styles or stigmata to provide yellow saffron. At one time it was freely grown around Saffron Walden, Hertfordshire.

The flowers of all species are easily damaged by sudden storms; they may of course be protected by panes of glass, but this is an unsightly remedy. It helps if they can be grown through some carpeting plant such as the smaller acaenas or thymes, or shingle, all of which will guard the frail flowers from splash. In fair quantity they do much to charm us when the days get short. I think *Sternbergia lutea*, in effect a yellow crocus, needs a sunny place in limy soil; its variety *angustifolia* seems to be the most reliable in flower. The contrast of the dark green shining leaves is most appealing.

Having given us bright yellow strawberry flowers over silvery foliage all the summer, *Potentilla eriocarpa* carries on into the autumn in a well-drained position in sun; the same may be said of the dark yellow *P. cuneata* (*P. ambigua*) and the hybrid 'Tonguei', whose flowers are of apricot-orange with a crimson flush in the centre.

Of all the autumn flowers I suppose the Himalayan gentians exert the greatest pull on alpine plant enthusiasts. To start with they give us true blue, in abundance, when growing well. They all demand a moist position in soil which contains plenty of humus and must be lime-free except for *Gentiana farreri*. But those who garden on limy soil need not despair; at Ingwersen's nursery – in spite of being on lime-free soil – a special demonstration is given every year that they will thrive in troughs and containers in full sun so long as they are watered regularly. This is surely the answer for limy gardens, for who could resist their vivid colours and free growth, so easily divided in spring? I used to grow *G. farreri* in an area of limestone scree, well mixed with peat, and it grew remarkably well, enough to serve as a model for a painting, as may be seen in this book. One of the ways of assessing the garden value of a group of plants is to take note of the number of hybrids and forms that have been named and remain in cultivation. The Himalayan gentians of the *ornata* group are noted for many. They all grow much better in the north of Britain than in the south-east; in fact we all wallow in the rich blue tones at the Royal Horticultural Shows in September and October when exhibits – of great beauty – come from Edrom Nurseries, Coldingham, Berwick. From the darkest blue *G. ornata* – which has never been widely grown – through rich and royal *G. veitchiorum*, the hybrids 'Inverleith', 'Devonhall', × *stevenagensis*, × *macaulayi*; × *hexafarreri* (*G. hexaphylla* × *G. farreri*) and 'Blue Bonnets' in light blue and 'Bernardii' in dark blue and many more, one's eyes eventually fasten on *G. sino-ornata*, still the most sumptuous and easily grown of the lot. Beside it, plant its white form and the picture is complete. No other race of alpines can hold a candle to the glories of these gentians in early autumn; all they ask is lime-free, humus-laden soil, preferably coupled with coolness in the air and at the root, and division every year or two in spring. Even without *G. sino-ornata*, they would be praised, but it needed this species, found by George Forrest and introduced in 1910, to catch the popular imagination with its splendour and ease of growth. Even by 1925 Farrer could write that it 'forms vast hassocks of erect azure trumpets in any low rich cool level of the garden'. It grows to perfection at Sheffield Park Garden in Sussex where the soil is cool and retentive of moisture.

During the splendour of autumn colours one gets satiated with red and yellow – not always ideal with blue flowers; I find the variegated form of *Cotoneaster horizontalis* turns to a pleasing pink and lasts a long time. This form is not so vigorous as the type species.

With the gentians, and also appreciating coolth and humus, is the autumn-flowering saxifrage, *Saxifraga fortunei*. Its white flowers, in airy sprays, unfortunately succumb to the first touch of frost but contrast well with the blue gentians. The foliage becomes richly tinted too, at its best in 'Wada' and 'Rubrifolia'. A miniature form for very small gardens is called *S.f. incisolobata*.

While all the gentians mentioned above are of true blue, they hover on the prussian blue side of the spectrum, whereas the hardy creeping plumbago, *Ceratostigma plumbaginoides*, has flowers of a hard cobalt blue. When it is grown in a sunny slope its foliage assumes purplish tones and even red in autumn, and the contrast is spectacular. I have mentioned the white gentian as a good contrast; to this I would add the white form of *Cyclamen hederifolium* (*C. neapolitanum*), which

*Gentiana farreri*, Kansu-Tibet, 1914.
Watercolour by the author in 1928
of the authentic species, growing
in peaty scree, but not lime-free.

*Primula reidii* var. *williamsii*, native of
Nepal, 1954. More vigorous and fragrant
than *P. reidii*. For cool, peaty position
and a pane of glass in winter.
Watercolour by the author, 1986.

*Silene keiskii* var. *akaisialpinum*.   Japan.
Suitable for cool positions on the rock
garden. Watercolour by the author, 1986.

*Pinguicula grandiflora*.   Western Europe
including S.W. Ireland, in wet sphagnum
moss. Watercolour by the author, 1986.

breeds true from seeds. And almost as soon as the flowers have faded in October, the beautifully marbled leaves appear.

The purist would hardly call the Californian Fuchsias, species of *Zauschneria*, true rock plants, but if I had the space I would at least include one or two of the best for their brilliant colour. They have somewhat tubular scarlet flowers held over leafy plants up to a foot in height. My own particular favourite is *Z. cana* (*Z. microphylla*), whose narrow leaves are a silvery grey; a wonderful contrast. In more luxuriant green is *Z. californica* and a particularly good, large-flowered form bears the name of 'Dublin' or erroneously 'Glasnevin'. There is a good white, and a new clear pink from the United States called 'Solidarity Pink', which appears to be settling well over here. The running rootstocks of all thrive in a hot, retaining wall or on sunny uppermost ledges. Zauschnerias are now included in *Epilobium*.

A few more plants include some with autumn foliage tints; the tiny feathery *Aruncus aethusifolius*, for instance; the khaki-yellow grassy leaves of *Libertia peregrina*; the black-green of little *Geranium sessiliflorum* 'Nigrum', and the astonishing maroon-black of *Ophiopogon planiscapus nigrescens*. I used not to think much of this, but since it has spread into generous carpets in gardens there is no denying the value of its dark tint for sun or shade. It would be ideal against the silvery foliage of some achilleas or artemisias. It would act as a foil to the white berries of that little bush *Margyricarpus setosus* and the rich tones of red and purple which occur through much of the year on *Nandina domestica*, the dwarf forms of which are so appealing for sheltered positions. Good orange-red leaf colour is found in *Prunus pumila depressa*, a prostrate shrub. The large Bugle, *Ajuga* 'Jungle Beauty' was brought from the United States some twenty years ago by James Russell; I do not know its origin. When it grows well its leaves resemble small bergenia leaves and are evergreen as a contrast to most other ajugas. Beth Chatto received another Bugle with larger coppery purple leaves named 'Catlin's Giant', also from the United States. It bids fair to become popular.

At the approach of autumn several conifers turn to a soft plum colour; likewise that little evergreen shrub *Cyathodes colensoi* from New Zealand, which I find perfectly hardy. In cold weather, its tiny leaves turn to a soft lilac-grey. Splashes of reds and purples occur on the leaves of *Galax urceolata* (*G. aphylla*) and the small *Bergenia stracheyi* and its white-flowered form which I think we can allow on the larger rock garden.

One of my great autumn pleasures is to clear up the last of the fallen leaves to reveal the rich green of the London Pride section of *Saxifraga*, embracing all the forms and hybrids of *S. geum*, *S. hirsuta*, *S. spathulata* and their relatives, even tiny *S. cuneifolia*. In the moist days the foliage glistens in dark colour and the crisp outline of the leaves is a good contrast to other verdure or stone. The same may be said of the vigorous spreader *Waldsteinia ternata* and various asarums, particularly the plain dark shining green of *Asarum europaeum* and the beautifully marked leaves of *A. hartwegii* (which seems to be trying to shame cyclamen leaves), *A. speciosum* and *A. asaroides*. It is a good thing that these plants have such beautiful leaves; we should not bother if their flowers were their only attraction. Globularias, the little creeping fern *Blechnum penna-marina*, the broad blades of *Speirantha gardenii*, and the hummocks of hard moss-like leaves of *Azorella trifurcata* all come into their own at the

177 *Saxifraga fortunei* in October. In the author's garden.

178 *Erodium guttatum*, white flowers with maroon eyes; in flower from June to October, like others of its close relatives. In the author's garden.

179 *Polygonum vaccinifolium* prefers a cool root-run, and produces spikes of pink flowers from early August until autumn.

180 The seed heads of *Acantholimon venustum* are almost as beautiful as the rose-pink flowers, and of similar shape. In the author's garden.

181 *Geum montanum* seed heads in late summer.

182 Pink berries of *Myrtus nummularia* in autumn.

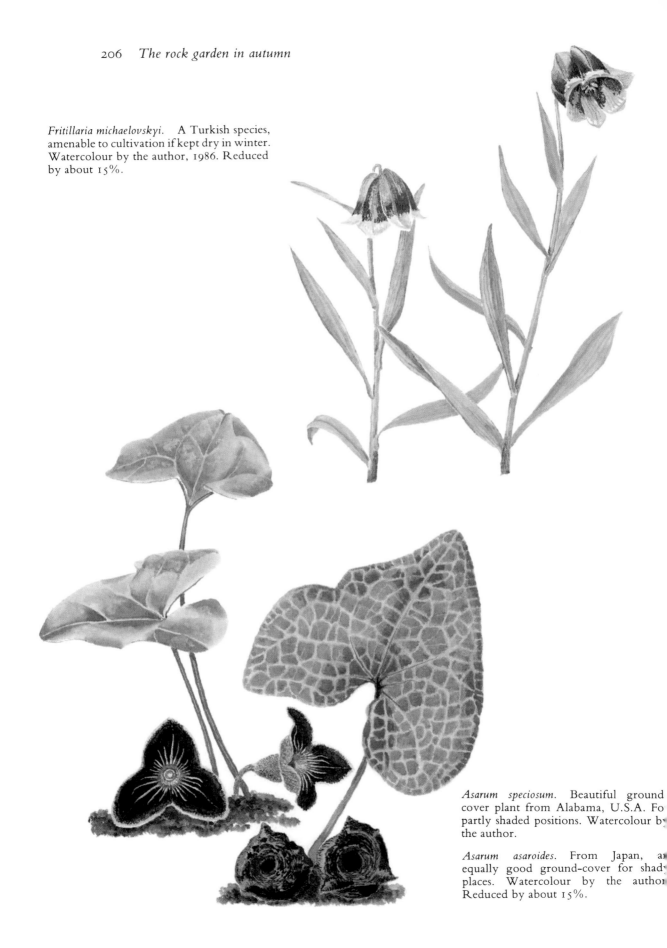

*Fritillaria michaelovskyi.*   A Turkish species, amenable to cultivation if kept dry in winter. Watercolour by the author, 1986. Reduced by about 15%.

*Asarum speciosum.* Beautiful ground cover plant from Alabama, U.S.A. Fo partly shaded positions. Watercolour b the author.

*Asarum asaroides.* From Japan, a equally good ground-cover for shad places. Watercolour by the author Reduced by about 15%.

*Phlox mesoleuca* 'Arroyo' (top left); *P.m.* 'Mary Maslin' (lower middle) and forms of *P. nana*.   All may be referable to *P. triovulata*. Natives of Texas and New Mexico; species known since 1888. Watercolour by the author, 1986. Slightly reduced.

approach of winter. *Daphne laureola phillipi* from the Pyrenees is a dense dwarf bush with dark glossy leaves, bearing green fragrant flowers in spring.

Berries should not be forgotten; I cannot think of any so bright and red as *Cotoneaster microphyllus cochleatus*. The very dark small leaves are about the same size as the berries and its growth creeps freely, repeating each hummock of soil or stone. Against its red and black-green leaves the strange, bright, khaki-brown of *Hebe ochracea* 'James Stirling' stands out; other highly desirable if more dwarf species in a variety of greyish and other greens are *H. buchananii* and *H. epacridea*. Somewhat in the same class is *Leiophyllum buxifolium*, but for lime-free soil; its flower-buds form, like those of skimmias, in autumn and the whole plant is attractive.

There remain the silvers and glaucous leafed plants which are never better than in autumn. The silvery-grey feathers of *Tanacetum densum amani* rival Mori's prostrate form of *Artemisia stelleriana* in their silver white and both rival the little erect bushes of *Euryops acraeus*. They are best in scree or on particularly well drained soil, but *Achillea ageratifolia* is not so particular. A real ramper is the dwarf variant of *Cerastium tomentosum*, known as *C. biebersteinii* or *C. columnae*, with small silver grey leaves. And for those who garden in cool but not cold climates there are the splendid New Zealand celmisias. The largest and most spectacular is *Celmisia spectabilis*, with broad sword-shaped silver-white leaves.

As for plants with glaucous leaves I need hardly do more than mention *Sedum*; among the species already mentioned are several good kinds to be joined with *S. spathulifolium* and its forms: 'Cape Blanco' (very grey) and 'Purpureum', a soft grey-purple. I think we might perhaps be allowed a small variegated plant which always attracts attention. *Arabis ferdinandi-coburgii* 'Variegata', which makes a small spreading mound of narrow green leaves edged with white; during the last two mild wet autumns the dark green of the type species has been spangled with pure white flowers during November.

The plants now have to endure the rigours of winter. As mentioned before, some of them with very woolly leaves thrive best if they are kept free from rain by means of a pane of glass. Otherwise one must remember two cultural details. One is that frost may loosen the soil and so loosen the roothold of shallow-rooting plants; they need firming at the advent of spring. The other is that summer watering and winter's rains tend to leech out the goodness from the soil. One should be ready with a little slow-acting general fertiliser, mixed with gritty soil (or chips or peat, according to the situation), to be spread around or tucked under plants which expose too much 'neck'. And I need hardly mention again the necessity of keeping the rock garden free of fallen leaves.

# 11
# Growing alpines
# without rock gardens

It is best in this life, I told myself, to love what you get and really
to see what you are looking at from your work bench.

Donald Culross Peattie, *Flowering Earth*, 1948

Having left aside all pretence – in this chapter – of making a natural rock garden, we can indulge ourselves in visualising the many ways in which we can grow and enjoy alpines in the garden generally. They can be made to fit in a number of schemes. There are many strong and hearty growers among alpine plants which can be grown in the open border, so long as the soil is well drained. We often see such plants as thrift, pinks, *Arabis*, *Aubrieta*, alpine phloxes, *Iberis sempervirens*, Sun Roses, *Saponaria ocymoides*, pulsatillas, potentillas, veronicas, from many different parts of the world, growing happily along the front of sunny borders, hanging over the brick or tile edging. There they give early floral colour and this is no mean advantage if the rest of the border is devoted to later-flowering herbaceous plants and shrubs. Mingled with tiny early-flowering bulbs they can add materially to the floral delights of the spring months. These remarks apply particularly to those borders which lie along a gravelled or paved path, or – if bordering a lawn – have a paved edge; there the plants can flow forward, adding grace and abandon to the planting. Many of these larger, stouter, easily grown rock plants are just those which are found in the checklist at the end of the book.

Let us start with the patio on to which we step directly from the house. This is conventionally the place for containers for plants. While I should not like to be without my heliotrope for fragrance, my pelargoniums and many other summer favourites, the patio has almost endless other possibilities. There are various pots, troughs and stone sinks to be considered, the interstices of paving, and retaining walls.

We might consider the paving first. Unless the patio is large, plants in the paving can be a nuisance, upsetting the balance of tables and chairs. But to rub one's shoes over a mat of thyme gives a delightful fragrance. In out of the way corners choicer plants can be grown, provided there is good drainage beneath. In cool shady corners, *Mentha requienii* will give a lovely whiff of peppermint as will the larger *M. pulegium* in sunny places.

With regard to stone troughs, these should be placed on brick piers, or mounted on a low wall or other support, to get them nearer the eye – and away from dogs and cats. Their use can be traced back in Joe Elliott's booklet on the subject, which he wrote for the Alpine Garden Society, to a Mrs Mary Saunders in Yorkshire. (As we go through the chapters of this book it will be seen what a great influence the county of Yorkshire has had on our pursuit.) Old stone pig troughs are now becoming scarce and costly, domestic stone sinks are almost non-existent. In the history of the cultivation of alpine plants they have had a wonderful day, since Clarence Elliott first exhibited them at Chelsea Show about 1925. Substitutes are, however, available; any kind of deep pot or container which is resistant to frost will do. Some people today use the glazed white kitchen sinks now available in some quantity owing to the change-over to steel sinks. But a glazed white object in the garden is not attractive. If the shiny surface is roughened by chipping away little pieces the outsides can be coated with a mixture of one part furnace ash or clean sand, one part cement, two parts dry peat. This is known as 'hypertufa' and after a year or two it assumes an earthy appearance. By making two wooden boxes to the required dimensions, one to fit into the other leaving a $2\frac{1}{2}$ inch space between, the same mixture can be filled into the space; when the mixture has set really firmly, the boxes can be removed and the result is a home-made stone-like trough. It is important to insert inch-thick pegs between the boxes to provide eventual drainage holes, or to carve them out with brace and bit after the hypertufa has set.

Whatever sort of container is selected, be sure that your first and second thoughts are once again concerned with drainage. There must be an adequate hole or holes in the bottom. Place crocks and dead leaves over the holes and fill with a mixture of potting soil lightened with grit. A few drooping dwarf plants such as *Thymus serpyllum* 'Minus', *Dianthus arvernensis*, *Helianthemum alpestre serpyllifolium*, *Gypsophila fratensis* and *Phlox douglasii* will help to grace its sides. A few small pieces of tufa or other rock to give it height and tight crevices for compact plants such as *Campanula waldsteiniana* and *C. tommasiniana*, the smaller silver saxifrages and compact sedums like *Sedum middendorfianum* and *S. ewersii*, will turn any container into a thing of delight. In some of my pots and containers I grow a collection of houseleeks, varieties of *Sempervivum*, of different sizes and colourings. They are a perennial attraction and do not object if they are not given water in periods of drought. It is also the best place to grow plants which inspire slugs with inordinate affection: the large-flowering dwarf *Campanula raineri*, puckish *C. zoysii* and the crimson-backed daisy, *Anacyclus depressus*, *Physoplexis comosa*, and others.

## *Retaining Walls*

As a finish to the edge of a patio there is the possibility of a low wall. This is an admirable support for containers of any sort, not only for close inspection but to get the tiny plants out of reach of feet and dogs. If the wall can be made the width of a brick's length – normally nine inches – there is a chance of making a narrow trough along its length. If the trough is made between bricks placed on edge, with drainage holes left here and there, many good little sedums, sempervivums and other sun-lovers will grow. It would be still better to make two walls, perhaps 1–2 feet apart, and fill in the space with prepared mixture. There we should have the luxury of looking at many plants near to the eye; clump-formers or spreaders hanging over the side, and something would be in flower from spring to autumn if a careful choice be made. Such a scheme would make containers unnecessary. Because frost will tend to make the soil swell and force the bricks apart, 'tie bricks' or metal ties must be built into the walls to prevent this expansion.

# *Raised Beds*

Raised beds need not necessarily be associated with the patio. They can be incorporated in the main garden design. The first raised bed I saw was in the garden of Mr F. Dickson Park in Hertfordshire in 1936 (see Fig. 192); excellent modern examples are to be seen at Kew. Valerie Finnis has a range of raised beds, supported by sleepers, holding her renowned collection of plants, near Kettering, Northamptonshire.

Their making is not difficult. It is best to use some walling stone, such as the limestone so common in the Cotswolds, or broken pieces of paving, or bricks. Retaining walls – with only a soil mixture between the courses – are best made with a slight batter of about three inches per foot, each block slightly behind the one below. Not only does this give added strength but it also ensures that rain or applied water finds its way into the bed; this is almost impossible unless the blocks slope downwards and inwards as well. The fact that the bed may be two feet above ground ensures good drainage, but if the soil below is clay some extra drainage should be arranged.

Having marked out the shape of the bed – which can be rectangular or curved, or a combination of both – and having the blocks to hand, have also a heap or bags of prepared potting soil with about one-third of pea-gravel or other washed shingle mixed thoroughly in it. About three-quarters of an inch of the mixture should be put between each course and be sure to have some suitable plants ready for insertion at the same time. After each second course or so, fill up with soil and make firm. It is an excellent way of growing plants; there is the choice of aspect, shade for ramondas, haberleas, ferns, etc. and the sunny side for *Saxifraga longifolia* and most other rock plants, dwarf pinks, campanulas, acantholimons, phloxes and many others. Some small plants with a running rootstock, such as *Campanula cochlearifolia*, thread their way prettily between the stones.

And then there is the entire top surface of the raised bed to be used, so that the advantage of the scheme in a small garden is manifest – the growing space has been more or less doubled. The top of the bed can have a few small rocks and tiny shrubs to give a variety in height, and it is indeed a tricky plant that will not thrive. On the shady side some extra peat can be worked into the soil because most shade-lovers appreciate humus.

In many gardens on sloping ground there will be no need to make raised beds; retaining walls will be needed to hold up banks. These are absolutely ideal for the provision of places for alpines, both in the walls and on top of them. The rules for construction remain the same throughout. The watchwords should be solidity, a gentle batter, prepared soil for use between courses of stone or brick to about one

183 Two stone troughs; the front one is built up with tufa limestone and contains *Phyteum comosum*, *Saxifraga grisebachii* 'Wisley Variety', *Equisetum scirpioides*, *Gentiana saxosa*; the second has *Wahlenbergia serpyllifolia* 'Major' and *Primula marginata*. In the author's garden.

184 (*Left*) A Welsh limestone trough, filled with alpine and other plants, *Calceolaria biflora*, primulas and saxifrages, with *Campanula portenschlagiana bavarica* growing amongst the supporting stones.

185 (*Right*) A novel way of using an integrated stone millwheel, supported by a pine stump. *Dianthus, Penstemon, Sedum spathulifolium* 'Cape Blanco'. The alpine roots penetrate the interstices of the stone millwheel.

186 A large stone sink set with *Saxifraga* 'Esther', *Gypsophila fratensis*, *Phlox douglasii*, lewisias, and *Crassula sarcocaulis*. Built by the author.

inch, good soil likewise for filling in the back to a depth of about one foot, and in a wall of more than one foot in height it is necessary to have plants in readiness for planting during the building. Later insertion will only be possible by the use of tiny seedlings or rooted cuttings or divisions. In really old, high walls, where it would be impossible or unwise to prise up the rocks or bricks to insert plants, seeds can often be blown into cracks with a puff of breath off a curved card.

Unless the garden is quite small, in which case one plant of each kind will probably be all that a keen collector of alpines will need, it is a good plan to adopt an informal method of planting. This is shown admirably in Gertrude Jekyll's *Wall and Water Gardens* of 1901; her diagram is reproduced here (Fig. 189). This repeats her usual predilection for drifts rather than spots of colour and is a good maxim to follow. As elsewhere when cultivating alpines by covering the level planting ground with washed shingle or other appropriate small grit, moisture is conserved and weed-seeding is reduced to a minimum.

Sometimes low walls are arranged around portions of the garden which are sunk either for effect or shelter. My own tiny sunken garden was made for two purposes: to have some shelter from wind and to provide walls facing two aspects for the growing of two classes of alpines. These two classes are those that would thrive best facing north or south. Instead of making a wall with a batter, I arranged rather square blocks of sarsen stone in two tiny terraces, setting the upper one ten inches back from the lower; thus I had two beds in which to plant alpines besides the interstices between the stones. The soil mixture for the north-facing little borders contained a fair proportion of peat, and to the south-facing I gave some extra grit. This sunken garden was made not only for the reasons given above, but because after some twenty-five years of being starved of alpines I wanted to grow ramondas and haberleas again. I acquired all species of the former and also pink and white forms. They settled in well but I had not realised that the little sunken area would act as a frost pocket; as a result buds form but seldom open. It has been a great disappointment in most years. On the south-facing side the borders would be thoroughly baked in the summer. On the north-facing ones the plants chosen appreciate a cool moist soil, so on both sides I sank three-inch land drains at the back at intervals of about three feet, vertically, covering them with pieces of flattish stone. It is easy to fill them with water during times of drought, and the water soaks into the subsoil where the roots can reach it, which is better than trying to water the ledges. There are two snags. During severe weather land drains crack unless well covered with rock, and the tops of the pipes should have had perforated zinc covers. The water could still be applied through this, otherwise the pipes form death-traps for the handsome violet-black garden beetles, which eat so many grubs and slugs.

## Underground Watering

While on this subject, I must add a word about underground watering. In hot dry regions, and on southern slopes, and when the subsoil is sand or gravel, it is invaluable. The scheme brings us back to the subject of the moraine, i.e. a scree with water flowing through the shingle from the snow melting on higher ground. There is no doubt that this underground form of watering is infinitely better than applying the water overhead; moreover it does not tend to wash the top shingle and soil away and is immediately where the roots want it.

There are two schemes. One is very easy; the ready-perforated plastic tubes stocked by most garden sundriesmen are buried in the soil face downwards a foot behind the wall, or a foot below the top surface of the bed or scree, with an attachment to a tap in needful times. Half-an-hour or so of running water will be all that is necessary to moisten thoroughly even a large and deep bed. The other scheme involves the use of three-inch diameter (or thereabouts) plastic pipes which can be perforated with hammer and nail at every six inches on the sides. They are laid a foot or so down in the soil; the far end is sealed off and the upper end is left curving up above the soil, to be filled with water in times of drought. It is necessary to fit a removable cap to the upper end in order to avoid letting *any* silt or debris go into the pipe when filling, which would block the holes.

In places of extreme heat some shading may be necessary in the form of removable lath frames or plastic netting.

## The Slab Garden

Joe Elliott tells me that it was Captain Simpson Hayward of Icomb, near Stow on the Wold, Gloucestershire, who first demonstrated this idea, and few visitors to Hidcote can realise that the fine Coffin Juniper (*Juniperus recurva coxii*) grew originally on a large slab of slate. Its roots have undoubtedly reached over the edge of the slate to the solid ground. The slab was built up with small rocks and gritty soil and originally grew some good alpines. My illustration of an articulated stone millwheel, supported by the sawn-off tree trunk, originally made up by my old friend R. B. Purves at the Mansion House Hotel, Evesham, is another example of a highly successful 'slab'. *Anacyclus depressus*, well out of reach of slugs, grew remarkably well there.

## Tufa

Let us now consider tufa. As explained in chapter 3, this is a very new rock and is formed by limy water from mineral springs dripping over debris of all kinds in caves. I did not include this stone in chapter 5 because it has no occurrence in this country as an outcropping rock; it has no stratification and can therefore be used without any rules, simply as an invaluable medium in which to indulge one's fancies in growing alpines. It is obviously limy but, strangely, even some calcifuge plants thrive in it. Its light weight makes it easy to handle and when brought from underground it is very soft, but hardens with age. When fresh, holes can be gouged out by means of a broad chisel held in the hand; later a hammer may be needed; or a brace and bit can be used. The holes should be made with a definite downward slant. The size varies according to the size of the plant to be inserted. If pot-grown stock is being used, holes of three-inch diameter and some six inches deep are

188 Raised stone beds in the garden of Francis H. Cabot, Cold Spring, New York, showing not only how a wide variety of alpine plants can be given shady or sunny positions in the walls but also how the planting space of the garden can be increased.
*Courtesy: F. H. Cabot: photo, Joel Spingarn*

187 (*Middle left*) *Anacyclus depressus* growing on the millwheel in Fig. 185.

189 (*Middle right*) Getrude Jekyll's diagram showing how planting should be arranged to achieve the best results. From *Wall and Water Gardens*, 1901.

190 (*Right*) The ideal planting of a retaining wall can only be achieved by insertion at the time of building. In Eleanor Spingarn's garden, West Redding, Connecticut, United States of America. Campanulas, *Geranium dalmaticum*, dianthus, primula.
*Courtesy: Joel Spingarn*

191  A retaining wall of tufa in the garden of Francis H. Cabot, Cold Spring, New York. Encrusted and Kabschia saxifrages find ideal homes.
*Courtesy: Joel Spingarn*

192  A raised bed, built of Cotswold walling stone in a Hertfordshire garden about 1936. All manner of plants find congenial homes not only in the walls but in the specially prepared soil with which the bed is filled.

193  A sloping shed-roof, covered with 2–3 ins of gravelly soil and a few rocks, and planted with a collection of sedums and sempervivums in the author's garden.

194  Random flints and old river-bed stones built successfully into a raised bed for alpines (with cement) by Alan Bloom at Bressingham, Norfolk.

needed. Smaller holes will suffice for seedlings and rooted cuttings, which are generally to be preferred. The tufa debris from the holes should be mixed with twice its bulk of potting soil for working in round the roots when planting. Pot-grown stock should have most of the soil shaken or washed from the roots. After planting, the whole block should be well watered. Brian Halliwell, Assistant Curator at Kew, has produced an admirable leaflet on the subject, and recommends that the block of tufa be laid on a tray of sand which can be kept permanently moist; the tufa will absorb the moisture. In my own garden I have set a good lump just into the soil; it graces – perhaps that is not quite the right word! – the small paved sunken garden together with the pots of sempervivums. I make a point of watering the tufa overhead and the surrounding soil of an evening in hot weather. There is one trouble about bedding the tufa in the soil – access by slugs and snails. But if it be surrounded by small stone chippings and given an occasional scattering of slug killer pellets, the danger is minimised. In due course the tufa will become green with moss in all depressions.

Anyone's appetite for choice small alpines can be assuaged by having a really large lump of tufa which would make a bold and interesting feature in the garden, perhaps six feet or more long and two to three feet wide. It is best to site such a lump when originally designing the garden; it cannot be put just anywhere. But it can conveniently be introduced into formal or informal areas in sun or shade so long as it is not overhung by trees.

There is no doubt that whether in a small or large garden, a lump of tufa can be a great joy when studded with dwarf rosette-plants or the airy sprays of silver saxifrages. I do not think that anyone has investigated how far the plants' roots penetrate, but I should be surprised if they do not use the entire block, given time.

## Alpine Houses

Many of us have been conversant with glasshouses for alpine plants for many years. Most specialist alpine plant nurseries have them either for propagation or display. The usual plan is to have a low-ridged house with sunken paths and some sort of staging on either side, raising the plants to a level where side ventilation can have best effect. Some houses used to have wooden slats for support on benches; others would have metal supports covered with slate or corrugated iron and then be covered with pea-shingle. The dry wood tends to encourage red spider. The shingle helps to keep the pots and pans cool and moist. Some shading is required in the summer months in England, the most usual being a spray of lime, or (great luxury!) roller blinds.

In our national and university botanic gardens the plants are usually grown in pots and pans in frames and brought into the house when in bud. If there is space available, the alpine house is the ideal place to enjoy early-flowering – and of course autumn-flowering – bulbs, particularly crocuses which are so quickly damaged by a sudden shower of rain. And the fragrance too: it is not until little plants are raised nearly to nose level that one finds so many are deliciously scented. How many of us, for instance, have detected the scent of *Androsace pyrenaica* or *A. lactea*, or crocuses for that matter? The winter-flowering *Crocus laevigatus fontenayi* is particularly fragrant and has a long flowering period.

I referred earlier to the dangers of slugs and snails, dogs and cats, but there are also the birds, bless them. A blackbird (in particular) can ruin the choicest plants in a second if it thinks it can hear an insect burrowing beneath. Wire netting placed over a tufa block, trough or pot – or the doors and vents of an alpine house – may be necessary in some districts, especially in winter and spring.

Recently the alpine plant department at Wisley has been undergoing renovation. The area is on a slope towards the north; some splendid retaining walls have been built to make level standing ground for troughs, frames and glasshouses. One wall is of the moisture-holding Sussex sandstone, the other of warm-coloured Cornish and Devon slaty rock, which is not absorbent. One of the difficulties of growing the choicer alpines in the south of England is the variable winter weather which may change overnight from a muggy dampness to sudden frost or snow. The walls provide excellent sites to combat the untoward dampness, and facing north as they do they offer some coolness in extreme heat in summer. Many of the plants at Wisley are those recognised as desirable subjects for retaining walls, others have been deliberately chosen from an experimental point of view. Of course the ramondas are well represented; to see them in flower carries my mind to a woodland garden bounded by a very old mortared brick wall in which they seed themselves abundantly. (It is not far from Ambleside in Cumbria; in the moist acid woodland *Rubus spectabilis*, the Salmonberry of western North America, luxuriates and produces an August crop of delicious red or yellowish raspberry-like fruits. But beware, it is terribly invasive and grows to six feet in height.)

At the time of writing, one glass house at Wisley has been set out with lumps of the Cornish and Devon slaty-stone and the soil, specially mixed loam (two parts) and grit (one part) with an admixture of slow-acting fertiliser, is covered with 'scalpings' of the same material. In it are many already established and thriving plants. *Paraquilegia grandiflora*, which used to grow well in a trough at Hidcote; tiny cushion-formers such as *Dionysia*, *Androsace* and *Draba*; the exquisite white *Dicentra pusilla*, *Campanula raineri* – so much loved by slugs; the winter-flowering *Ranunculus calandrinioides*, and those two well-known plants which will specially benefit from the dry air and stony surface, *Asperula suberosa* and the powdered foliage of that beauty of spring, *Primula marginata*. For with a glass roof and sides, lavishly set with louvres, the air in this house will be as dry as can be, while a miniature stream, it is hoped, will combat the attacks of red spider, besides providing in one corner special damp conditions for the tricky *Ranunculus glacialis*. The old alpine house is being reconditioned to receive plants flowering in season, growing customarily in pots and pans. This harks back to the culture of alpines in the eighteenth century when these rare new plants were first grown in pots in frames. It is wise to sink all such pots and pans to the rims in ashes or sand which prevents them from drying out too soon. It is quite a skilled job to set them all level, without which refinement, watering would have an irregular effect.

# The Kew Alpine House

I think to augment this chapter I cannot do better than set all my readers longing for the resources at Kew. Since 1977 we have been able to enjoy the fruits of much thought, expense and expertise both inside the new alpine house and outside it, where there are rock banks for sun- and shade-loving plants. To walk into the house in spring or early summer is like entering the premises of a most *recherché* vendor of precious stones encased in gold and platinum. Every plant seems to be a jewel, all are tended with great and loving care by Tony Hall.

I think the best thing I can do is to let Mr Halliwell use his own words from the Alpine Garden Society's Bulletin for 1983. To Mr Halliwell and the editorial board of the Bulletin I tender my best thanks for this permission to reprint.

In 1974 it was decided to build a new house for alpine plants on a site to the west of the Jodrell Laboratory, with work commencing late in 1975. This house was to be a break with tradition and would be in the form of a rock garden built under a glass cover with plants growing *in situ*.

The completed house is some 40 ft. square, approximately 9 ft. to the eaves and is surmounted by a high pyramidal roof, rising to about 27 ft. at its highest point. As an architectural feature, the house is surrounded by a water-filled moat. In the portion of the house that projects over the moat is a series of louvres through which it is hoped that air entering in summer would be cooled and moistened. The moat collects rainwater from the roof and when full the overflow goes into an underground storage tank to be used for watering. 55% of the surface area of the pyramidal roof is provided with ventilators which is probably the greatest amount of ventilation possible for any glasshouse. When fully open these ventilators are approaching the vertical. They are connected to wind and rain sensors so that if gales spring up they will close, or should it rain they will fall below the horizontal so as to shed water.

Heating pipes have been mounted on the inner walls of the moat within the house. It may be necessary in extremely severe weather to use them to raise the temperature slightly, but they are more likely to be needed in cold damp periods during the winter to dry the air and to produce a more buoyant atmosphere when air conditions are stagnant.

The rock work within the house is of rectangular blocks of Sussex sandstone built against the moat walls. In the north-east corner is a waterfall which, by means of a short stream, supplies a small pond. Beds constructed around this pond are to accommodate plants which require moist soil conditions. One of the plants growing here is *Parnassia foliosa* var. *nummularia* from Japan. Only a few cms. high, it has several kidney-shaped leaves on a flower stem which supports a white cup-shaped flower whose petals are feathered. In crevices around the waterfall are a number of small ferns such as *Asplenium flabellifolium* from Australia and New Zealand.

In contrast, the south-east corner has been built for plants from dry areas. Growing here are one or two high altitude succulents, including *Coryphantha vivipara* from Wyoming. The south-east corner is occupied by a scree where the New Zealander *Cotula atrata* with maroon-red button flowers can be seen. Along the west side of the house provisions have been made for calcicoles with the well-known south-west European *Saxifraga longifolia* carefully positioned in a vertical crevice. Between this area and the scree is a narrow peat gulley which provides a home for *Primula reidii williamsii* from Nepal.

The dominant feature of this house is a high sided metal bench. To its base have been fitted coolant pipes similar to those in a domestic refrigerator.

These pipes have been covered with sand to a depth of 12 in. into which plants in pots are plunged. There are two areas: the smaller is kept at between 34–48°F and is used for the cultivation of arctic alpines whilst the larger, with a sand temperature of 41–69°F, is intended for tropical montane plants.

Arctic alpines have not proved to be an easy group of plants to cultivate because of the difficulty of providing artificial growing conditions. In nature these plants are dry and dormant under a snow cover throughout the winter which may be for a period of six or more months. When the snow melts, the surface soil thaws even though a few inches below the surface there may be a region of permafrost. Once these plants emerge from the snow, they have to grow, flower, produce and ripen seed before the snows return. The arctic and antarctic regions are lands of the midnight sun when night or rather twilight is of no more than an hour or two's duration.

Pioneering work with this group of plants began in the Danish Botanic Gardens in Copenhagen. Plants were stored throughout the winter in a refrigerated basement below an insulated glasshouse. In spring plants were brought up into the light so that their growth cycle could take place. Kew has followed on with the work begun in Copenhagen with a more sophisticated but simpler system. In October plants are transferred from the alpine house to a cold store, protected from drying out by plastic covers and stored in darkness at a temperature of 22°F. They are returned to the house in April and replunged into the temperature-controlled sand. Above the bench is a bank of lights which are attached to a time clock so that they come on automatically. These are used to extend day-length, which is gradually increased as spring passes into summer until there is a night of no more than four hours. In the three years that this bench has been in use, experience has been gained in the cultivation of this difficult group of plants. Amongst the successes achieved has been to flower two arctic primulas: *P. egalikensis* from Greenland and Alaska and *P. scandinavica* from Norway and Sweden; this last species resembles our own Scottish native, *P. scotica*, which is also here.

Alpine plants from Arctic regions are difficult to grow, but so are the alpines from the high mountains of the tropics. In these regions there is virtually no change in seasons and day length remains constant at twelve hours. Nightly the temperature falls well below freezing but by midday it can be very warm. Although there is nightly frost, the soil may not freeze and in spite of fluctuating air temperatures that of the soil remains more or less constant. The temperature which is maintained on this bench as has already been mentioned is between 41–69°. The plants which are growing here seem to be less affected by day length than do those in the arctic alpine section. Whilst originally it had been intended to reserve this portion of the bench for the cultivation of tropical montane plants, the range has been extended to include species from many mountain regions of the world. Mount Kenya, which is on the equator, has provided two species of *Lobelia* which are extremes of size: *L. lindblomii* is prostrate with tiny bluish flowers, whereas *L. sattimae* can exceed 3 m. with stout stems and flowers mostly hidden between large leafy bracts. It is probably impossible to imagine a more complete contrast in location than the Falkland Islands on the Antarctic fringe. From almost sea level comes one of the most handsome of its genus, *Sisyrinchium filifolium* with large white pendant flowers. *Calceolaria darwinii*, from Chile and Patagonia, is a choice plant for a cool shady rock or peat garden and is much easier of cultivation in the cooler north than at Kew. On this bench its cultivation seems to be easier and has resulted in plants producing a greater profusion of flowers.

This refrigerated bench is a modern development which should make it possible to succeed with certain difficult groups of plants which previously have defied successful cultivation.

The new alpine house is surrounded on three sides by an 8 ft. brick wall, which hides a complex of old glasshouses and frames. Beds have been constructed against these walls, and climbing plants grown to disguise the bricks. To the east of the house is a paved area where garden seats can be positioned. Against the outer moat wall rock banks have been built using the same Sussex sandstone. These are about 3 ft. in height and of similar breadth and whilst pockets between rocks are not extensive there is plenty of planting space for a large collection of plants, many of which are uncommon or rare. There is *Senecio gerberifolia* from Mexico, which has handsome grey-felted leaves and yellow daisy-like flowers. Between rocks has been planted a number of plants of *Campanula piperi*, a crevice plant which is endemic to the Olympic Mountains of Washington State just south of the Canadian border.

While few of us could ever contemplate going to such great lengths of expertise, to say nothing of the expense, any small unheated glasshouse, so long as it is well ventilated, can be made to serve as an alpine house. I think it gives untold delight early in the year because at that time the tinies of the alpine world can be protected from storms and splashing rain which can so quickly ruin the little flowers.

## Some Plants for the Alpine House

Soon after Christmas, *Saxifraga × kellereri* will be putting up its croziers of pinkish flowers, the minute but large-flowered *Primula allionii* will be showing bud, and surely on a bench, raised nearer to eye-level, is the place to appreciate the extra-ordinary assembly of blues and greens and creams and oyster-tints of the hybrid *Iris* 'Katharine Hodgkin'.

Time was when the Royal Horticultural Shows of early spring had whole exhibits devoted to saxifrages. Those gorgeous, crimson-velvet, arching spikes of *Saxifraga grisebachii* 'Wisley Variety' and the pale yellow of *S. luteoviridis* would be showing; both are, like *S. × kellereri*, members of the Engleria Section, while members of the short-stalked Kabschia Section are poking up buds from their compact grey cushions. *S. burseriana* in its many forms such as 'Crenata' and 'Gloria' in white, and yellow hybrids (probably descended in part from *S. aretioides*) like 'Lutea' and the incomparable 'Faldonside', are all gems of the first water. The notable pink hybrids following all derive their colour from the much later flowering *S. lilacina*; the first was raised at Kew early in this century and named after the raiser: 'Irvingii'. It is still to be enjoyed, though to some it seems outclassed by later raisings such as 'Jenkinsae' and 'Arco-valleyi', and also by the pure pink almost stemless 'Cran-bourne' and Farrer's richly coloured 'Myra'. After all these are over, *S. lilacina* flowers; alone among them it seems to prefer a part-shaded position if grown outside. The creeping British native *S. oppositifolia* has green leaves, and selected forms like 'Latina' in light pink (now seldom seen) and 'Splendens', a ruby-pink, are to be preferred.

Before all these are really over we have the great race of primulas following. If

I were to choose one, it would be *Primula marginata*, for its sweetly scented flowers of lavender-blue have the perfect setting in the toothed, powdered leaves. A hybrid, 'Linda Pope', is justly famous for its size and beauty, in cool lavender, whereas another famous hybrid, 'Marven', is much darker. To walk into an alpine house filled with these early primulas is to enjoy to the full their delicious fragrance. And, as I have written earlier, the protection given preserves the farina or powdering of the flowers; specially good in this way are the various types of auriculas, whereas the *P.* × *pubescens* hybrids, 'Mrs J. H. Wilson', 'The General' and all the rest have little farina on flowers or leaves, but all are fragrant. The alpine house is the place, too, to enjoy *P. edgeworthii*, whose leaves are covered in farina, a perfect setting for the lavender flowers with yellow eyes.

Hummock-forming, high alpine androsaces – *Androsace pyrenaica*, *A. helvetica*, *A. carnea* and many more – are the better for being under glass. And all the tiny early crocuses benefit likewise; frail little *Crocus fleischeri*, whose white floral segments are so thin that you can see the orange stigmata through them, and all those opulent, globose-shaped flowers of *C. chrysanthus* and *C. biflorus*. In the hands of E. A. Bowles and others these two species have hybridised, producing colours from orange-yellow, cream, white, pale blue and indigo. They are only outclassed when one sees the very regal *C. imperati*, in rich lilac, whose outer segments are buff with royal purple featherings. The bright yellow *C. gargaricus* is another claimant for attention early in the year.

Lewisias make admirable pot or pan plants, and being in these containers it is easy to keep them comparatively dry for a while after flowering and in winter. The reward, when they are in multicoloured bloom, is well worth some trouble. Lastly let me mention *Acantholimon venustum*, a very rare plant because it is so difficult to propagate, but whose flowers are like little sprays of pink gladioluses held prettily arching over the spiny hummocks. It is almost as beautiful in seed.

*Thymus membranaceus*, *Campanula hypopolia*, *Origanum dictamnus* are some very beautiful later flowers; with them I should want to grow those superb phloxes from New Mexico State, variously known as *Phlox mesoleuca*, *P. nana ensifolia* and *P. triovulata*. My painting (see page 207) was inspired by seeing these brilliant but frail plants in the alpine houses at Wisley and Kew. The flame colour of *P. mesoleuca* 'Mary Maslin' needs to be separated from the softer tints for the best effect. They must all have full sun and sharp drainage, and slugs and snails be kept at bay.

There is of course no end to the plants that can be grown, and which probably grow best in alpine houses and unheated frames. I am not going to allow myself to be drawn into contemplating all of those exquisite bulbs – so many from the Middle East – which have to be dried off and given a summer baking. They are a special culture, all on their own, and frames specially for them have been built at Kew and Wisley in particular. But I should certainly grow *Fritillaria michaelovskyi* in pots or in prepared soil in an alpine house where its waxy quality can best be enjoyed. In the autumn the astonishing dark yellow of *Oxalis lobata* achieves its greatest brilliance and might have for a companion the new, white *Sternbergia candida*. A lovely spring bulbous plant is *Weldenia candida* and another *Iris cycloglossa*. But among other classes of plants than bulbous are those little perfections the smaller species of *Dicentra*, the Japanese *D. peregrina* (*D. pusilla*) and American *D. cucullaria*. They

195 (*Above*) Low retaining walls
providing homes for sun-loving
alpine plants: *Dryas drummondii*,
*Erodium guttatum*, *Origanum* 'Kent
Beauty' and *Saxifraga longifolia*
'Tumbling Waters' on the top
layer, with *Lithodora oleifolia*,
*Hypericum olympicum* 'Citrinum'
and *Campanula betulifolia* below.
The bowl is filled with various
sempervivums; these do not
require watering. In the author's
garden.

196 (*Left*) *Saxifraga × hostii* growing at
the lower edge of the shed roof in
Fig. 193.

197 (*Right*) *Onosma einerea* (*O.
alboroseum*) in a limestone crevice
in full sun.

have every bit of charm possessed by their larger relatives. The former is in cool pink, the latter white, with cheeky upturned segments. *Origanum amanum* astonishes for weeks with its lilac pink tubes and bracts; it is from Anatolia. Also somewhat tubular are the flowers of *Salvia caespitosa* carried over silvery leaves. It is obvious that many plants for alpine houses have woolly, silky and grey leaves; the dryness protects such foliage and hence I would grow *Origanum dictamnus* there. Its foliage alone warrants inclusion.

The woolly *Verbascum dumulosum* is rather large for our purpose, but the clear yellow flowers appear for weeks over the grey leaves; its hybrid 'Letitia', raised at Wisley, is even more showy and desirable. And for the amusement of one's visitors we must grow that little Australian plant with needle-like leaves and pale pink flowers whose pollinating mechanism is so intriguing, *Stylidium graminifolium*.

It is unfortunate that the New Zealand *Geranium traversii* is not hardy out of doors in Britain, even on a scree. It is best in an alpine house where its long succession of silvery pink flowers appear over silvery silky leaves. Dodging about the world as we do, this is the place to call attention to that gem among silenes, *Silene hookeri* from North America; the petals are so deeply incised that they appear to be ten in number.

There are hosts more plants which enjoy alpine house and frame culture, but that is not really what this book is about. Enough has been said, I hope, to indicate the joys of early and late flowers under cover.

## Window Boxes

If one has merely a flat to live in, the urge to grow plants can be assuaged by having window boxes. On a sunny sill the boxes would become unbearably hot for any plants except for sedums and sempervivums. In both of these genera there are, however, surprising variations in size and colour. Shady sills present little difficulty; the majority of Silver Saxifrages alone would content many of us but here again we resort to alpines and small woodland plants that in nature grow in shade. As to soil, use the mixture as for troughs and raised beds for sunlovers, and add peat for the shade lovers.

## The Planting of Alpines

Wherever they may be planted, alpines prefer to be moved during the growing season, and not in autumn, winter or during what often proves to be a period of drought in spring. As with all planting, it pays to make a hole much too large to take the root ball, preparing the soil with whatever extra ingredients we imagine the plant may need – grit, peat, etc. – and thoroughly soak the plants after planting even when the soil is damp. The watering ensures that the soil is in close contact with the roots. Should a period of hot sunny weather follow it is helpful to shade the plants either with branches of an evergreen stuck into the soil on the sunny side or with clay pots inverted over each plant and supported on inch-high pebbles. Inverted baskets are also useful. It is frequently recommended that the root ball of a pot-grown plant should be broken or loosened before planting, but I have never found this necessary nor desirable, except on scree or tufa.

# 12
# Dwarf and slow-growing conifers and shrubs

The supreme test of the rock-gardener's craft lies in the placing of his shrubs. . . . As a matter of fact, too much importance can hardly be set on the right placing of big and little bushes among the boulders – as by their wise disposition the schemes of the whole may be keyed up to grandeur and illusion, or reduced to a mean chaos.

Reginald Farrer, *Alpines and Bog-plants*, 1908

The Japanese realised long ago that a pine of a hundred feet in height was as out of place in a small garden as a pygmy juniper would be in the middle of the Black Forest, and they planted their trees with a due sense of proportion.

Murray Hornibrook, *Dwarf and Slow Growing Conifers*, 1923

During the last hundred years and more, conifers have become very popular in gardens, even an obsession in some. I think this is due to several reasons. In a country such as this, the British Isles, we have only three native species – the Scots Pine, which I class as the most beautiful of all pines and perhaps of all conifers, the English Yew, which is undoubtedly the most favoured hedging plant in historic gardens and indeed chosen by most people today for a really 'finished' hedge, and the Juniper, *Juniperus communis*, which gives us some valuable prostrate forms as well as the columnar Irish variety. (The species itself is an untidy wild plant and is not usually favoured in gardens.) Therefore we welcomed the many conifers from particularly the northern hemisphere, but also some from the southern, which thrive in our climate; they have given forms of varied growth for almost any position in the garden. Further, their colour variants are appetising. The whole group – which to be strictly correct we should term Gymnosperms rather than just conifers, since they do not all bear cones – lent itself specially to the collector in the arboreta of the nineteenth century as well as for garden furnishings. Lastly, they are in beauty throughout the year, almost without exception. While all this is undoubtedly true of the great conifers it also applies to the so-called dwarfs. Throughout this century they have become almost pets to many growers.

Murray Hornibrook formed the first real collection of them in Ireland in 1923 and later gave the plants to Glasnevin Botanic Gardens. There is no doubt that this initial very considerable effort by him, and his book *Dwarf and Slow Growing Conifers*, 1923, put the dwarf conifer in its rightful place in Britain and elsewhere. On the Continent these engaging plants had been favoured by nurserymen, especially in Holland, where the names of Koster and den Ouden are noted for their frequent occurrence. Botanists, too, such as L. Beissner in Germany, and enthusiasts and botanists in Britain and the United States – W. J. Bean, W. Dallimore, A. Rehder, L. H. Bailey, C. S. Sargent and others – had all contributed descriptions, if not collections.

To revert to Murray Hornibrook, he and I corresponded about them and I was able to provide him with *Thuja orientalis* 'Meldensis' which he had lost. Later I sent him rooted cuttings of the form of *Sequoia sempervirens* which had originated as a prostrate 'witches' broom' on a tree in the University Botanic Garden at Cambridge. I was the first to take cuttings of this broad-leafed variant – now known as *S.s.* 'Cantab' – but which when established throws up vigorous erect stems. A few specimens of his collection still grow at Glasnevin but many have outgrown their positions while others have disappeared. Other good collections were formed by Hew Dalrymple and also by Rogers & Son, both near Southampton. There is no doubt that their spell worked itself into the mind of Alfred H. Nisbet, whose collection in Hampshire was in due course given to the Royal Horticultural Society at Wisley. They were planted rather closely on a raised bed and once again have outgrown their positions. This collection was succeeded and exceeded by that of Humphrey Welch at Devizes, Wiltshire; his book *Dwarf Conifers* is the standard work today and resolves a lot of taxonomical tangles. The collection has been taken over by Mr Van Klaveren and it is still run as a demonstration garden and nursery. A very large collection is to be found also at the Hillier Arboretum, Hampshire, formed largely by the enthusiasm of Sir Harold Hillier. It is sad that, apart from his *Manual of Trees and Shrubs*, the booklet entitled *Dwarf Conifers*, published jointly by the Alpine Garden Society and the Scottish Rock Garden Club, is his only major contribution to the gardener's library. Hillier recorded for us the early collection made by James Noble in California, presented to the Golden Gate Park, San Francisco, in 1960.

There is no doubt that there are big collections in Europe, witness the firms of Jeddeloh at Oldenburg in West Germany and Gimborne at Utrecht, Holland, and also in the United States, where the name of William T. Gotelli of New Jersey is prominent. The Gotelli collection is now housed by the National Arboretum, Washington.

At the present time in the British Isles I think the largest and most diverse collection is in the area above the Valley Garden in Windsor Great Park. Together with the Heather Garden – which already included many genera of conifers – this covers an area of some twenty acres of hungry soil, undulating owing to the extraction of gravel and fully exposed to sun and wind except for some bushy screening. It is therefore an ideal spot for the plants to keep as compact as possible and to develop their brightest tints. This remarkable collection has been built up since 1978 – and is still growing in extent – under the direction of John Bond, and is a place of pilgrimage especially during late autumn, when the plants' tints are spectacular, enhanced by certain shrubs of warmer colouring. There is no doubt that owing to the resources at his command, this collection is in prime condition and clearly labelled, and thus is of the greatest value to the keen student. It has been designated the National Collection by the National Council for the Conservation of Plants and Gardens. The assembly is not restricted merely to one specimen of each kind; as a rule there are several of each, often widely dispersed, giving us the benefit of seeing several thousand plants under differing conditions. I should not have felt it desirable nor possible to have prepared this chapter without several long days studying in this area.

In better, alluvial soil at Bressingham, Norfolk, Adrian Bloom has also a varied collection in his garden and nursery. Whereas any form is welcomed at Windsor, Adrian tends to go in for the brightest variants in yellow and glaucous tints. Both collections have as associates heathers of various types and a few other dwarf shrubs and plants, the heathers at Bressingham adding bright scarlet foliage to the winter scene. There is no doubt that these classes of plants can easily foster the spirit of the collector in their devotees.

At first sight a garden devoted to heathers and conifers might seem to be an ideal to be striven for. It would be considered as permanent planting and 'colourful' throughout the year. But we cannot all grow heathers to perfection and dwarf conifers *grow*, sometimes only too well; heathers, likewise, are best while young.

The association of conifers with the rock garden goes back to Reginald Farrer and beyond. One reason is because we have seen on the high hills gnarled and aged pines and other trees, windswept and dwarfed, rooted in cracks of the rock, their branches hugging the ground. There is also at the back of our minds – certainly of mine – the thought of those dwarfed specimens of wayward windswept beauty in Japanese gardens where they are associated with rocks. And then there is the wonderful contrast that the dark green kinds give to grey rocks. In particular this applies to pines. In her *Flowers and Gardens of Japan*, 1908, Florence du Cane devotes a delightful paragraph to the value that the Japanese place on pines, particularly at the New Year. She notes that for over eight hundred years it has been the custom to plant *Pinus thunbergii*, the rugged 'male' pine, on the left of the garden gate with the softer and more graceful species, *Pinus densiflora*, representing the 'female', on the right. While this may perhaps not have much significance for a European, it indicates how pines have become associated specially with rocks in Japan, for no Japanese garden is without rocks.

We must all be prepared for change in this world and in no section of horticulture has there been such a transformation as in conifers. The brilliant colours treasured today – bright yellow, steely glaucous tones, as well as every conceivable tint of green – are amplified by the tones assumed by some in the winter which include plum-purple and something nearly approaching orange. (This is echoed in general among trees, shrubs and plants where every variegated form of leaf-colour variant is treasured, propagated and cossetted.) Without doubt there are several different types of rock gardens which give pleasure to their owners, and on some of them these colourful forms would be welcomed to cheer the scene throughout the year, in addition to the many plants grown specially for their flowers.

I venture to suggest that this is not the ideal when we are trying to create as natural a piece of rock-scenery as possible. Here, surely, the rock must be the *dominant feature*, against which plants must be used *as a foil*, and especially those of dark green. We are attempting to place the rocks to look as if they had been there since the dawn of time; how could we defile their beauty with a 'golden' conifer? Let us leave these until later.

There is another matter to be considered also, and I drew attention to it in my book *The Art of Planting*. It is the fact that unless we are skilled with the knife and secateurs – like the Japanese experts – conifers of any size will outgrow their positions in due course. They are easily spoiled, and their enchanting outline destroyed if they have to be reduced in size by cutting back. They grow *inexorably*, even the most dwarf of them. Those which are difficult to propagate by cuttings – cedars and pines, and certain kinds of *Abies* and *Picea* – are grafted, with the result that they are on stronger rootstocks. Sometimes these rootstocks, supporting only a few feet of top-growth, may be as much as eight inches across at ground level and will prise open any crevice between two rocks. Against all this impending disaster has to be balanced the pleasure and satisfaction that each plant has engendered during a decade or two. Then we have to harden our hearts, expending much energy to remove the whole thing by the root and start again.

The fact is that we like our plants to grow, and a so-called dwarf conifer will 'go to it' with a will. Some growers keep their plants on the move, severing the roots every year, or keep them in pots sunk below the rims in the ground to curtail growth. But either method has its dangers in times of drought, and the natural elegant growth is inclined to be forfeited. Some of the prostrate junipers can be controlled by the knife almost indefinitely, without spoiling their natural appearance. It is a case of removal of the longest shoots from the inside of the plant as often as is necessary. By thinning and pruning, some other dwarfs can be somewhat controlled, averting the evil day as long as possible.

Many of the slower growing conifers are formal in shape; they may be dome- or ball-shaped, conical, or columnar. It cannot be said that any of these really fit the scenic rock garden. They are at variance with what would have happened to them on a poor-soiled, windy slope. Formal-shaped conifers, whether small or large, are best used in formal gardens unless they simply form part of an arboretum or collection of plants. They are the darlings of the nursery; charming though they undoubtedly are, their place even in a formal garden would be better taken by topiary – which more or less retains its intended shape and size if carefully clipped. Looking at the matter from a natural point of view, we should find the tallest, most slender trees in sheltered valleys and the prostrate growers on mountain tops. A rule such as this is worth bearing in mind when adding shrubs of any sort to a rock garden. A photograph in this book (see Fig. 201) shows how slow-growing conifers have outgrown their positions and instead of adding just a dark foil to the rocks, have achieved a dominant position, completely destroying the sense of scale.

It seems to me that we have to be very circumspect in our use of these dwarf and slow-growing conifers if we are to avoid the tragedy of uprooting a plant that has outgrown its position, or to avoid the distress of seeing daily a size and shape that is foreign to our scheme.

98 *Tsuga mertensiana*, dwarfed by wind near Mount Shuksan, N. Washington, United States of America, at about 5,300 ft. These little trees have great character but would of course revert to forest giants if transferred to the garden.
*Courtesy: Brian O. Mulligan*

99 Dwarf and slow-growing conifers in the Valley Gardens, Windsor Great Park. *Juniperus horizontalis* 'Bonin Island' in foreground; left *Abies procera* 'Glauca Nobel' and *Juniperus horizontalis* 'Bar Harbour'. Right, *Chamaecyparis pisifera* 'Filifera Aurea' and *Ch. lawsoniana* 'Minima Glauca'.

100 Dwarf and slow-growing conifers in the Valley Garden, Windsor Great Park. Left *Juniperus squamata* 'Nana', *Pinus sylvestris* 'Westonbirt', *Juniperus sabina* 'Von Ehren'. Centre *Pinus mugo* 'Mops'. Right *Abies procera* 'Glauca Nobel' and *Juniperus horizontalis* 'Bar Harbour'.

The choice of a little plant should be swayed by what I may perhaps call movement. If a carpeting juniper or *Microbiota* should flow down a valley between two outcrops of rock, a sense of movement will be achieved. Likewise some of the dwarf pines – and none better than forms of *Pinus mugo* – will with a little pruning and selection of branches develop into a windswept shape which again suggests movement. And a drooping small *Tsuga* – *T. canadensis* 'Dumosa', for instance – may also suggest the movement of a weeping willow by a pool.

If in a rock garden of half an acre, as at Sizergh Castle, Cumbria, some dwarf variants of *Picea abies* have reached ten feet across, how could we plant them in our smaller gardens of today? They already dominate and almost ridicule the superb limestone at Sizergh, though as examples of so-called dwarfs they are nothing short of magnificent.

The great trouble about all this is that if one does not choose the real dwarfs, the plants fairly soon get out of scale; on the other hand one has to wait long before real dwarfs have any effect. Perhaps it would be best to plant some of the less dwarf ones to have reasonably quick effect but to keep some others, real dwarfs, growing slowly in pots, for use when the day of reckoning arrives. I have only touched on this subject; it would require almost a book on its own to classify and describe the sizes, shapes, colours and rates of growth of the smaller conifers in order to make selection more easy. It is, however, a vital subject and nobody could do better than make a visit to the Valley Garden and to the Savill Garden (where the extreme dwarfs are grown), both at Windsor, to assess their values and beauty.

Considering that we have already looked at many evergreen alpine plants in the preceding pages, only a few conifers are needed on each rock garden, to give decided contrast. We should remember Symons-Jeune's dictum that 'the contrast of common plants is better than "alpines" ' and that 'peppering a rock garden with dwarf conifers is fatal'. He was also a great believer in contrast of plain surface – i.e. rock, scree or a carpet of any one plant – against the mixture of plants elsewhere. I think Kingdon Ward had this in mind in his remark that the 'rock garden is most effective when rocks are hinted at by a turbulence in the coloured tide of flowers which flows over them'. But this of course depends on whether you are making your rock garden to accommodate a large collection of plants, or whether you are mainly aiming at the beauty of a rock outcrop. Either can satisfy in the extreme.

Holding to my suggestion that we are principally concerned in this book with the creating of a natural landscape rock garden, I will now list a few really dwarf conifers for small gardens.

## I Small rounded hummocks, suitable for placing generally among rocks on open slopes and screes.

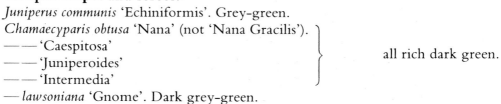

*Juniperus communis* 'Echiniformis'. Grey-green.
*Chamaecyparis obtusa* 'Nana' (not 'Nana Gracilis').
——'Caespitosa'
——'Juniperoides'    } all rich dark green.
——'Intermedia'
— *lawsoniana* 'Gnome'. Dark grey-green.

*Chamaecyparis pisifera* 'Nana'.
—— 'Plumosa Compressa'
*Juniperus horizontalis* 'Grey Pearl'. Erect, bushy, grey-green.
*Chamaecyparis pisifera* 'Filifera Nana'. Dark green.
*Picea abies* 'Gregoryana'. Mid green.
—— 'Little Gem'. Mid green.
—— 'Pygmaea'. Mid green.
—— 'Humilis'. Mid green.
— *mariana* 'Nana'. Grey-green.
*Pinus mugo* 'Gnome'.
   *leucodermis* 'Schmidtii'. Rich dark green.
*Tsuga canadensis* 'Armistice'. Soft green.

**2 Small rounded hummocks, but more spreading than the above.**
*Picea abies* 'Nidiformis'. ⎫
—— 'Procumbens'    ⎬ Mid green.
—— 'Pumila Nigra'    ⎪
—— 'Tabuliformis'    ⎭
*Pinus parviflora* 'Adcock's Dwarf'. Silvery grey-green.
— *sylvestris* 'Ackerley Edge'. Grey-green.
—— 'Burghfield'. Grey-green.
— *mugo* 'Humpy'. Dark green.
*Abies balsamea* 'Hudsonia'. Very dark green.

**3 Sn:all to medium, arching, or tree-like if pruned, to stand away from rocks or by pool.** They will need pruning, and thinning to give good effect.
*Cedrus libani* 'Nana'. Dark green.
— *brevifolia*. Mid green (only for use while young).
*Chamaecyparis lawsoniana* 'Nidiformis Compacta'. Soft green.
*Podocarpus nivalis*. Dark green.
*Tsuga canadensis* 'Compressa'. Soft green.
—— 'Minima'. Soft green.
—— 'Bennett'. Soft green.

**4 Conical and upright for limited use against an outcrop or large rock; they should not exceed one-third of the height of the rock or outcrop. (They are of value in a landscape so long as they occur once and not repetitively.)**
*Juniperus communis* 'Compressa'. Slender, grey-green.
—— 'Suecica Nana'. Stout cone-shaped, grey-green.
*Chamaecyparis obtusa* 'Ericoides'. Feathery grey-green, plum-colour in winter.
*Picea glauca* 'Laurin'. Fresh green, pyramidal.

**5 Tabular growth, for general positions where a horizontal line is required.**
*Chamaecyparis obtusa* 'Kosteri'. Brownish green.
—— 'Repens'. Rich green.
*Pinus strobus* 'Nana'. Grey-green.
*Juniperus squamata* 'Pygmaea'. Grey-green.
*Taxus cuspidata* 'Nana'. Very dark green.

201 *This is what happens to a noble rock garden when the planting gets out of hand.*

202 (*Left*) *Picea abies* 'Gregoryana'. One of the more reliable dwarf spruces. Windsor Great Park.

203 (*Right*) *Chamaecyparis pisifera* 'Nana Aurea Variegata'. A reliable dwarf hummock. Windsor Great Park.

204 *Juniperus horizontalis* 'Grey Pearl'. Little bushes of informal outline for the smaller garden. Windsor Great Park.

205 *Juniperus communis* 'Prostrata', two forms in foreground, with *Pinus mugo* 'Corley's Mat' beyond. Windsor Great Park.

206 *Chamaecyparis lawsoniana* 'Nidifera Compacta'. A mass of drooping twigs. Windsor Great Park.

207 *Pinus mugo* 'Corley's Mat', Slow spreading, dark green. Windsor Great Park.

**6 Compact, prostrate growth, for use as ground-cover over gentle slopes.**
*Cedrus libani* 'Sargentii'. Soft green.
——'Prostrata'.
*Juniperus procumbens* 'Nana'. Light grey-green.
—*taxifolia lutchuensis*. Mid green.
—*sargentii*. Greyish.
——'Viridis'. Bright green.
——'Compacta'. Greyish.
——'Glauca'. Glaucous grey.
——'Blue Moon'. Glaucous grey.
—*horizontalis* 'Wiltonii' ('Glauca Nana', 'Blue Rug'.) Glaucous.
*Tsuga canadensis* 'Cole's Prostrate'. Grey-green.

**7 Vigorous prostrate growth, for use as ground-cover on slopes and on the flat.** Those with upturned growing tips are specially effective on slopes. They may cover as much as ten feet square in the same number of years.
*Juniperus communis* 'Depressa'. Grey-green.
——'Sibirica'. Glaucous grey-green.
——'Hornibrookii'. Grey-green.
—*sabina* 'Broadmoor'. Grey-green.
—*procumbens* 'Nana' ('Bonin Island'). Grey-green.
—*conferta*. Bright green.
——'Emerald Seas'. Light glaucous green.
*Microbiota decussata*. Brownish green.
*Juniperus virginiana* 'Chamberlaynii'. Grey-green.
—*horizontalis* 'Bar Harbour'. Glaucous green.
——'Douglasii'. Grey-green, purplish in winter.

**8 Growth prostrate while young, but building up with age. Suitable for general open positions.** The pines are particularly good in effect on rock gardens.
*Juniperus sabina* 'Tamariscifolia'. Grey-green.
*Pinus mugo* 'Corley's Mat'. Creeping stems, upturned shoots, dark green.
—*mugo* 'Mops'. Dark green.
—*sylvestris* 'Hillside Creeper'. Creeping stems, upturned shoots, grey-green.

In the main, brighter-tinted varieties are larger in growth than the above and give winter cheer to many a shrub border. In brightest yellow is *Pinus sylvestris* 'Gold Medal' – a globose bush of mustard colouring. *Chamaecyparis pisifera* 'Filifera Sungold' runs it close for colouring. *P. sylvestris* 'Moseri' is dark green in summer, but burnished with gold in winter. *Abies lasiocarpa* 'Golden Spreader' seems to 'burn' in full sun and should be given part shade. *Juniperus communis* 'Depressa Aurea' is a mixture of bronze and grey in winter, yellow in spring.

All of the above and all of the glaucous forms I am about to mention are at their best in open sunlight.

Among the brightest glaucous blue forms (apart from forms of *Picea pungens* which are not reliably dwarf, almost always developing a leading shoot after some years) are *Juniperus squamata* 'Blue Carpet' and *Abies procera* 'Glauca Prostrata'. *Pinus parviflora* 'Adcock's Dwarf' makes a compact, bushy little tree and is the most dwarf of the few forms of the Japanese species; glaucous grey, short needles. Almost any form of *Pinus pumila* is desirable.

I could enlarge this chapter almost indefinitely, so many are the forms that I could choose. But I have probably written enough to confound the novice, enthuse the enthusiast and given pointers even to the confirmed addict! And I have not even mentioned several genera, in particular *Thuja* (which provides orange colouring in winter, from *T. occidentalis* 'Rheingold') and *Cryptomeria*. The fault of this genus is that its dwarfs are mostly so dense that not only are they rather shapeless but they collect the snow and tend to rot at the top. The innumerable compact formal dwarfs – globose or conical – of many forms of Lawson's Cypress and also of other species of *Chamaecyparis* I have left severely alone.

It should always be remembered that one is seeking to reproduce a scene from nature in one of her wilder moods, so anything savouring of smugness is to be avoided and plants should be selected for each situation of a form which would be expected in just that situation in the wild. For this reason the globose forms and others of a neat and formal outline are in a general way the least useful.

This is the place, I think, to add to the above groups of conifers a number of dwarf and slow-growing evergreen shrubs. These are specially useful in the foreground of plantings, often having leaves larger than those of the conifers, except in Group 1, and thereby adding to the perspective of the view. The numbers refer to the corresponding numbers and group descriptions of the conifers.

(1) *Empetrum nigrum*. Tiny leaves, dark green.
　*Hebe vernicosa*. Rich green.
　— *cupressoides* 'Boughton dome'. Grey-green.
　*Leiophyllum buxifolium* 'Nanum'. Dark green.
　*Buxus sempervirens* 'Suffruticosa'. Bright green.
(2) *Sarcococca humilis*. Dark green, suckering.
　*Gaultheria cuneata*. Dark green, suckering.
　*Vaccinium vitis-idaea*. Dark green, suckering.
　*Aucuba japonica* 'Nana'. Bright, shining green.
(5) *Ilex crenata* 'Golden Gem'. Yellow tinted.
　*Rhododendron impeditum* and relatives. Grey-green, some purplish in winter.
　— *saluenense* and relatives. Dark green, some purplish or grey in winter.
　*Daphne cneorum*. Dark green.
(6) *Cotoneaster congestus*. Dark green.
　*Euonymus fortunei* 'Kewensis'. Dark green, tiny leaves.
　*Jasminum parkeri*. Dark green, tiny leaves.
　*Coprosma petriei*. Tiny leaves, bright green. Fruits purplish.
(7) *Arctostaphylos uva-ursi*. Dark green.
　*Cotoneaster microphyllus cochleatus*. Dark green.
　— *dammeri*. Dark green.
　*Euonymus fortunei* 'Highdown'. Dark green.
　*Genista sagittalis*. Dark green.

For tabulated details of most of the above, see my book *Plants for Ground-Cover*.

# *13*
# *Paths and ponds*

Work where you can in the spirit of nature, with an invisible hand of Art.

Wordsworth

I have already made some suggestions in regard to paths – how they must be laid in a practical direction and be of suitable surface for whatever use may be made of them. Let us now consider them more deeply.

In a natural rock garden of any size the path needs to be sympathetic to its surroundings and it must be decided whether it is to be what we might call an ornamental path, leading just to and through outcrops, pool and other features in other parts of the garden, or whether it is to be a simple service path, or a combination of both. If the former, it could of course be of mown grass, but I feel this is somewhat out of place and too artificial among rocky outcrops, scree and pool. No grass substitutes such as thyme or camomile are really practical because they take little wear and have to be hand-weeded frequently.

Ideally the path should be what one might call continuous stepping stones of the same rock as the outcrops, but many kinds of rock would be unsuitable, uncomfortable and even dangerous. A paved path of different material would be out of place. We therefore are left with gravel; strictly this should match the outcropping rock in colour even if it is of a different nature, and whatever shingle is chosen it should not be of uniform screening but of random-sized pebbles. The larger pebbles can be raked to the sides where they will link up with the rocks themselves. One big advantage of using some sort of gravel is that it does not have to follow one level and is easily kept free of weeds by using a residual herbicide in early spring.

Some gravels and shingles are of a limy content and it is wise to ascertain this before purchasing; the same of course applies to any soil that has to be imported.

If possible it should be contrived to make the actual rock-placing to act as steps if it is decided to take the footpath through the rock garden. Otherwise on a gravel path outlying rocks can be introduced to achieve the same effect. There is in most gardens a position in a natural design where all the harmonised lines, outcrops, important shrubs, pool and the divergence of paths meet. Here it is good to take a leaf out of the Japanese book and establish a wider area of paving, or one great slab, which they would call a viewing stone. Nearby a comfortable boulder can be introduced as a temporary seat.

Stepping stones are also needed across a large scree or through a bog garden, where they must be made doubly firm.

Turning now to the peat garden, once again if the path is a main access for a barrow, it could well be of acid or neutral gravel, but I should much prefer shredded bark, which is now becoming available from forestry sites, and which lasts a surprisingly long time. If there should be pine trees in the vicinity, pine needles will be equally long-lasting. Logs are frequently used for steps, and sawn, circular sections of tree trunks make admirable 'stepping stones'.

## *Pools and Ponds*

I do not feel I can go thoroughly into the construction of pools in this book; it is a major undertaking, must be extremely well done, and the matter is fully covered in numerous books about the practicalities of gardening. But let me put a few important points forward. A pool intended to look natural in a natural rock or peat garden *must* be in the lowest place of all. This needs to be decided at the outset. The soil removed will be mostly poor subsoil and needs to be buried well below the position of the largest outcrop or bank. Not only do water pipes have to be led to the spot, but a means of emptying the pool must also be envisaged. On sloping ground this presents no real difficulty because the water can be siphoned out. On flat clay soil it presents great difficulty. The whole of the water-works needs to be considered before any rock-building or earth-moving is started. The sides of the pool or pond, and the base, need to be constructed of concrete, reinforced with wire-netting and nowhere should the concrete be visible. This can be achieved by arranging its position so that rock – in its right and rightful bed – overlaps it where suitable. Where the pool does not lie under the rocks, certain plants can be grown to hang over the sides. It may seem to be stating the obvious, but the greatest values of a pool are (1) the reflection of sky or plants in the water, (2) its flatness, and (3) the upright line of rushes. The last two, in complete contrast with all else in the rock garden, give repose and stability. With regard to reflection, the whole idea of having water in a garden is to see it; so often water lilies and other plants are allowed to spread, obscuring the lovely flat surface. I think that two-thirds of the water of any pool, pond or lake should always be free of foliage of any kind.

Most people, if they have a pool, will imagine moisture-loving plants growing around it – water forget-me-nots, mimuluses, primulas and the like. But no concrete pool will be surrounded by moist soil unless the soil runs over the concrete edge, being held from going farther by another concrete edge, below water level. The intervening space will become filled with mud and by capillarity the moisture will be attracted upwards into the bank and positions between rocks. However the scheme is achieved, the surface of the soil should always slope down into the depression, and be mixed with heavy loam and some sand if on a freely draining subsoil; to prevent erosion during times of heavy rain it should be well covered with plants.

Just occasionally an owner is blessed by the possession of a natural stream. It should be watched for a whole year before any attempt is made at rock building or planting and local advice should be taken. Only the very best-behaved trickles and streams remain at a uniform content throughout the seasons. Some become dry during the summer, others may develop into a raging torrent after heavy rain or snow. In some places it is necessary to arrange a spillway for excess water higher up the stream. Something of the same may happen in a pond of natural water; its margins may shrink in dry weather.

Today one can buy irregular-shaped, ready-made plastic pools. In many ways they are a great help but tend to be too shallow for the water to keep clear and I always prefer a well-made concrete affair. Shade from waterlily leaves or a neighbouring outcrop of rock or a bush will be found helpful in keeping the water clear of algae.

## Artificial Watering

Since the dragging of a hose pipe would be inimical to all but the smallest rock gardens, this is the place to mention the advantage of having water laid on at the time of building. There is nothing so misery-making as to watch one's plants suffering from lack of water during hot spells. The ideal is a switch which, at a touch, will float a film of mist over the rock garden for hours on end. But, as with the construction of pools, I feel I cannot go fully into this matter. There are numerous specialist firms who will advise. Perhaps the most sophisticated and advantageous method – if watering is required in a peat garden in a semi-shaded position – is to have the nozzles suspended from tree branches, but such an opportunity cannot occur with a true rock garden. Almost invisible 'pop up' nozzles are perhaps the best approach to actual rain. Mains water is sometimes strongly alkaline and this should be borne in mind in a garden where lime-haters are grown. Finally let me add that one good soak of several hours' duration per week is worth more to the plants than a nightly sprinkle.

208 Alpine plants and dwarf shrubs growing in well drained soil and forming an informal but highly interesting outline along a path of shingle.

209 (*Left*) Concrete slabs were made on gravelly soil, so that when reversed their texture was the same as the surrounding soil, making effective but unobtrusive stepping stones.

210 (*Right*) a 'toy' rock garden on a flat lawn. It would have been better had the pool been made lower so that the concrete verge could have been covered with creeping plants.

211 In this garden the rock was built in the pool, thus conveying moisture upwards. The concrete verge needs covering and the water lilies are too large a variety for the scale of the rocks which do not show distinct stratification.

212 The Westmorland rocks are well sorted into like textures. The concrete verge to the pool should be covered with rock or creeping plants.

# 14
# *Restoration and maintenance*

Beautiful things, perhaps, are never quite so perfectly beautiful as
·when they have passed beyond the untrustworthy criticism of
eyesight into the safe guardianship of memory.

Reginald Farrer, *Among the Hills*, 1911

If we recall the dozen or so great rock gardens which were annually made at the
Chelsea Show – to say nothing of perhaps an equal quantity at Southport – it
is obvious that we own in this country hundreds of these great works of art.
This is because most exhibits were bought and re-erected in the purchasers' grounds;
some indeed ·were sold several times over, and each re-creation would have been
slightly different, to suit each site and local conditions. In addition to these direct
results of exhibition work, many other rock gardens of varying sizes have been
made. The older efforts are mostly neglected and forlorn, the expertise in building
and planting is misunderstood; hands are held up in horror at the thought of all
that back-breaking and time-consuming hand-weeding – if indeed hand-weeding
can be practised among the overgrown 'dwarf conifers' and seedling shrubs, bram-
bles, birches and sycamores that inhabit the once-proud outcrops of noble rocks.
As like as not, the ponds and watercourses no longer run on account of the disruption
of rock and concrete by frost and tree roots. I have seen and heard of many and it
is a disquieting spectacle or thought.

Occasionally today the very rich commission the building of a rock garden, but
as a generality I am writing about the great works of art put up between about
1930 and 1960 – some thirty years of great endeavour when the flowering of this
latest of garden arts reached its apogee. For there is no doubt that we have watched
the flowering and fading of this unique, English, garden art without raising a finger
to arrest its downward progress. And not only are we losing the great naturally-
inspired creations of beautiful rock, but also those incredible masterpieces by Messrs
Pulham. Together they are as much period pieces as any other form of art. Like
buildings they have to be tended and restored on the spot; one cannot take a rock
garden to an expert to be restored in his workshop. Bearing in mind the complexity
of the art – and I hope my earlier chapters will have brought home the knowledge
that is required to build, maintain, plant and appreciate a rock garden – I suggest
that only the application of normal expertise is needed to save these garden

masterpieces. To my mind it is not an impossibility to restore and to tend them with a minimum of work. This is what it all rests upon, of course, the amount of work involved in restoration and maintenance. Few people today will contemplate the vast expense of carting tons of rock from one county to another and I have touched upon the ethics of this matter in an earlier chapter. But we have these period pieces about the country and it makes me shudder to think of the compilations of rock in a great garden, which on the property being sold for 'redevelopment' have been broken up and used as hardcore for the new service roads. There is no doubt that since the formation of the Garden History Society nearly a quarter century ago, numerous facets of horticulture have received due thought and research and have been covered by many writers and lecturers. Horticulture and its history has been given a tremendous uplift and many gardeners and historians are today actively concerned in conservation. The rock garden has not received its due by these worthy folk – perhaps because it forms too recent a picture in garden art. I propose therefore that in this final chapter we should look at the possibilities of restoration and preservation – and let it be fully understood that I am only concerning my thoughts with those rock gardens which owe at least half of their importance and beauty to an initial understanding of geology. The others cannot be valued as real 'period pieces'.

## *Restoration*

Undoubtedly the first thing to do is to clear out all overgrown 'dwarf' conifers and shrubs, seedling trees and other rubbish. It will then become apparent how much their roots have disrupted the rocks and the watercourses and pools, if any. The soil will probably be impoverished and it is advisable to have it analysed at the start so that the necessary enrichment can be applied intelligently after the clearance of weeds. As like as not, much of the top soil will have been weeded away over the years and will need replacing with fresh, analysed soil. Unless stretches of turf are simple and have been well maintained and are not composed of invasive species, it will be advisable to treat the whole area with a general weedkiller such as Roundup, regardless of any living plants. Only by making a completely fresh start can we feel confident of future ease of maintenance. It will probably be necessary to apply the weedkiller for two seasons to make sure of a complete clearance, especially if the weeds contain such troublesome things as couch grass, running thistle, bindweed, ground elder and horsetail – to name some of the worst.

While this preparatory work is going on an assessment can be made of the extent of reconstruction needed. Rocks will be out of their proper alignment, probably having been forced apart by coarse roots and their extraction. Only careful observation on the spot will reveal which rocks need realignment in accordance with the rules of stratification. Some top-heavy rocks may have been placed insecurely during building; any such 'key' rocks may need a shovelful of concrete to keep them in place. Ponds and watercourses are noted for damage by frost. Cracks can seldom be repaired satisfactorily by patching; this requires more fundamental work and may require complete replacement. The same sort of cracks are not likely to recur on new construction on what is now firmly consolidated ground. And let me stress that in an artificial construction, while concrete may be vitally necessary, it should never be visible. It should be obscured by the rocks or covered with evergreen creeping growth.

It may well be that parts of the landscape need attention to drainage. This is more than likely in the scree, if any. It is best to excavate a scree completely and to examine its drainage system. The shingle should be washed and screened and restored in suitable mixture (as explained in chapter 8), and particular care should be taken to ensure that the larger pebbles and stones which formed the top layer are reserved for the surface as 'window dressing'. It matters not what shingle constitutes the bulk of the scree.

## Maintenance

After a year or two's work as described above – not an unreasonable time, surely, for the restoration of a great work of art – we should be ready for the surface work. Following the policy of covering all areas vacant of rocks with either ground-covering plants or with rock chippings, we need to decide which of these complete labour-savers shall be used, and where. Obviously, to give the most natural effect all ground surrounding outcrops and escarpments of rocks should be covered with shingle: it is there that the soil is visualised as not only at its most hungry and gravelly but also at its most shallow – barely covering the greater upthrust of rock from below which should all along be in our imagination. These areas need to be excavated for about three inches, enough depth to accommodate the weed-proof covering of shingle. There are not likely to be sufficient shingle and broken stones on the site and it is ideally desirable to get a supply of material of the same geological formation as has been used for the rock building. In finishing off, it should be borne in mind that it is the larger pieces of stone that reach the bottom of the shingle-slides, while quite small screenings can be used towards the top.

Occasionally it may be permissible and advisable to reinstate the stretches of turf. Never should this be anything but the finest of bowling-green quality, devoid of invasive grasses, and I should prefer to sow species of dwarfest grasses on the spot. Seldom will it be desirable for the resulting turf to be so level that a cylinder mower can tackle it, but with today's rotary mowers and strimmers much can be done where the shingle-slides have given way to ground-covering plants and these in their turn lead to the surrounding finish of turf. Even so, mown turf always looks artificial in such surroundings and is best avoided, in preference to dense ground-cover, creeping shrubs and the like, sprinkled in spring and autumn with dwarf bulbs.

Enough has been written in earlier chapters, I think, to indicate that the planting of a rock garden is as much an art as that of construction. It requires a wide knowledge of suitable plants and their cultivation and an awareness of their effect in maturity, shapes, form, colours (of foliage and flower and season) and general suitability. A landscape rock garden is not the best place for growing all those delicate, demanding, choice little plants that are more suitably accommodated in raised beds, troughs and alpine houses. We are dealing with what purports to be an outcrop of natural rock in natural surroundings. In every instance it is the rock that is the *raison d'être* of the whole work, and no planting should detract from its majesty. The dwarf shrubs and plants, the shingle slopes, the tranquil pools or chattering rills should enhance the beauty of the rock.

With all this in mind we can go forward along the lines suggested, knowing full well that we shall be restoring a national asset in a way that will not burden us with endless maintenance, if done well.

# Conclusion

Among those who have actually read as far as this page there may well be some who skipped over the earlier chapters; they would be the ardent plantsmen. Others may have found the chapters devoted to plants somewhat tedious. Yet others may only have been interested in the instructional chapters; those would have as their principal interest the joy of making something. All would, I hope, be unanimous in thinking of this little book as basically a history, with many facets welded perhaps into an easily digested whole. And to remind ourselves of the value of history I cannot, I think, do better than finish with a short quotation from the essay on Arles in Hilaire Belloc's *Hills and the Sea* – a book deeply steeped in history in all its aspects:

> History ... once a man has begun to know it, becomes a necessary food for the mind, without which it cannot sustain its new dimension. It is an aggregate of universal experience, nor, other things being equal, is any man's judgement so thin and weak as the judgement of a man who knows nothing of the past.

# Bibliography

All titles are published in London unless otherwise stated.

Bailey, L. H., *The Standard Cyclopaedia of Horticulture*, New York, 1927.
Blaikie, Thomas, *Diary of a Scotch Gardener*, c. 1775.
Britten, James, *European Ferns*, 1879–81.
Chambers, Sir William, *A Dissertation on Oriental Gardening*, 1772.
Correvon, H. & Robert, P., *The Alpine Flora*, 1912.
Cox, E. H. M., *The Plant Introductions of Reginald Farrer*, 1930.
*Dictionary of Gardening, The*, Royal Horticultural Society, 1951.
*European Garden Flora*, 1984–.
Evans, Alfred, *The Peat Garden and its Plants*, 1974.
Farrer, Reginald, *Alpines and Bog Plants*, 1908.
   *My Rock Garden*, 1909.
   *Among the Hills*, 1911.
   *The Rock Garden*, 1912.
   *The Dolomites*, 1913.
   *The English Rock Garden*, 1925.
Flemwell, G., *The Flower Fields of Alpine Switzerland*, 1911.
*Flora Europaea*, 1964.
*Floral World and Garden Guide, The*, Ed. S. Hibberd, 1866–77.
Foster, H. Lincoln, *Rock Gardening*, Portland, Oregon, U.S.A., 1982.
*Garden History*, The Garden History Society, 1972–.
*Garden, The*, founded by William Robinson, 1871–1927.
*Gardeners' Chronicle, The*, 1841–.
*Gardeners' Magazine, The*, Conducted by S. Hibberd and others, 1875–1916.
*Gardeners' Magazine and Register, The*, conducted by J. C. Loudon, 1826–43.
Godfrey, W. H., *Gardens in the Making*, 1914.
Graham, Dorothy, *Chinese Gardens*. No date.
Heath, F. G., *Garden Rockery*, 1908.
Hill, Jason, *The Curious Gardener*, 1932.
Ingwersen, Will, *Manual of Alpine Plants*, 1978.
Irving, Walter, *Rock Gardening*, 1925.
Jones, Barbara, *Follies and Grottoes*, 1974.

*Journal of Horticulture, Cottage Gardener* and *Country Gentleman*, 1861–80.

Longus, *Daphnis and Chloe* [translated from the French version of Jacques Amyot of the Greek of Longus and 'the Shepherd's Holidaie'] by Angell Daye, 1587.

Lothian, James, *Practical Hints on the culture . . . of alpine or rock plants*, Edinburgh, 1845.

Loudon, John Claudius, *The Suburban Gardener and Villa Companion*, 1838.

  *An Encyclopaedia of Gardening*, 1825.

Main, James, *The Villa and Cottage Florists' Directory*, 1830.

Mathew, Brian, *Dwarf Bulbs*, 1973.

M'Intosh, Charles, *The Flower Garden*, 1838.

Meredith, Lewis B., *Rock Gardens*, 1910.

Miller, T. G., *Geology and Scenery in Britain*, 1953.

Miller, Naomi, *Heavenly Caves*, 1982.

Murray, Lady Charlotte, *The British Garden*, 3rd Edition, 1808.

*Paxton's Magazine of Botany*, Ed. Sir Joseph Paxton, 1834–49.

Pulham, J., *Picturesque Rock Garden Scenery, Ferneries*, etc., or *The Pulhamite System of Forming Rocks*, c. 1877.

Robert, P. A., *Alpine Flowers*. 1938.

Robinson, William, *Alpine Flowers for English Gardens*, 1870.

Rockley, The Lady, *Historic Gardens of England*, 1938.

Smee, Alfred, *My Garden: its plan and culture*, 1872.

Smith, Charles H. J., *Parks and Pleasure Grounds*, 1852.

Symons-Jeune, B. H. B., *Natural Rock Gardening*, 1932.

Thacker, Christopher, *Masters of the Grotto*, Tisbury, 1976.

Thompson, H. S., *Sub-alpine plants of Swiss woods and meadows*, 1912.

Ward, F. Kingdon, *Common Sense Rock Gardening*, 1948.

Woodbridge, Kenneth, *The Making of Stourhead: Henry Hoare's Paradise*. The Art Bulletin, March 1965, Vol. XLVII, No. 1, The College of Art Association of America, Reprinted by The National Trust.

Wooster, David, *Alpine Plants*, 2nd Series, 1874.


Books on pool construction etc:

Royal Horticultural Society Wisley Handbook: *Water Gardens*, 1986.

*Stapely Book of Water Gardens,* David and Charles, 1985.

# Index

## INDEX of PEOPLE, PLACES and SUBJECTS

## INDEX AND CHECK LIST OF PLANTS

Because it would have been impossible to have given all the facts necessary to intending planters in my somewhat discursive pages, I have thought it well to provide a list of those facts in easily assimilable form. Further details can be obtained from catalogues and books devoted entirely to plants. This index therefore indicates by means of letters in columns the following facts:

Column

1   D = deciduous } some small plants seem to hover between the two categories
    E = evergreen

2   One word indicating the general flower colour

3   W   = winter flowering
    Spr = spring flowering
    ES  = early summer flowering } an approximate guide, much influenced by weather and geographical position
    S   = summer flowering
    Aut = autumn flowering

4   C   = clump-forming, or what one might describe as self-controlled growth.
    GC  = surface ground-covering plants, to exclude weeds if growing satisfactorily.
    inv = plants which are invasive and spread by underground roots. These can be troublesome and are not necessarily suitable for ground-cover.

5   The first figure indicates the approximate Height of the plant when in flower in inches. The second figure indicates the approximate Width apart for planting in inches.

6   C = cuttings
    D = division
    L = layers } Details of the most appropriate method of propagation
    R = root cuttings
    S = seeds

7   Page reference number

| | Evergreen or Deciduous | Flower Colour | Flowering Season | Habit | Dimens in inches | Propa- gation | Page |
|---|---|---|---|---|---|---|---|
| *Acaena buchananii* | D | Cream | S | GC | 4 × 18 | D | 153 |
| — *inermis* | D | Cream | S | GC | 4 × 18 | D | 153 |
| — *microphylla* Fig. p. 146 | D | Cream | S | GC | 2 × 18 | D | — |
| *Acantholimon glumaceum* | E | Pink | S | GC | 5 × 12 | C | 161, 178 |
| — *oliveri*, see *A. venustum* | | | | | | | |
| — *venustum* | E | Pink | S | C | 9 × 9 | CS | 178, 222 |
| *Achillea ageratifolia* | E | White | ES | GC | 6 × 12 | D | 208 |
| *Adenophora bulleyana* | D | Lilac | S | C | 18 × 12 | S | 184 |
| *Adiantum pedatum* | D | Fern | — | C | 12 × 12 | DS | 125 |
| — *venustum* | D | Fern | — | GC | 6 × 18 | D | 129, 169 |
| *Ajuga* 'Catlin's Giant' | E | Blue | Spr | GC | 12 × 18 | D | 204 |
| — *genevensis* 'Brockbankii' | E | Blue | Spr | C | 8 × 8 | D | 184 |
| — 'Jungle Beauty' | E | Blue | Spr | GC | 12 × 18 | D | 204 |
| — *reptans* varieties | E | Blue | Spr | GC | 8 × 12 | D | 184 |
| *Alchemilla conjuncta* | D | Cream | ES | GC | 9 × 12 | D | 152 |
| *Allium beesianum* | D | Blue | S | C | 10 × 5 | DS | 122 |
| — *cernuum* | D | Fern | | C | 12 × 8 | DS | 125, 182 |
| — *cyaneum* | D | Blue | S | C | 5 × 4 | DS | 122 |
| — *cyathophorum farreri* | D | Mauve | S | C | 8 × 6 | DS | 122 |
| — *glaucum* | D | Mauve | LS | C | 12 × 8 | DS | 182 |
| — *narcissiflorum* Fig. 134 | D | Pink | S | C | 9 × 6 | DS | 182 |

| | Evergreen or Deciduous | Flower Colour | Flowering Season | Habit | Dimens in inches | Propa- gation | Page |
|---|---|---|---|---|---|---|---|
| *Allium* (cont.) | | | | | | | |
| — *ostrowskianum* | D | Pink | ES | C | 8 × 6 | DS | 182 |
| — *senescens* | D | Pink | S | C | 6 × 6 | DS | 182 |
| — *triquetrum* | D | White | ES | C | 9 × 6 | DS | 182 |
| *Alyssum saxatile* | E | Yellow | Spr | C | 10 × 18 | CS | 107 |
| *Anacyclus depressus* | E | White | ES | C | 5 × 9 | S | 210 |
| *Andromeda polifolia* 'Compacta' Fig. 76 | E | White | Spr | bush | 9 × 12 | CL | — |
| *Androsace alpina* Fig. p. 175 | E | Pink | Spr | GC | 4 × 10 | CL | 181 |
| — *carnea* | E | Pink | Spr | C | 2 × 2 | DS | 112, 222 |
| — *helvetica* | E | White | Spr | C | 2 × 3 | CS | 107, 222 |
| — *lactea* | E | White | Spr | C | 5 × 4 | S | 106, 107, 217 |
| — *lanuginosa* | E | Pink | ES | GC | 9 × 24 | CLS | 164 |
| *Androsace lanuginosa leichtlinii* | E | White | ES | GC | 9 × 24 | CL | 164, 181 |
| — *pyrenaica* | E | White | Spr | C | 2 × 3 | CS | 217, 222 |
| — *sarmentosa* | E | Pink | Spr | GC | 5 × 10 | CL | 181 |
| — — *chumbyi* | E | Pink | Spr | GC | 4 × 10 | CL | 181 |
| — — *yunnanensis* | E | Pink | Spr | GC | 6 × 12 | CL | 181 |
| — *sempervivoides* | E | Pink | Spr | GC | 4 × 10 | CL | 181 |
| — *villosa* | E | White | Spr | C | 3 × 5 | DS | 107 |
| *Anemone alpina,* see *Pulsatilla* | | | | | | | |
| — — *sulphurea,* see *Pulsatilla* | | | | | | | |
| — *flaccida* | D | White | Spr | C | 6 × 6 | S | 169 |
| — *pulsatilla,* see *P. vulgaris* | | | | | | | |
| *Antennaria dioica* | E | White/ pink | ES | GC | 5 × 10 | D | 108, 153 |
| — *plantaginea* | E | White | S | GC | 8 × 18 | D | 156 |
| *Anthericum liliago* Fig. p. 166 | D | White | ES | C | 18 × 12 | S | 184 |
| — — *major* (*A. algeriensis* of gardens) | D | White | ES | C | 18 × 12 | S | 184 |
| — *ramosa* | D | White | S | C | 18 × 12 | S | 184 |
| *Anthyllis hermanniae* | E | Yellow | ES | bush | 12 × 36 | CS | 149 |
| *Aphyllanthes monspeliensis* | E | Blue | S | C | 10 × 10 | DS | 184 |
| *Aquilegia alpina* 'Hensol Harebell' | D | Blue | ES | C | 24 × 18 | S | 165 |
| — *canadensis* | D | Red, yellow | ES | C | 18 × 10 | S | 165, 188 |
| — *chrysantha* | D | Yellow | ES | C | 36 × 12 | S | 125 |
| — *glandulosa* | D | Blue | ES | C | 10 × 10 | S | 165 |
| — *viridiflora* | D | Green/ brown | ES | C | 15 × 10 | S | 165 |
| *Arabis ferdinandi-coburgii* | E | White | Spr | GC | 5 × 6 | D | 208 |
| *Arcterica* (*Pieris*) *nana* | E | White | Spr | bush | 6 × 6 | CS | 168, 172, 193 |
| *Arctostaphylos nevadensis* | E | Pink | ES | GC | 6 × 24 | DLS | 148 |
| — *uva-ursi* | E | Pink | ES | GC | 6 × 24 | DLS | 148, 235 |
| *Arisaema candidissimum* | D | White | S | C | 18 × 18 | D | 122 |
| *Aristea africana* (*A. cyanea*) Fig. p. 139 | E | Blue | ES | C | 9 × 9 | DS | 108 |
| *Armeria caespitosa* (*A. juniperifolia*) Fig. 153 | E | Pink | Spr | C | 5 × 8 | C | 178 |
| — *juniperifolia* (*A. caespitosa*) Fig. 153 | E | Pink | Spr | C | 5 × 8 | C | 178 |
| — *maritima* varieties | E | Pink | ES | GC | 9 × 12 | CDS | 184 |

| | Evergreen or Deciduous | Flower Colour | Flowering Season | Habit | Dimens in inches | Propa-gation | Page |
|---|---|---|---|---|---|---|---|
| *Campanula* (cont.) | | | | | | | |
| — *garganica* | D | Lavender | ES | C | 6 × 12 | CS | 164 |
| — *hypopolia* | D | Lilac | ES | GC | 4 × 10 | CDS | 222 |
| — 'Joe Elliott' | D | Purple | S | C | 5 × 6 | D | 137, 178 |
| — 'John Innes' Fig. 118 | | | | | | | |
| — *kolenatiana* Fig. 119 | | | | | | | |
| — *piperi* | D | Lavender | S | inv | 2 × 6 | D | 165, 221 |
| — *portenschlagiana bavarica* | D | Violet | S | GC | 8 × 15 | C | 164 |
| — *pulla* Fig. 123 | D | Purple | S | inv | 4 × 10 | D | — |
| — *raineri* | D | Lavender | S | C | 3 × 4 | CS | 210, 218 |
| — *sarmatica* | D | Lilac | S | C | 12 × 12 | S | 184 |
| — *saxifraga* | D | Purple | S | C | 4 × 5 | S | 178 |
| — *stansfieldii* | D | Lilac | S | C | 6 × 8 | CS | 164 |
| — *tommasiniana* | D | Lavender | S | C | 8 × 8 | CS | 164, 165, 210 |
| — *tridentata* | D | Purple | S | C | 4 × 5 | S | 178 |
| — *waldsteiniana* | D | Purple | S | C | 5 × 6 | CS | 164, 210 |
| — 'W. H. Paine' Fig. 139 | D | Violet | S | C | 5 × 9 | C | 164 |
| — *wockii* 'Puck' | D | Purple | S | C | 5 × 6 | CS | 164 |
| — *zoysii* | D | Lavender | S | C | 3 × 4 | CS | 210 |
| *Cassiope* 'Muirhead' and 'Edinburgh', bushes | E | White | Spr | C | 9 × 12 | C | 168 |
| *Celmisia coriacea* Fig. 147 | E | White | ES | C | 8 × 8 | DS | — |
| — *spectabilis* Fig. 130 | E | White | ES | C | 12 × 12 | DS | 133, 208 |
| *Cerastium biebersteinii* or *columnae* | E | White | ES | GC | 4 × 24 | CD | 208 |
| *Ceratostigma plumbaginoides* | D | Blue | A | inv | 9 × 24 | D | 160, 201 |
| *Ceterach officinarum* | E | Fern | — | C | 5 × 8 | DC | 169 |
| *Cheilanthes gracillima* | E | Fern | — | C | 4 × 6 | DS | 169 |
| *Chimaphila umbellata* Fig. p. 142 | E | White | ES | C | 5 × 8 | DS | 108 |
| *Chionodoxa grandiflora* | D | Lavender | Spr | E | 5 × 5 | DS | 113 |
| — *luciliae*, see *C. siehei* | | | | | | | |
| — *siehei* | D | Blue | Spr | C | 8 × 5 | DS | 113 |
| *Chrysanthemum nipponicum* | D | White | Aut | C | 18 × 12 | D | 200 |
| *Clematis alpina* 'Frances Rivis', climber | D | Blue | Spr | — | | CL | 149 |
| — *tenuiloba* | D | Purple | Spr | GC | 9 × 12 | CS | 107 |
| *Codonopsis meleagris* | D | Opal | LS | C | 18 × 18 | S | 122, 184 |
| — *vinciflora*, climber | D | Lavender | S | — | 48 × 12 | S | 165 |
| *Conandron ramondioides* (tender) | E | Blue | Spr | GC | 10 × 18 | DS | 116, 120 |
| *Coprosma petriei* | E | — | — | GC | 2 × 18 | CL | 235 |
| *Coptis trifolia* | D | White | Spr | C | 5 × 5 | DS | 61 |
| *Cortusa matthioli* | D | Purple | ES | C | 10 × 10 | DS | 61 |
| *Corydalis cashmiriana* | D | Blue | Spr | C | 6 × 6 | DS | 124, 193 |
| — *caucasica* | D | Cream/lilac | Spr | C | 6 × 8 | DS | 156 |
| — *cava* (*C. bulbosa*) | D | Lilac | Spr | C | 6 × 8 | DS | 156, 184 |
| — *solida* | D | White/mauve | S | C | 6 × 8 | D | 184 |
| *Cotoneaster congesta* | E | White | ES | GC | 48 × 24 | CDL | 235 |
| — *dammeri*, red berries | E | White | ES | GC | 48 × 24 | CL | 148, 235 |
| — 'Gnome', red berries, bush | E | White | ES | GC | × 48 | CL | 148 |
| — *horizontalis*, red berries, bush | D | White | ES | GC | 36 × 72 | CLS | 149 |
| — — 'Variegata', bush | D | White | ES | GC | 24 × 48 | CL | 201 |